The TVEI story

The TVEI story

Policy, practice and preparation for the workforce

Roger Dale, Richard Bowe, David Harris,
Mark Loveys, Rob Moore, Chris Shilling,
Pat Sikes, John Trevitt and Vicki Valsecchi

Open University Press
Milton Keynes · Philadelphia

Open University Press
Celtic Court
22 Ballmoor
Buckingham
MK18 1XW

and
1900 Frost Road, Suite 101
Bristol, PA 19007, USA

First Published 1990

British Library Cataloguing in Publication Data

The TVEI story: policy, practice, and preparation for the workforce/
1. Great Britain. Technical & vocational education.
Programmes: Technical & Vocational Education Initiative
I. Dale, Roger
373.0113

ISBN 0–335–09563–1
0–335–09562–3 (pbk)

Library of Congress Cataloging in Publication Data

The TVEI story: policy, practice, and preparation for the workforce
Roger Dale . . . [et al.].
p. cm.
Includes bibliographical references (p.) and index.
ISBN 0–335–09563–1 (Hb.) – ISBN 0–335–09562–3 (Pb.)
1. Vocational education – Great Britain – Case studies.
2. Technical education – Great Britain – Case studies. 3. Industry and education – Great Britain – Case studies. I. Dale, Roger.
LC1047.G7T85 1990
370.11'3'09401 – dc20 90–7638 CIP

Typeset by Scarborough Typesetting Services
Printed in Great Britain by St Edmundsbury Press Ltd
Bury St Edmunds, Suffolk

Contents

About the authors

The TVEI story was jointly edited and authored by:
Roger Dale, Department of Education, University of Auckland.
Richard Bowe, Centre for Education Studies, King's College London.
David Harris, Faculty of Education, Wolverhampton Polytechnic.
Mark Loveys, Bushfield County Middle School, Milton Keynes.
Rob Moore, Homerton College, University of Cambridge.
Chris Shilling, Department of Sociology and Social Policy, University of Southampton.
Pat Sikes, Department of Education, University of Warwick.
John Trevitt, Department of Adult and Continuing Education, University of Hull.
Vicki Valsecchi, Independent Education Consultant.

Preface and acknowledgements

This book is very much a collective endeavour. The idea for it came after we had been meeting together for around 3 years to examine jointly the problems and opportunities of carrying out local evaluations of the Technical and Vocational Education Initiative (TVEI). The group's origins were in the contracts offered to the Open University, following Roger Dale's voluntary involvement from the very beginning with one of the first 14 local education authorities (LEAs) involved in the scheme, to carry out local evaluations of TVEI pilot schemes. In the end, the group was involved with seven local evaluations. Six of these form the core of this book. The seventh, the final pilot scheme in the Initiative, began too late for information to be included in this book. That Open University group of evaluators consisted of (at various times) Roger Dale (who convened this group), Richard Bowe, Mark Loveys, Rob Moore, Simon Sandberg, Pat Sikes, Mike Taylor and John Trevitt. They were augmented quite soon after the group was set up by David Harris and Vicki Valsecchi, who were evaluating another first round project and wished to become part of a larger group, and by Chris Shilling, then a PhD student at the Open University, whose work drew on his experience of observing a second round TVEI scheme (the eighth scheme referred to throughout the book).

The group was an open one. It was joined at various times by a number of visitors, including people from local authorities and schools where the local evaluations were being carried out. Its main purpose was to enable a fairly far-flung group of evaluators to meet to exchange information, ideas and suggestions that would enable us to produce the best possible local evaluations of TVEI. All the Open University evaluations were set up on the same theoretical basis and the same contractual terms. These are described at length in the book, but essentially involved a qualitative, process-focused, problem-making rather than problem-taking approach as the theoretical basis, and a commitment to joint identification with the local authority of priority areas for examination.

Eventually we began to recognize that the strategy of group meetings was bearing fruit as the information we each brought to meetings began to fit together in a pattern whose coherence was given by our broad joint approach. We decided that it would be useful for us in the short term and, we hoped, for others in the longer term if we were to put our findings together in a book. In a sense, that was where our troubles began. Our main commitment had to remain with actually carrying out the local evaluations, and issues arising from these continued to take priority at our (now more frequent) group meetings. In addition, the original group had begun to break up as the earliest contracts came to an end and as people moved on to other jobs. At this point, much research and writing had to be carried out by group members now working in institutions other than the Open University. We still managed to meet regularly, though, and took joint responsibility for editing the book and individual responsibility for the writing of separate chapters. Roger Dale wrote the introduction and Chapters 2, 4 and 7 (the latter being a joint piece with David Harris and John Trevitt); Richard Bowe wrote Chapters 5 and 10; Mark Loveys wrote Chapter 11; Rob Moore wrote Chapter 3; Chris Shilling wrote Chapter 8; Pat Sikes wrote Chapter 6; and Vicki Valsecchi wrote Chapter 9. In a very real sense, though, each chapter remains the result of a collective endeavour; drawing on group discussion and data gained by others in the group. Furthermore, it was only possible to sustain the idea of producing a book as a result of the secretaries who worked with us at the Open University, and with each of whom the whole group got on with extremely well. In succession, Dot Purdon, Diane Ward and Ann McFarlane provided the essential continuity that enabled the project to keep going. Their connection with the TVEI group was only a very minor part of their work, but they never allowed that to interfere with this commitment to and practical support of the project. The support of Glyn Evans, at Southampton University, was also invaluable in the months before the completion of the final manuscript. It is literally true that without their efforts this book would never have seen the light of day.

This is even more true of Kate Laughton. Kate agreed to join the group to edit the book at a time when our commitment, inspiration and especially our application were flagging. Within a very short time she had grasped the situation and shown us how we could and should proceed with the production of the book. She rapidly became a fully contributing member of the group and deserves as much credit for the outcome as any of the listed authors. Indeed, it was the group's wish that her name should appear as co-author of the book, and the fact she declined in no way lessens either the genuine indispensability of her contribution or our appreciation of it.

Many people have made helpful comments and suggestions on the group's work and on drafts of the chapters. First among these must be the two people who were full members of the group but whose subsequent careers prevented them from putting pen to paper. Mike Taylor was the first person to be appointed to carry out a local evaluation in the Open University and his views inevitably informed the subsequent work of the group in crucial ways. Simon Sandberg was a member of the group for a shorter time but made an important contribution through his energy and originality, to say nothing of his irreverence. Both affected the development of the project for the better and we are very grateful for their help.

Other friends and colleagues in the Open University and elsewhere helped us to improve this book by their comments and suggestions as the project developed. Particular thanks are due to Rosemary Deem, Geoff Esland, David Finegold, Denis Gleeson, Gary McCulloch and Jenny Ozga. We have received a great deal of support and assistance in the local evaluations from people in the TVEI Unit of the Manpower Services Commission (MSC), especially Gaynor Cohen and Terry McIntyre of the Evaluation Group who were always friendly, supportive and helpful. Several of us have had extended and productive conversations with Malcolm Deere, the doyen of TVEI Regional Advisers, that have done much to sharpen our view of TVEI and its development.

A great debt is due to those we worked with on the ground. Almost without exception, the teachers, headteachers, LEA officers and elected members that we met and whose work we 'evaluated' treated us with courtesy and cordiality. Meeting them became a pleasure as well as a duty, and if they gained as much from it as we did then we have succeeded with one of our major aims. Our greatest debt of all, however, is to the local co-ordinators of the TVEI projects we worked with. They were the crucial figures in providing information about local schemes and in enabling us to link our evaluations constructively to the respective schemes and the organizations and bodies involved in them.

It will be seen that we have acknowledged the contribution of a large number of people and that they come from rather different backgrounds with rather different perspectives on TVEI. This makes it all the more important, as well as more correct, to point out that not one of them is responsible for what is written in this book and that all of them would disagree with parts of it.

PART 1

BACKGROUND

CHAPTER 1

Introduction

This book aims to tell one version of the story of the Technical and Vocational Education Initiative (TVEI). TVEI was in many ways the most important educational innovation of the post-war period. It signalled the final collapse of the settlement instituted by the 1944 Education Act, and prepared the ground for the settlement that is currrently being installed in its place. It changed the relationship between schools, local authorities and central government in ways that will be difficult to reverse. Schools and pupils within them were quite explicitly treated differently from each other. For the schools that were involved in the pilot scheme, it proved a catalyst to changes in what they taught, how they taught it and how they assessed pupil performance. The pilot schools laid themselves open to a scrutiny of their practices and processes potentially as searching and intensive as a full inspection, but much more frequent. TVEI was an innovation officially so successful that its pilot stage was being extended within months of it starting, and that at the conclusion of the pilot stage £1 billion was allocated for its extension to all the schools in the country.

The TVEI story might be judged a success story indeed. However, it will be our argument in this book that much the greatest successes and consequences of TVEI are to be found in its effects on the control and processes of schooling, rather than in its effects on the curriculum or on the young people who experienced it. Consequently, it is worthwhile to list here very briefly what we see as TVEI's main achievements. First, and very clearly, TVEI altered fundamentally and irrevocably the administration and control of education. It represented an unprecedented, unanticipated, unwelcome and entirely novel intervention into the previously self-controlled world of the secondary schools by a body that not only had no previous record there, but that symbolized values that were anathema to many people working in those schools. And yet at the end of the 5-year pilot phase of TVEI, that intervention, if not necessarily more welcome, had become an accepted part of school life, and the methods of control it introduced had been taken up throughout the education service. TVEI prepared the way for the centralization of the education service that was continued by the 1988 Education Act, and the method it pioneered of schools bidding for earmarked funds was being used to direct schools into desired directions and to ensure that no central funding could be 'captured' by the teachers and diverted to 'subversive ends' of any kind.

Secondly, while it did not come to constitute a 'bridge' between school and work, it did lead schools to become more closely involved in the preparation of the workforce. In any case, the kind of bridge that was in the minds of some people at the outset of TVEI, a device for ensuring simultaneously a smooth and rewarding entry into work for all young people and the efficient meeting of industry's 'needs', was never a real possibility. Schools do not have and cannot attain the capacity to meet industry's 'needs' in any direct way. To describe TVEI's 'failure' to build such a bridge then, as a failure may be rather unfair. However, it should be noted that such claims were made, and it was frequently those schools who failed to achieve what was not possible rather than those who did not recognize the impossibility of the task who were blamed. However, the message of all the chapters in the second part of this book is that, however indirectly, even unintentionally, the TVEI pilot scheme did lead schools to become more closely involved in the preparation of the workforce than they had been previously. TVEI may not have had dramatic effects on the curriculum or on pupils' ability to get jobs, but it did have an effect on the 'vocabularies of motive' that schools used to justify what they did, to the extent that it became very difficult not to refer to the 'instrumental' purposes and effects of any practice, proposed or actual.

Thirdly, schools did seize the opportunities TVEI provided for well-funded curriculum development (in its widest sense) to bring about changes they considered desirable in themselves. It enabled them to modify practices to which they had been tied only by the inability to produce alternatives. For it was this inability to change them, rather than any professional commitment to them, that led schools to retain forms of organization, curriculum, pedagogy and assessment that offered them convenience and the comfort of habit in place of professional stimulation, and offered very much less to their pupils than they would have wished, or felt themselves capable of. As a consequence, TVEI did, if by no means entirely for the reasons desired or envisaged, change often for the better, the school experiences of those who were involved in it.

Therefore, judged by its own originally stated criteria, which emphasized changes in schooling to give much greater weight to technical and vocational education, or by what we see as its fundamental aim, to shift the centre of gravity of secondary education from the academic to the vocational, it had limited success. For instance, the Director of TVEI in its extension to all schools in the country, in setting out a list of yet to be achieved aims that was to build on the achievements of the pilot phase, produced a programme that itself looked remarkably like the kind of detailed specification of objectives that might have been expected at the outset of TVEI (Jones, 1989). Such a specification never emerged because of the speed with which TVEI was set up. Instead, it developed 'on the hoof', and it is a central part of our argument and of the TVEI story that it was during this process of specification, largely carried out by dedicated (in both senses of the word) people involved in TVEI centrally, in LEAs and in schools, that the seeds of TVEI's curricular heritage, and to a lesser extent, its administrative success, are to be found.

By the time of the Education Reform Act of 1988, TVEI had moved from being the prodigal and the favoured child to one more or less deserted by its parents. The dominant parent, the Manpower Services Commission (MSC),[1] had changed her name and seemed to have lost interest in the child TVEI as she bestowed her favours on younger, more needy and more trendy offspring. The MSC had provided quite well for the child TVEI's future, though there were serious doubts about whether these resources would be adequate to meet all the child's needs as it grew. More importantly, TVEI's other parent, the Department of Education and Science (DES), had decided that the time had come to take a greater interest in schools. In changing what was to happen to them, he paid very little attention to TVEI or to what he had learned from her upbringing. To put it less opaquely, the Education Reform Act and the National Curriculum it sponsored owed little if anything to the TVEI experience. Indeed, it was difficult to tell how a full TVEI programme as originally envisaged – could be fitted into the National Curriculum.

The metaphor of the child is a most appropriate one for the story of TVEI that we shall be trying to tell in this book. We aim to follow it from unexpected conception through the extraordinarily short gestation period and the turbulent infancy that so marked its later development, to the period of prodigality when it sometimes threatened to become a spoiled brat, and the increasing maturity that preceded its comparative neglect. Our focus is restricted to the pilot phase of TVEI. That phase is still not complete in some areas, including some of those where we studied TVEI, but our story effectively ends with the announcement of the extension of TVEI to all state secondary schools in 1986.

This book has two major aims. We want both to tell the TVEI story and to draw its morals, and therefore we provide a description of the conception and operation of TVEI in eight local authorities. The focus here is on TVEI as a particular kind of educational policy initiative, on how it has gone about achieving its aims in practice and on the effects and the effectiveness of the educational processes it set in motion. This aim is explicit throughout the book and is the basis of its organization.

The second aim is much more implicit and will rely to a greater extent on readers making inferences about the implications of TVEI for their situations, actual and foreseeable. While it remains relatively indirect in the text, however, this second aim was central to our thinking about what to include in the book, in terms of topics and level of treatment. While we feel there is a pressing need for a systematic analysis and description of TVEI in operation (which we do not feel exists in any coherent form in any of the rapidly growing literature on TVEI) – and we try to fulfil that need – we do not see the development of a theoretical account of TVEI as an end in itself. TVEI has educational and political importance, as well as theoretical importance, and we have borne this very much in mind in the level and extent of our discussion. However, we also insist that both its educational and political importance can effectively be laid bare only by means of a coherent and systematic analysis of TVEI.

The consequences of under-theorized or *ad hoc* responses to TVEI in both political and educational spheres became increasingly evident as the Initiative developed. Politically, it was greeted with the fear that it meant MSC control of education, a fear that never entirely disappeared. Educationally, a major source of hostility was that it would inevitably bring about the narrowing of the curriculum and the reintroduction of selection. Neither of these things has come to pass. TVEI *may* have shown how greater central control of schools can be achieved, though this is a claim we would qualify (in a nutshell, for we will develop this argument later, a system that has proved effective in bringing about a restricted amount of change through operation at the margins of schools is by no means guaranteed to be equally successful in bringing about a widespread transformation of the whole of secondary education).

What we are seeking to provide, then, is a comprehensive account of the installation and operation of TVEI that will enable realistic and informed estimates to be made of the likely impact of future runners from the same stable – in particular, of course, the National Curriculum. We are as concerned to indicate what did not happen and why, as we are to provide a catalogue of TVEI triumphs and disasters. While we are concerned to register some of these things, we are more concerned with why and how they came about. Without this any lessons to be learned from TVEI would be confined to *ad hoc* copying and imitation. And to do this we need an effective analysis as well as a description of what happened in TVEI.

The book has two principal foci, the content and the structures of TVEI. The focus on the content of the Initiative is directed to the educational processes associated with it rather than to its outcomes. There are two reasons for this. First, a quantity of evidence is available from the TVEI Unit itself regarding the gross characteristics of the scheme, i.e. the numbers taking part, curriculum offerings, the numbers staying on after 16, and so on. But more important than this, it is exceptionally difficult to identify the quantifiable outcomes of TVEI, such as how far it contributes to young people's employability, whether it has made the curriculum of a particular participating school[2] more relevant, or increased the number of external examination passes. Very simply, this is because the absence of any effective or realistic control group makes it impossible to attribute any of these outcomes to TVEI alone, or even mainly to TVEI.

Consequently, the content focus is on those processes at the level of the local education authority (LEA) and the school which we have been able to monitor, and which we know are responses to TVEI. Of course, these processes have undoubtedly themselves had an effect on pupils' experiences of schooling, but again exactly what differences they have made is impossible to say. As one TVEI student said when asked whether he thought he was better off on TVEI, 'I don't know, because I don't know what the alternative would have been like.' Our major emphasis, then, is on the processes of development from the guidelines which framed the LEAs' original submissions, to the experiences of the pupils, especially the programmes, styles, decisions and organizations which transformed national guidelines into classroom practice. Our second focus is on the effect of categorical funding. It is, of course, not wholly separate from the first, but we are particularly interested in how submissions and contracts were drawn up, monitored and implemented.

The different local evaluations we were involved in were all guided by the same broad approach and set of principles (enshrined, incidentally, in the contracts for the work agreed with the LEAs), and we jointly arrived over the course of many meetings at a framework for the analysis of TVEI in practice. This approach is described more fully in Chapter 4, but in essence it involved not taking the problems – and solutions to them – faced by LEAs and schools within TVEI as they presented themselves. Rather, we attempted to locate them with the processes of TVEI as a whole, and in the effect they had on the continuing lives of the LEAs and schools involved in the Initiative. The kinds of problems and solutions generated within TVEI, the forms they took and the ways they were interpreted were a result of the various parties drawing on their own preferences, priorities and capabilities to cast them in forms that were least threatening to their aims for TVEI and what they were willing to invest in the achievement of those aims – in a word, to make them their own. The difference between this notion of people involved in TVEI seeking to make its problems and solutions their own by selective definition and interpretation and the notion of 'ownership' that became very prevalent in the later days of the TVEI pilot phase, is worth pursuing briefly because it does throw some light on one of the ways we thought our approach could be distinguished both from the more 'official' views of TVEI, and from those evaluators and commentators on TVEI who tended to take TVEI problems more at face value, or at least to isolate them from the processes that generated them. 'Ownership' in latter TVEI-speak came to denote an acceptance of the responsibility for a part of a TVEI programme by one of the involved parties (usually a school or a group of teachers) that confirmed its acceptance and adoption. Until 'ownership' was accepted, the programme could not be effectively installed, and the problem of TVEI was how to bring about this sense of ownership. In this way, ownership essentially involved the acceptance of some other party's definition of a problem and its solution, and implied something quite different from what we meant by a group making a problem its own.

What most clearly underlay our view of TVEI problems and solutions, then, was a view of them as political and professional problems rather than managerial and technical problems. We did not assume that implementing TVEI was an exercise in managing people and organizations to bring about the most effective achievement of a known and agreed set of goals – which was, in essence, the official view of the initiative. Rather, we saw it as a political process of bringing about change in a particular set of conditions and through the medium of existing professional practices and processes. These professional practices and processes were not immutable, but neither were they infinitely variable or readily incorporated into technical solutions to managerial problems.

In essence then, one approach is *qualitative, localized* and *formative.* Qualitative because the focus from the start has been on processes rather than outcomes, with a particular emphasis on how TVEI coalesced with the existing provision at all levels of the education service, and on the historical development of each project. Localized, because beyond establishing the 'natural history' of the project, in each case the principal foci of investigation were selected and agreed with the local project director or his or her surrogate (such as an evaluation steering committee). Because the schemes were also so different from each other, this meant considerable variation in both the range of topics covered, and the intensity of coverage of any single topic. From the point of view of this book, this is both a weakness and a strength. It is a weakness in so far as we do not always have complete 'sets' of information on any particular topic. But this is more than compensated for by the possibility it affords of showing the full complexity of TVEI, and of linking different approaches, strategies, processes and programmes in the same area of TVEI activity. Existing comparisons of TVEI in different LEAs have tended to assume that they are comparing like with like. It is fundamental to our approach that TVEI means very different things in different authorities and it is our aim to explain both the sources and consequences of that variation (though there is both coherence within the variations, and limits to it).

The approach was formative, because in our view the first audience for the local evaluations of the scheme was the practitioners involved in it. Hence our decision to emphasize those aspects of our work that may be of most use to schools and LEAs in the future, just as our local evaluations were framed by a selection principle that made feedback to the practitioners a major priority.

This much we share but, beyond this, we each have our different strengths, interests and theoretical positions. We feel we have capitalized on, rather than been obstructed by, our different experiences, knowledge and approaches, because this is a collective endeavour. We are no more writing about eight distinct TVEI schemes than we are writing about TVEI as a monolithic innovation. We share the belief that there are common threads to TVEI, but that these can be very differently interpreted in different places. The topics covered in the later chapters of the book have different histories, and followed different trajectories in the eight LEAs. TVEI did not have the same effect on all aspects in all places. TVEI is both more than, and less than, the sum of its parts, and this book is devoted to elucidating that, rather than to being a vehicle for discrete theoretical forays or detailed accounts of single TVEI schemes. Both would necessarily be abstracted from what we feel is the necessity of producing a holistic account of the Initiative.

It is mainly for this reason that we have organized the book by theme rather than providing separate case studies for the eight LEAs we were involved with. (Some of us were involved in more than one LEA, and two of us worked at different times in the same LEA.) On the one hand, there is a growing number of individual authority case studies in TVEI that tend, almost inevitably, to abstract them from the larger national picture and to make comparative appreciations of how particular issues might be tackled rather difficult. On the other hand, there are studies which homogenize the findings from what are known to be a disparate set of TVEI schemes and, consequently, produce results that are distinctly of limited value to anyone wishing to study the impact of any particular programme in a particular context. In addition, to have provided fully detailed accounts of the relevant histories of each of the LEAs, how they became involved in TVEI, what structures they set up to handle it, etc., would have required a separate book. Our commitment was to write about TVEI as it operates in schools and its wider political impact, rather than to focus narrowly on its consequences for educational administration (though they are, of course, a necessary part of the overall picture and are referred to when it seems relevant to do so).

We also wanted the LEAs we worked with to remain anonymous, often for political reasons. For instance, we agreed with the individual authorities that, if they were identified, they would be allowed to view the manuscript before publication. As the project was already behind schedule, we did not want to delay any further. Also, however, a number of individuals who had passed information on to us in confidence, could have been identified if the authority had been identified. The main reason for retaining anonymity, however, was that the lack of it would contribute little, if anything, of value to the reader. Also, without providing the fully detailed accounts alluded to earlier, the effect could have been misleading and possibly damaging to the LEA. The accounts would have been partial, in both senses of the word.

The book then, is largely made up of chapters that focus on particular issues generated in and for schools and LEAs by their participation in TVEI. In each of these areas we have looked at the TVEI requirements of schools and teachers, what they made of them and how they responded. As has already been mentioned, not all issues were of equal prominence in all LEAs, but we have tried to pool our knowledge of how issues were handled in different schemes in order to meet our first aim of producing a description of TVEI in practice that seeks not to homogenize different experiences but to show them as different locally based responses, drawing on different interpretations of and responses to TVEI, and different resources and strategies for coping with the problems TVEI posed.

Our approach may most easily be characterized by contrasting it with much other existing writing on TVEI. One indication of the growth and change in the nature of the literature on TVEI comes from an examination of references to the initiative reported in the British Education Index (BEI) between 1983 and 1988. In 1983, there were only two references to TVEI and these described the setting up of the scheme. In 1984, there were 10, still largely descriptive. The number of references increased to 17 in 1985, and these contained several articles arguing the merits of TVEI. In 1986, there were again 17 articles listed, with an increasing trend towards describing TVEI in practice, e.g. how it could be used in particular subject areas. The trend continued in 1987, when 24 references were cited, and when TVEI was listed separately in the BEI for the first time; but in 1988, the last year for which we were able to obtain information, there were only six references to TVEI.

Of course, the BEI is selective, and we would expect it to emphasize the practical implications of TVEI. However, even among those articles not listed in the BEI, the dominant emphases are descriptive/prescriptive/good practice, rather than analytical or critical. However, TVEI has spawned a fair number of analytical and critical articles as well (to which most of us have contributed outside this book), many of which proceed from a stance similar to that which we adopt. The major difference between these articles and what we are trying to do here, however, is that we seek a coherent approach across a range of topics in the same set of LEAs. Most of the other academic papers on TVEI, by contrast, tend to be based on 'one-off' studies of a particular issue or a particular scheme, or of particular issues in a particular scheme. Though such articles have produced a range of important insights, it has not been possible for these to be developed systematically across schemes and topics. What we have then are *collections* of variously disparate pieces, rather than a grounded and integrated attempted to tackle TVEI as a whole.

However, the majority of papers on TVEI are not academic or analytical. Descriptions of the scheme by its national and local organizers abound. Of particular importance are the statistical accounts provided by the TVEI Unit itself and by the NFER, on the basis of the questionnaires sent to schools as part of their national evaluation. The style of the NFER reports tends to provide an overall picture of the issue under review and to supplement that description by accounts of good practice. These highly descriptive, nationally derived reports inevitably blur the differences between schemes and cannot begin effectively to tackle the reasons for those differences. These accounts, which are largely paralleled by a number of accounts of individual local schemes, do not in effect attempt to lay bare what is distinctive about TVEI, but effectively treat it as just another curriculum innovation. They assume consensus over aims and equivalence of conditions for their achievement (though this assumption clearly disappears in descriptions of individual schemes). As we note elsewhere, they represent an essentially managerial response to the evaluation of TVEI (indeed, they are quite open about this; the 'Perspectives on TVEI' series produced by NFER has as its subtitle 'A set of papers exploring management themes within TVEI'). These accounts seek both to establish the degree of adherence to/success in achieving the taken for granted goals of the Initiative and to indicate *by reports of good practice, rather than by an analysis of reasons for 'failure'*, how the success rates may be improved.

These essentially descriptive accounts, then, actually contribute to the definition and achievement of what they are describing. This is even more the case with another series of 'in-house' publications. The 'TVEI Network' (in a magazine format) and the more 'academic' 'TVEI Developments' series, published by the TVEI Unit, can be seen as being aimed at creating and sustaining the TVEI family. These series are major means of giving an identity to TVEI that transcends its different local identities. Indeed, they can be seen as the major public means of defining TVEI on the hoof. They are filled largely with accounts of how TVEI is being carried out in various places and with various groups. TVEI pupils feature prominently in 'Network' while the 'Developments' series is made up very largely of accounts by local co-ordinators and teachers reporting on their experience of devising and/or implementing TVEI curricula, or teaching or assessment methods in various sets of circumstances.

Both these sets of publications are heavily imbued with curricular and pedagogic evangelism, with energy and commitment taken as evidence for change. There is little if any discussion of the *conditions* of successful change; rather, a persistent presentation of the need for change and the possibility of achieving it under TVEI.

As we have suggested, a key function of 'Network' and 'Developments' is to discursively locate TVEI more precisely. In essence, they are contributions to the continuing negotiation over 'what is TVEI'. For instance, as we point out below, plausible cases can be made for both the two key, but contrasting, arguments for expanding technical education as progenitors of TVEI – the 'get the best brains into technology' case, and the 'give them something interesting and "relevant" to keep them quiet' case. However, if the balance of the reports in 'Network' and 'Developments' is any kind of accurate indication of how TVEI has operated in practice, it is clear that the latter, 'social control' version of technical education has been dominant.

The key themes running through the series are *process, experience* and *management*, which is hardly surprising given their avowedly practical bias. But this does mean that wider structural and contextual issues are almost totally neglected. Thus, while emphasizing educational 'processes' and 'experience', they are also directed unequivocally to instrumental ends ('national needs'). All pupils are to be admitted via 'instrumental' processes (e.g. rote learning), or admitted to 'personal-instrumental' ('career') ends of education.

What we think is distinctive about our approach is further elaborated in the rest of the book. Part 2 consists of a series of topic based studies compiled on the basis we have outlined in this introduction. In Part 1, we look first at the constitution of TVEI – the double meaning is deliberate – focusing on its political background. Chapter 3 examines the educational themes, discussion and background to which TVEI was heir, and in Chapter 4 we outline our understanding of how, from a common set of guidelines, TVEI became the many things it was in practice.

Notes

1. The MSC has in fact changed its name since the inauguration of TVEI, first to the Training Commission and then to the Training Agency. However, throughout most of the period of our study, it was known as the MSC, and that is how it will be referred to throughout this book.
2. To avoid clumsy and irritating repetition, we use the term 'school' throughout to cover both schools and colleges of further education, which were included in every scheme, except where there are relevant distinctions to be made.

CHAPTER 2

The constitution of TVEI

The Technical and Vocational Education Initiative, originally known as the N (New) TVEI was announced by the Prime Minister, Margaret Thatcher, in the House of Commons on 12 November 1982. She announced that 'in response to growing concern about existing arrangements for technical and vocational education for young people expressed over many years, not least by the National Economic Development Council', she had asked 'the chairman of the Manpower Services Commission [MSC] together with the Secretaries of State for Education and Science, for Employment, and for Wales, to develop a pilot scheme to start by September 1983, for new institutional arrangements for technical and vocational education for 14–18-year-olds, within existing financial resources, and, where possible, in association with local authorities.'

That announcement came like a bolt from the blue to all the most directly interested parties. Neither the DES, the LEA associations, the teacher professional organizations, nor even the MSC had been consulted before the announcement was made. It created an enormous furore not only by the manner of its delivery but also by what it appeared to threaten. The reference to 'new institutional arrangements', and to collaboration with local authorities 'where possible', gave rise to considerable fears that a new kind of institution was intended – or rather that something like the old technical school was to be revived. There were some grounds for these fears. David Young (then chair of the MSC, and together with Sir Keith Joseph and Norman Tebbit credited with producing the original plan) made it clear that the MSC were in the last resort (if LEAs did not cooperate in the scheme) prepared to set up their own schools, which he thought might even be called 'Young' schools (*Education*, 26 November, 1982).

However, local authority resistance crumbled very rapidly (though complaints about lack of consultation continued) and their collaboration in the scheme was assured with Mr Young's announcement that the membership of the National

Steering Group to be set up to run the initiative 'would reflect the key part the education service would play in the pilot projects' (*Education* 1982).

The TVEI scheme emerged as:

> a pilot scheme; within the education system; for young people of both sexes; across the ability range; voluntary. Each project must provide a full-time programme; offer a progressive four-year course combining general with technical and vocational education; commence at 14 years; be broadly based; include planned work experience; lead to nationally recognised qualifications. Each project and the initiative as a whole must be carefully monitored and evaluated. The purpose of the scheme is to explore and test ways of organizing and managing readily replicable programmes of technical and vocational education for young people across the ability range (MSC, 1984a).

In his letter to all education authorities in England and Wales, inviting them to submit applications, David Young amplified this framework by indicating that the general objective was to:

> widen and enrich the curriculum in a way that will help young people prepare for the world of work, and to develop skills and interests, including creative abilities, that will help them to lead a fuller life and to be able to contribute more to the life of the community.

Secondly, he suggested that:

> we are in the business of helping students to "learn to learn". In a time of rapid technological change, the extent to which particular occupational skills are required will change. What is important about this initiative is that youngsters should receive an education which will enable them to adapt to the changing occupational environment.

Its unique, secret and personal origins make it difficult to point with any conviction of accuracy to the sources and diagnosis that lay behind the TVEI proposal. Nevertheless, it is possible to infer a good deal about that diagnosis. It has two main elements. One is that what is taught in schools has to be changed. The other is that the process of changing what is taught in schools has itself to be changed. Both these elements were central to the 'Great Debate' on education of 1977, and they remained important, though not exclusive, components of the diagnosis which 5 years later produced the TVEI.

If that debate itself was a watershed in the post-war history of English education, it was because the settlements enshrined in the 1944 Education Act were beginning to breakdown. Central to that debate were the very questions about the purpose and control of education which were still there for TVEI to tackle some years later (and which originally only showed signs of resolution in the 1988 Education Reform Act: see Dale, 1989[1], esp. ch. 7). Deriving from this breakdown, the three themes of standards, accountability and economic reponsiveness dominated the education debates of the late 1970s, and produced a responding flurry of action and rhetoric. The initial responses were guided by the perceived need for the DES to take greater control over the education system. LEAs were required to provide information about their arrangements for the management of the curriculum to the DES, who on the basis of responses received, announced that they would move towards creating a national framework for the curriculum. This heralded a spate of papers from Her Majesty's Inspectorate (HMI) and the DES on the curriculum that continued through the rest of the Callaghan government and the early years of the Thatcher government (for details of these papers, see Fowler, 1988). Significantly, however, these documents contained little, if anything, to suggest a more vocational orientation to the curriculum. Rather, they were concerned to establish a core curriculum entitlement for all pupils, which would include a technological/vocational element as a necessary part of a balanced education, no different in kind from any other. That is to say, these documents represented a refinement of existing traditions and a will for increased central control rather than a major reorientation of the curriculum. Indeed, the DES resisted pressure towards linking 16–19 education more closely to economic needs. As Ted Wragg (1986: 11,12) reports on the basis of his work as specialist Adviser to the Parliamentary Select Committee on Education in 1976:

> the DES seemed singularly unenthusiastic about most aspects of the 16–19 school-to-work debate . . . [their] attitude seemed to be: profess ignorance about the whole thing, mention a ludicrously long time scale like 20 years, talk in telephone numbers about the cost and with luck the whole issue will waft away on the next breeze.

The other facet of the process of installing central control over the education system was to increase control by means of the enhanced accountability of the teaching profession. The influence of the teaching profession over what went on in education had already begun to decline before the institution of the Great Debate, under the influence of falling school rolls (and consequent loss of union 'muscle'), the ideological onslaught on the alleged consequences of a teacher-dominated system, encapsulated in the Black Papers, and a general feeling of dissatisfaction that education had failed to deliver what it had promised, socially, politically and economically, and for which it had claimed ever-growing funds. In particular, the education system had at the very least done little to forestall or inhibit the country's economic decline. And this apparent failure of the education system was laid very much at the door of the teachers, especially following the William Tyndale affair, which led to teachers being identified as the major culprits in this situation. This was possible in large part because of the 'licensed autonomy' which gave them great influence over the kinds of changes that should take place in the education system (see Dale, 1989, ch. 8).

A clear recognition of the perceived need to curtail 'teacher power' was inscribed in the very format of the Great Debate. As Bates *et al.* (1984: 199) puts it:

> the Great Debate reflected a trend towards defining and limiting the boundaries of teacher autonomy. The very initiation of a public debate on education, involving the unprecedented consultation of industrial organizations and parents as well as educational organizations, served as an explicit reminder to the teaching profession that the curriculum was not solely their responsibility to determine. . . . Thus the Great Debate, irrespective of its content, simply as a means of intervening in education helped to change the political context in which educational issues were discussed.

That teachers' licensed autonomy affected not only the process of educational change, but also its content was a central theme of the Great Debate. A clear tension was discerned there between teachers' professional interest and the interests of the wider society, and especially of industry. This professional interest led to an over-emphasis on the academic and a matching neglect of the vocational aspect of schooling.

The argument that it is essential to change this emphasis, and the stress on the 'need' to bring education and industry closer together, to attach the former more closely to the needs of the latter has, of course, been the object of a 'recurrent debate' (Reeder, 1979) in English education over the course of this century. This is not the place to go through that debate, which is discussed in Chapter 3 and developed more fully in Reeder (1979) and Esland and Cathcart (1981), while useful accounts of American experience which suggests that education is called in to solve a range of social and economic problems, are given in Grubb and Lazerson (1981) and McGowan and Cohen (1977).

Beck has convincingly argued that through the second half of the 1970s, industry's contribution to this recurrent debate took a dual form. On the one hand, larger employers and, significantly, the Department of Industry were putting forward the criticism that the education system's longstanding academic bias 'had played a major part in creating and maintaining the situation in which wealth creation, the profit motive and engineering were accorded less status in Britain than in most other manufacturing countries' (Beck, 1983: 221). On the other hand, a campaign against alleged declining standards and discipline, generated mainly in the press, pointed to the negative consequences for pupils' attitudes to work and authority of progressive teaching methods, teacher autonomy and certain aspects of comprehensive reorganization.

However, it was quite clear that it was not enough merely to advise, counsel and tinker. Stripped of its academic bias, the education system would not automatically revert to some pristine 'economy-friendly' state; a positive alternative was required. This alternative, heavily implicit in the Great Debate, and explicit before and after it, remained the reorientation of education in more vocationally relevant directions.

At least two other factors led to the need for its supplementation. First of all, though the diagnosis was at least superficially clear, very little had happened between 1977 and 1982 to shift schools in the required direction; many of the criticisms contained in the Great Debate and Green Paper still held good. Secondly, over that period there had been a quite dramatic increase in youth unemployment, as well as continuing expansion of 'high-tech' industry. Both these factors were incorporated into the diagnosis which we can infer underlay TVEI.

While most of the elements of the diagnosis which produced TVEI were common currency, they had had rather little impact on the education system. Privately sponsored programmes like Project Trident, which concentrated on providing work experience for school pupils, and Young Enterprise, which aimed to show them how business worked, had had some impact (see Jamieson, 1986), but neither they nor any more official efforts seemed likely to bring about the kind of redirection of the education system called for in the Great Debate and Green Paper.

There are a number of reasons for this. Among the more important are:

1 The DES's constitutional position prevented it from making central interventions in the school curriculum. It had therefore to rely on what it could achieve by means of advice, persuasion and whatever pressure it could bring to bear.

2 The funding base of schools made them less vulnerable to the kind of incursions that the MSC had been able to make into the curriculum and structure of colleges of further education.
3 It is by no means certain that the DES's own field representatives and organic intellectuals, the HMI, were convinced either of the correctness of the diagnosis or of the value and appropriateness for schools of the approaches contained within MSC youth programmes.
4 The schools and teachers had always quite explicitly opposed attempts to divert them in a more employment-related direction. They, too, did not accept the diagnosis, which they felt made them scapegoats for the nation's economic decline.

Thus, while the problem of the kind of education required by the diagnosis outlined above was being taken seriously, and a range of possible solutions was available, the problem of school, teacher and education system autonomy and accountability remained. There was not in the existing framework a way of reorienting schools in the desired direction. That is why the MSC had to be given the job of delivering TVEI. The failure to move education in a more vocationally relevant direction was not only due to a lack of enthusiasm on the part of the DES and education professionals. It was due, more fundamentally, to the mode of political rationality its constitutional position symbolized. For even if radical change had occurred, it was by no means sufficient to achieve even the reorientation of education implied by the Great Debate, let alone the new targets set for it by an increasingly confident and increasingly dominant and coherent brand of Thatcherite Conservative policies. And the reason for this lay not in the abilities or the motivations of the politicians, but in the relationship between education and politics; the radical educational message could not be delivered through existing political forms and modes of political rationality. The kernel of the argument is that up to 1984, and specifically the introduction of TVEI, Conservative governments had effectively been attempting to implement policies with a supply side (structural mode of political rationality) bias, through the medium of a system still largely following a conjunctural mode of rationality that had grown up alongside the demand-led education system of at least 30 of the previous 40 years. This distinction is summed up by Claus Offe (1981: 127) as follows:

> Conjunctural policies would seek to maximize the adequacy of policy *reponses* to problems as they emerge and appear on the agenda; the concomitant expectation is that such problems and demands will remain within a range of manageability defined by existing capacities of state action and their continuing improvement. Structural policies, in contrast, become the predominant mode of intervention as soon as this expectation is no longer supported by experience. They are adopted in response to conditions of economic and institutional crisis. In response to such crises, the physical and economic parameters of production and the institutional parameters of interest representation, which together constitute the nature of the problem, become subject to redesign. The shift is from policy output and economic demand management to the shaping of political input and economic supply – from 'state intervention' to 'politicization'.

The MSC was very clearly much more in tune with a structural mode of political rationality and supply side politics than the DES, and indeed it might be argued that

TVEI, set up and run in the schools by MSC, symbolized and heralded the replacement of a conjunctural with a structural mode of rationality in the politics of education. It centralized control over the allocation of resources and the recognition of demands, and directed them to clear politically, rather than professionally, selected targets. TVEI's most important feature in this context is the 'bid and contract' system of 'categorical funding', which TVEI extensively piloted. Under this system, central government made resources available for specified purposes, and invited LEAs to submit detailed bids for these resources. The bids then became the basis of a contract between central government and the LEA. It is worth noting here that though the DES was traditionally reluctant to embrace anything like a structural mode of political rationality under Sir Keith Joseph, it took some distinct steps in that direction and, following the success of TVEI as a funding mechanism, has adopted the bid-contract system for the whole of its financing of in-service education of teachers.

Of course, there is a long history of attempts to bring education more closely into line with the apparent requirements of the economy. The roots of the efforts to reconcile 'secondary' and 'technical' education, and the consequences of the failure to do so, have been very well charted by McCulloch (1986; McCulloch *et al.*, 1985). As he puts it:

> TVEI might be interpreted as in the tradition of the Bryce Report of 1895, the Spens Report of 1938, and the Crowther Report of 1959. All sought to reconcile technical with secondary education by stimulating a distinct kind of "secondary technical education" (McCulloch, 1986: 40).

However, 'reconciliation' of these two strands of education has rather more limited connotations than those we wish to suggest are associated with the kind of hybrid TVEI represents. It is not so much a question of the reconciliation of these two separate strands of secondary education as of the different assumptions held in the two contributing traditions about what it is assumed a public education service should be, and is capable of, doing, i.e. assumptions about the *mandate* for the education system and about its *capacity* fulfil that mandate. We want now briefly to compare MSC and DES assumptions about the scope of education policy and the consequences of their hybridization in TVEI.

Over the past 10 years, the dominant mandate has been that contained in the 1976 Green Paper, *Education in Schools*. This document both prefigured and required the kind of hybridization of education-training for employment whose culmination is TVEI. Essentially, that mandate called for a much greater emphasis on the preparation of workers and citizens than on the development of individual talents.

This was a mandate for the education service prepared within the education service, albeit with unprecedentedly extensive and unprecedentedly welcome input from outside the education service. The MSC, then a relatively small organization, was not a significant factor in drawing up the mandate nor in the plans for its fulfilment. However, MSC was at that time beginning to work in adjacent areas, and there is considerable overlap between the *Education in Schools* mandate for education and MSC's developing approaches to the problems of training and youth employment. The Holland Committee, for instance, recommended the creation of the Youth Opportunities Programme to guarantee some form of work experience to all unemployed school leavers.

Thus, there is clear overlap in the mandates of the two organizations in respect of the education and training of young people. There are, though, distinct differences in their capacity to fulfil this mandate. This applies not just to the broad, overall conception of 'vocational education', but also to such issues within it as gender equality, the management of the curriculum and teachers' careers.

There are, then, crucial differences between (and within) the political and administrative discourses of DES and MSC. The nature and consequences of these differences can be clarified by examining the two bodies' respective conceptualizations of the scope of a public education service.

Though there is some overlap in the education and training mandates of the DES and MSC, there are very important differences of interpretation and emphasis between the DES and MSC. These differences have two, linked bases. The first lies in the different traditions of which they are part. In giving reasons why the MSC's work 'is still largely separate from that of the DES and the local authorities that maintain schools and employ teachers', William Taylor (1985: 109) lists the following:

> Administratively, training has been linked with employment rather than education. Politically, governments have been somewhat less than satisfied with the way secondary schools have dealt with their older age groups. Financially, it has been difficult to earmark for particular purposes the funds made available to local authorities. But more fundamentally, the separation reflects the way in which history, economic circumstances and social structures have given us a heritage of values, attitudes and assumptions that constitute education and training as two separate metaphors, a heritage which continues to influence our thought and our practice.
>
> It is not difficult to identify the values conventionally associated with these two metaphors. Education is often depicted as soft, person-centred, moralized, academic, critical, contemplative, radical in attitude but traditional in form, theoretical, norm-referenced, enclosed, a consumption good rather than an investment. In contrast, training is represented as hard, task-centred, materialistic, practical, oriented towards action, criterion-referenced, pragmatic, innovative in structure but conservative in substance, unselective, open, a valuable national investment.

The second basis of the difference of interpretation and emphasis is the 'policy obligations' of the DES and MSC. These are perhaps best set out in the lists of objectives of the Department of Employment and of the DES which appear, symbolically, on the inside front and back covers, respectively, of the *Working Together* White Paper. For instance, while the DES is *obliged* to 'ensure a broad and balanced curriculum for all pupils', the DE(MSC) is not – though that is not to say that in its forays into education it will not seek to do so, as it claims to have done with TVEI. Similarly, it is not an obligation, let alone a prime aim, for the DES to encourage the development of an enterprise economy – though again it *may* choose to meet its aims in part by doing so. The main relevant difference between the two departments for our present purpose is that while the DES is obliged to pursue all three broad targets for education, the MSC is not; while education is an end in itself for the DES, for the MSC it can only be a means to achieving its (MSC's) own objectives. We are not suggesting either that every action of the MSC and DES can be directly related to their policy obligations, or that either of them are entirely monolithic (we know that neither is), merely that they are subject to different fundamental pressures.

To return to the mandate contained in the 1976 Green Paper; its fulfilment provided two major problems for the education system. The first was that the system itself was identified in the Green Paper as one of the obstacles to the mandate's fulfilment. The degree of autonomy of the education system, schools and teachers, and the ways that autonomy was alleged to have been used, made the system as much part of the problem the new mandate addressed, as the key means of fulfilling it. The mandate indeed implied not only changes in the orientation of education policy, but changes in the way it was formulated and implemented too – not only changes in the content and purpose of education but also in the way those changes were devised and introduced into the system.

The formulation and implementation of policy – in particular, the inability of the DES to institute system-wide change – comprised the second major problem. The DES was not able to compel compliance, only to persuade and pressure in various ways (Ranson, 1985). It was this inability to fulfil the 1976 Green Paper mandate – together with massive rises in youth unemployment – which brought MSC, via Prime Ministerial initiative, into the educational system at school level for the first time in 1983.

There are perhaps even greater potential differences between the DES and MSC in terms of their capacity and *modus operandi* than there are in their traditions and policy obligations. In understanding TVEI, differences between the DES and MSC in this area – and the way they are hybridized – are at least as important as differences in interpretation of the mandate. The capacity and *modus operandi* of the DES and MSC differ significantly in a number of ways.

1 The DES is a Department of State headed by a Cabinet Minister politically accountable through Parliament to the *electorate*. It operates according to a structured, bureaucratic rule-following model. The MSC, on the other hand, is a corporate body, made up of people representing particular *interests*, particularly the two sides of industry. This means both that MSC is a coalition of potentially competing interests, and that any decisions and actions it takes can be assumed already to have the approval of those they affect (in so far as they are represented on the Commission); those actions and decisions do not have to go through further consultative, participative discussion stages – which is one of the reasons that the MSC is able to act much more quickly than the DES:

> MSC . . . is no advisory body, but a public board charged with executive responsibilities. . . . When a commissioner commits himself/herself to a particular programme, policy, or line of action, he/she is also committing many more people and organizations

> in the world outside. This commitment . . . is the key reason why so many far-reaching developments have taken place so quickly under the Commission's auspices (Holland, 1986: 88).

2 The MSC's operating model differs from the DES's. Rather than being bureaucratic and process-orientated, it is technocratic or even commercial. For the MSC, achieving results is the criterion of action, while the DES is bound by the need for accurate rule-following. The DES can only bring about major change by changing the rules, i.e. by introducing legislation; for the MSC it is a much more straightforward matter of changing the substance in the most immediately effective way.

3 Until relatively recently, it had been assumed that the DES could only operate through the local education authorities, whom it could not in any case compel to follow a particular path; perhaps the best known example of this is the failure of Shirley Williams as Secretary of State at the DES to get local authorities to spend, for the State's purposes, the £7 million she had earmarked for in-service training.

4 Certainly, in the education area, MSC has operated more like a firebrigade than a police force. It is essentially a crisis-management organization. It could withdraw altogether from education and has no built-in continuing commitment to the area. Thus not only is it able to introduce different kinds of programmes, it is also able to do so less hampered by the ramifications they may have for the rest of the service or by the need to continue supporting them if they appear initially to be unsuccessful.

5 Associated with this is the different pattern of funding available to the two bodies. The MSC's funds are for particular programmes, typically contracted for by providing agencies on terms laid down by the MSC. Its budget is not immutably tied up in continuing financial obligations which take up almost all its resources, unlike the DES, with its major commitments in the area of school building and higher education, for instance. The DES has, then, been financially as well as constitutionally restricted in the kind of intervention it could make in the education service.

6 A further financial difference is that the DES needs (from the Secretary of State) approval *before* committing expenditure, whereas the MSC is accountable only *after* spending the money. The corollary of this, however, is that the MSC has to do far more monitoring, auditing, etc., of projects *after* they are set up (and this has been a major source of irritation to teachers and schools in TVEI).

7 The MSC is much more likely to intervene from the supply-side, whereas the DES's tradition has been much more demand-led funding. The MSC provides funds whose levels are known beforehand for specified programmes aimed at identified objectives, and subject to monitoring. The DES has traditionally been much more reactive (within its constitutional limits), responding to pressures and suggestions within the education system, rather than using fully what powers it had to steer the system.

8 Another difference in the mode of intervention lies in the source of the resources used. Though this is beginning to break down, certainly informally, DES assumptions have traditionally been that state education will be wholly state-funded.

MSC assumptions are quite different, and deliberately so. Efficiency of performance and cost-cutting through competition are much more important in determining which bodies will carry out the work than a commitment to state provision.

9 These various constitutional and financial differences combine in the different types of activity and intervention the two bodies make. This difference can be summarized as the difference between what Claus Offe calls 'allocative' and 'productive' types of state activity, and it is worth expanding on the distinction a little. Offe's distinction is usefully summarized by Jessop (1982: 110–11):

> Allocation involves the use of state resources to secure the general framework of economic activity and/or to provide general public services in accordance with general constitutional or legislative codes which effect the prevailing balance of political forces. Production involves direct state-sponsored provision of material resources as a precondition of crisis-avoidance or crisis management where there is no general code that can be applied and decision rules must therefore be developed in order to determine more effective action by case. Offe then argues that, although rational-legal bureaucratic administration may be appropriate to the allocative activities of the state, it is inadequate to the demands of state productive activities in so far as they are oriented to the attainment of particular objectives rather than the general application of pregiven rules.

This distinction encapsulates much of the difference between the DES and the MSC, and the ramifications of MSC sponsorship, in terms of substance, style, purpose and method, that mark TVEI as a form of education policy at least as effectively as the funds it provides.

What, though, did TVEI amount to in practice? What numbers of schools, pupils, LEAs were involved, and just what did their bounty amount to? A total of 66 LEAs applied to be included in the project and 14 were chosen (the originally planned number was enlarged to ensure better geographical coverage). A central feature of the scheme is that these authorities then signed contracts with the MSC for the delivery of the project outlined in their application. These projects were all drawn up to match the guidelines contained in David Young's letter, but they differed considerably from each other in philosophy, numbers of schools involved (though most schemes included between five and eight schools and colleges of further education) and the number of pupils to be involved (though the funding basis assumed five annual cohorts of 250 pupils per authority). Some of these differences and their implications are elaborated more fully below. Each local project is responsible to a local steering group made up of representatives of both sides of industry, educational interests, voluntary organizations, and so on. The steering groups report to the TVEI Unit in the MSC and to the local authority.

Twice as many Conservative as Labour authorities applied: some Labour authorities refused to submit bids on the grounds that the scheme would both be divisive by reintroducing some form of selection into comprehensive education, and have a narrowing, excessively vocationalizing effect on the curriculum. These were the dominant criticisms of the TVEI scheme throughout its history. At first, the pilot nature of the scheme received a great deal of emphasis. Critics in the House of

Commons (where questions on TVEI were answered by both the Employment and Education ministers) and elsewhere, were typically told not to become too anxious or worried about what was after all only a small pilot scheme. And yet, scarcely 3 months after the announcement of the first group of pilot LEAs and before the projects had started, it was announced that the scheme would be extended, with another £20 million in addition to the original £7 million available to bring in another 40 or so LEAs in September 1984 (in the end, 48 more authorities – including 5 in Scotland – were accepted). And then, in October 1984, a further extension to the scheme was announced to start in September 1985. A further 12 LEAs took up TVEI then, and in a fourth round 29 more (including one deferred start) were added. The announcement of the extension brought in the remainder of the LEAs. All of the schemes in the second and subsequent rounds received funding of £2 million spread over 5 years, compared with the £51.5 million shared by the 14 originally successful applicants. The LEAs tended to spend the greatest proportion (60%) of their funds on extra staff, with around 25% on new equipment and buildings, and the remainder on the administration of the schools.

TVEI did not follow any of the three main routes of bringing about major educational change in Britain, either in the nature of its aims or in its methods. It was neither a programme drawn up by and in consultation with practising educators, aimed at improving the content and/or delivery of (parts of) the school curriculum (the Schools Council model); nor did it follow the Plowden Advisory Committee model, where representatives of a wide range of appropriate interests join with the 'great and the good' to scrutinize and recommend a series of more or less major changes; nor did it follow the model of legislative change, which encouraged comprehensive schooling, for instance, or raised the school-leaving age. Rather, it might be argued, it followed a business or commercial model, moving resources into a new 'line' when the existing one was proving ineffective. At the centre of its aims was improving the service to a particular group of customers, clients and consumers – it did not seek to improve the service to those already seen as (too) well catered for. Its mode of operation was executive rather than legislative or advisory. And it was singularly unencumbered either by the professional experts, or by the 'great and the good' – there are no latter-day Lords Vaizey or (Michael) Young in TVEI.

TVEI, then, was a political intervention, in the sense that it was introduced into the educational system from outside, albeit with the acquiescence or even encouragement of the Secretary of State for Education (though without even the knowledge of his department officials, or any other part of the educational apparatus, national or local). Though in the end the cooperation of the LEAs was secured – at least to the extent of making themselves contractually accountable for disposing of very large sums of money for specified purposes, it is clear from David Young's comments that the scheme would have been introduced anyway (though whether it could have succeeded without the cooperation of the education service is a matter of fascinating, if now futile, debate).

The final crucial feature of the constitution of TVEI we want to refer to is its size and scope. It now involves all of the education authorities in the country and provides unprecendentedly large amounts of money for those involved. Its objective was not merely the improvement or updating of a particular aspect of the school curriculum – although this is undoubtedly part of its intention – but the redirection and restructuring of the school experiences of a large proportion of pupils. This redirecting and restructuring was aimed at bringing schools into a closer relationship with the world outside them, especially, though not exclusively, 'the world of work'. This involved making 'the vocational' rather than 'the academic' the central purpose and criterion of what a considerable proportion of children learn in school. In both these aspects, then, its extra-educational, political origins, and its funding and ambitions, TVEI was quite unlike any curriculum innovation we have seen in this country before.

TVEI also differed from what has gone before in the pattern, process and pace of curriculum change it involved. It represented an obvious and deliberate break with the essentially incremental, apparently haphazard, pattern which had typified educational change. It represented as much a break with, as continual with, existing provision, seeking to renew or even replace it as much as building on it. Its size and its ambitions also pushed it towards being comprehensive rather than piecemeal.

The accepted pattern was challenged, too, through its operation at the margins of the school, both financially and educationally. That is to say, TVEI gained maximum 'bang for a buck' from all its funding being devoted to additional items, and none of it to the continuing basic cost of running the school, which accounted for nearly all the funding it received, leaving very little available for 'development'. Educationally, its funding and the conditions attaching to it meant that, at least formally, the school had to adjust to the innovation rather than the other way round.

The process of change was not wholly dependent on persuasion and the marshalling of voluntary effort in the schools involved. LEAs and schools were contractually accountable for implementing the changes they proposed to introduce. They had to be able to demonstrate that the material and human resources they had bought with TVEI money were being used, at least preferentially, with the pupils, and for the purposes specified in the contract. A second major difference was that formal authority for the direction of the project was vested not in the schools, the LEA or the MSC alone, but in the local steering group (on which, of course, all three parties were represented, along with both sides of industry). A third difference was that the projects were also monitored by members of an advisory team within the TVEI Unit. Finally, TVEI was introduced at quite unprecedented speed. Scarcely 9 months after the first, entirely unheralded announcement, the scheme was operating in 14 LEAs, who had had 2 months to prepare their applications and who learned that they had been successful barely a term before the programmes had to start. The pace hardly relaxed throughout the pilot phase, certainly in the schools, as the implications of very rapid decisions became transformed into timetable, resource, administrative and pedagogic problems, all requiring almost immediate responses.

Note

[1] This chapter draws heavily on material in Dale (1989).

CHAPTER 3

TVEI, education and industry

Introduction

TVEI emerged against the background of prolonged debate about the relationship between education and the economy. An influential current within that debate presents the view that to a major extent Britain's economic decline and the more immediate problems of youth unemployment could be attributed to failures within the educational system. TVEI can be seen as representing a particular type of response to the issues posed by such an analysis. The purpose of this chapter is to examine TVEI within the context of this wider debate and to explore the ways in which it might be seen as addressing the issues it defines.

The criticisms commonly made of education can be summarized as follows:

1 The educational system in this country has been dominated by a tradition of liberal education which has tended to be hostile to industry and commerce and to the practical application of knowledge. This has had the effect of deflecting the more academically able away from careers in industry, of stressing 'pure' rather than applied knowledge, of giving priority to the humanities over the sciences and technical subjects and of failing to prepare adequately the majority of pupils for 'the world of work'.
2 This approach to education has been supported conceptually by the ideas of philosophers such as Peters, Hirst and Dearden (often referred to collectively as 'the London School') who stress the *intrinsic* and non-instrumental value of education as a good in its own right. This view proposes a strong distinction between education and training and is, consequently, antithetical to *vocationalism* in education. Teachers who receive this view in their training tend to reject the idea that priority should be given to preparing pupils for working life. Indeed, it is

often argued, they might even see their role as opposing the narrowly instrumental and materialistic preoccupations of the industrial and commercial worlds. Such an approach is often associated with the influence of Leavisite ideas in the English curriculum or with 'child-centred' progressivism. In this, the teaching profession is seen as being profoundly out of line with the largely instrumentalist and pragmatic concerns of the great majority of pupils, parents and employers.

3 These 'liberal-humanist' values not only prejudice teachers against industry but promote 'the wrong attitudes' in young people. In general terms, the arts and humanities are given higher prestige than sciences, and even within science itself, pure research and 'the pursuit of knowledge' for its own sake is valued over and above practical application. An effect of this has been to encourage the 'drift away from science' in university applications. At the other end of the academic hierarchy, young people are not encouraged to develop the attitudes and disciplines required in work. They are unwilling to accept the routines and authority of 'the world of work' and do not acquire the basic skills which employers demand. In this way, the educational system has failed to deliver the skills that industry requires to remain internationally competitive.

4 This stress upon the 'intrinsic' value of education has been reflected, on the one hand, in the domination of the traditional academic curriculum by the requirements of university entrance and the priorities of academics concerned with 'the logic of the discipline' and, on the other, in 'child-centred', progressive preoccupations with 'self-expression' or the realization of 'inner potential'. In both these senses, the learning process itself has been divorced from the kinds of practical activities typical of 'the real world'. Hence the divisions represented in the curriculum have been reinforced by both traditional and progressive pedagogies.

5 The effects of liberal-humanist values and the more general ethos of the culture of education have been reinforced and effectively sustained by the relative independence of the educational system, the system of teacher training and the teaching profession. This has been most pronounced and, it is argued, most damaging, in the tradition of professional control over the 'secret garden' of the curriculum. Hence these cultural factors have been underpinned by institutional arrangements. These have rendered the DES relatively ineffective in imposing change on the system and prevented education from being employed as an instrument of government policy (e.g. in attempting to meet the problems of the economy by improving the supply of skilled workers).

Hence the criticisms of education have focused upon what is seen to be an unhealthy reinforcement of cultural prejudices by institutional arrangements which have had the effect of insulating teachers from the demands of parents and the requirements of government and the economy. The profession is seen as having had for far too long the freedom to indulge its idiosyncracies with relative impunity. Hence the need to bring about change in *what* teachers do, in what they teach and how they teach it, has come to be seen as a problem of how teachers as a profession are controlled.[1] Changes in institutional arrangements, especially in the relationship between schools and the central state, have become identified as the precondition for changes in curriculum and pedagogy. Such changes are represented in the more general reforms associated with the Educational Reform Act.[2]

The longstanding concern that education should be more responsive to the needs of the economy (expressed, for instance, in James Callaghan's Great Debate of the late 1970s), has been sharpened by the consumerist and supply-side emphases of Thatcherism. The major change which has occurred since the Great Debate has been the radical rejection of the claims of 'professionalism' and the ascendency of the view that they reflect no more than producer self-interest working against the interests of consumers (or 'clients'). Hence the increasing power of the central state over LEAs and the teaching profession, is being underwritten by increasing control by 'lay' groups such as parents and employers. The State and the Market (supported by the increasingly repressive and authoritarian climate generated by the right-wing press) are, between them, depriving the teaching profession and professional educationalists of what had been seen as their traditional prerogatives of determining the character of education.

In these terms, TVEI can be seen as a model for bringing about a complex set of interrelated changes.

1 It explicitly set out to change traditional academic hierarchies by shifting scientific and technical subjects to the centre of the curriculum. This is reflected in the practical support given to raise the status of areas such as CDT.
2 It directly related content to 'the world of work' and to the actual skill requirements of industry.
3 It promoted an experiential pedagogy which, it was believed, more accurately reflected the kinds of practical applications and problem-solving situations to be found in 'the real world'.
4 It significantly restricted the professional independence of teachers through its general administration by the MSC, through the strictures of the bid/contract system and by introducing employers into the management structure (e.g. in Project steering committees).
5 It attempted to develop 'appropriate' attitudes and values in young people by promoting 'enterprise values' through supporting areas such as business studies and activities such as mini-enterprise schemes.

In the same way that 'the problem' of education is seen in terms of the relationship between values, educational processes and institutional structures in the system at large, so TVEI, at the level of participating institutions, represented a 'solution' in terms of a restructuring of those factors. The mode of delivery was intrinsically connected with the form of curriculum and pedagogy. Essentially, the restructuring of the institutional arrangements of TVEI delivery can be seen as an experiment in a new way of enforcing prescribed curriculum change.

However, despite the internal coherence of this restructuring it is not the case that

TVEI resulted in a uniform and equally coherent pattern of curriculum change. Even within the relative rigours of the MSC delivery model, considerable scope emerged both for variety in the character of TVEI courses and for the maintenance of continuity with established liberal and progressive educational approaches. There are three major conditions which have contributed to this. These are elaborated elsewhere in the book but briefly they can be defined as follows:

1 Despite its genesis in the MSC and the strong influence of MSC thinking and practices, TVEI delivery has adopted a 'hybrid' form, i.e. it is an MSC programme *delivered* by LEAs.[3] Within the general framework of the bid/contract system, the MSC had to reconcile itself to the traditions and conditions of authority and school autonomy in the actual implementation of projects. Hence at a practical level, the form of their delivery remained negotiated rather than prescribed. The capacity of headteachers in particular to retain control over TVEI in their schools had been helped by MSC's own need to see TVEI succeed and an obvious reluctance to withdraw support for schemes which did not fully meet their criteria.
2 MSC's own version of experiential pedagogy (based in a behavioural objectives model of 'skill') and its stress upon 'relevance' and practical activities, resonated sufficiently with established progressive currents in secondary teaching (relating back to the raising of the school leaving age, the Schools Council and Newsom) for teachers to be able to 'recontextualize' TVEI within a familiar form of educational discourse. In this way, an 'educationalist' version of TVEI was constructed which in certain respects reproduced precisely those 'progressive' tendencies which the current reforms were aimed at eliminating.
3 In practice, the 'vocationalization' of schooling in TVEI was attenuated by the real problems of integrating educational practices with 'the needs of industry' at the local level. This reflects a number of factors, including the perennial problem of getting employers to specify what their needs actually *are*, their well-documented educational conservatism and a frequently expressed view that education is the job of the teachers and they don't really want to get involved anyway.[4]

The third of these raises a fundamental issue; namely, how far the MSC in fact either represents or can accurately reflect the views and interests of employers or (more abstractly) 'the needs of industry'. Underpinning this is the prior status of the kind of analysis of Britain's economic problems and more specific assumptions about education/economy linkage which MSC represents. To some degree, the failure to effectively realize the 'pure' TVEI model at the local level could be taken as indicative of the limitations of the initial analysis.

More specifically, TVEI can be seen as focusing the problem of curriculum change in terms of how control of the process can be taken out of the hands of professional educationalists. It provides a model of the kinds of institutional restructuring required to redefine teachers as simply the delivery agents rather than the controllers of educational change. At the same time, it can be seen as illustrating the limitations of this process and, in this sense, may have implications for a wider understanding of the effects of the Educational Reform Act.

We will now explore these issues in greater depth.

Curriculum change and the crisis of liberal education

As Reeder (1979), for instance, has pointed out, the debate about education and industry has a long history. Over the past 150 years, alleged failures of education are periodically invoked as explanations of national failure in economic affairs (or problems encountered in war). It may be that the present form of this debate has a new dimension in that it is strongly associated with a set of reforms which in large part set out precisely to remedy the deficiencies as currently defined. Although there has been a tendency to concentrate upon specifically 'educational' factors in the current debate, some writers have identified a broader and more deeply rooted malaise.

A particularly influential account of 'the problem' has been provided by the American historian Martin Wiener (1981). Essentially, Wiener identifies a widespread anti-industrialism and nostalgic ruralism within English culture as being responsible for 'the decline of the industrial spirit' which initially supported Britain's rise to industrial leadership. Although strongly implicating education in the inculcation of these anti-industrial values, Wiener himself does not write at length on education.

Mathieson and Bernbaum (1988) have related current vocationalist reforms to this wider perspective. They argue that any analysis which focuses too exclusively upon education is bound to be too restricted. The problems within education need to be explicated in terms of more general features of English culture and the structural interconnections between education and other social institutions. This is essential if reforms are to succeed:

> For over the last hundred years there have been intermittent periods of critical analysis which have drawn attention to the greater success of other nations' educational institutions in producing pupils and students who are well prepared to meet commercial, industrial and scientific needs . . . the relative failure of earlier critics to introduce effective reforms cannot be ignored. Their failure stands as a monument to the outstanding success of the British education system in embodying and perpetuating the values of Britain's dominant elites. It should serve to instruct contemporary critics and reformers who ignore these longstanding, deep rooted structural features of British society which have been responsible for the development of the educational system. Too many past reforming efforts have failed because the educational system has been viewed as a discrete unit, whose personnel act independently of other institutional arrangements in society and are supposedly uninfluenced by the values of its elites (Mathieson and Bernbaum, 1988: 127).

Hence, it is necessary to explicate the more detailed linkages between education and the wider cultural and social context.

Mathieson and Bernbaum go on to explore these connections in terms of the nineteenth-century model of the Christian gentleman and Coleridgian concepts of a 'clerisy' based around notions of 'an essentially artistic, creative view of human spirit' (Mathieson and Bernbaum, 1988: 128). They develop the links between these ideas and the influence, for instance, of Leavisite views on the English curriculum, as represented by Peter Abbs and David Holbrook, and in child-centred progressivism.

Ahier (1988), however, has raised a number of critical objections to the implications of Wiener's thesis at this level. He points out that Wiener's approach depends upon an 'holistic' and essentialist view of 'national culture' or 'world view' (see Ahier, 1988: introduction). As with Mathieson and Bernbaum, precisely *how* these anti-industrial values of the elite come to permeate society as a whole remains mysterious or, at best, is simply attributed to some 'disproportionate influence' of the elite upon society at large. The thesis implies that what happens in education is simply an automatic effect of elite ideology. Ahier (1988: 4) suggests that:

> There is a naive view of the relations between state education, national culture and the elite from which the cultural values are said to descend. The presupposition of a consensual national culture and a 'seepage' theory of elite influence is obvious . . .

In the course of his argument, Ahier also points out that varieties of 'ruralism' and anti-industrialism are also evident in other countries, including the USA.

Hence the Wiener type argument can be seen as presenting a number of problems *given* what it is being used to explain. Following Ahier, these problems can be summarized as follows:

1 It assumes an overly consensual view of 'the national culture' based in an essentialist notion of 'world view'.
2 It ignores differences, tensions and contradictions within 'the national culture'.
3 It ignores other significant material factors such as *international* economic circumstances.
4 It operates with a simplistic model of cultural transmission and elite dominance.
5 It simplifies precisely those complex structural linkages that Mathieson and Bernbaum invoke in order to extend Wiener's argument. Indeed, it can be suggested that an awareness of structural *complexity* is exactly what Mathieson and Bernbaum's argument lacks.
6 It overstates the distinctiveness of English culture in this particular respect, ignoring both the existence of 'ruralism' in other societies and also the extent to which a Mandarin disdain for practical activities has been a pronounced attribute of elites of economically more successful nations, e.g. Germany.[5] There is, in fact, a certain irony in observing how our major continental competitors have so often disparaged the British as 'a nation of shopkeepers'.
7 It could also be added that an additional dimension to the problems of this position is the actual *success* of British science, e.g. in terms of Nobel prize winners, significant innovation, etc.

A central implication of Ahier's critique is that if we take up Mathieson and Bernbaum's argument and in fact explore the wider linkages between education and national culture, Wiener's thesis actually becomes increasingly vulnerable. At the same time, the status of the educational reforms for which this type of argument provides the rationale, are weakened rather than secured.

Change, the curriculum and the credential

Wiener's thesis, and analyses of that type, suggest that the problems of British education are in some way simply an automatic effect of an inappropriate elite ideology. Deeper considerations, however, indicate that this essentialist approach, with its holistic concept of 'national culture', obscures precisely the tensions and contradictions which actually require examination. The development of TVEI marks a radical and symptomatic change in the way in which educational change is to be managed in this country. In the manner of its conception and in the form of its delivery and control, it measures the distance travelled from the Great Debate.

Contrary to Wiener's implications, the major peculiarity of the Liberal tradition in English education has been its ability to preserve itself as the 'official' educational ideology *despite* the fact that no substantial group in society supported it. Evidence massively indicates that only a limited social group other than professional educators had anything other than a thoroughly 'instrumental' attitude to education. Even the 'cultural capital' of academic elitism was (and still is) employed by upper-class groups in a thoroughly utilitarian fashion. Liberal rhetoric, with its characteristic stress upon 'intrinsic' values and virtues, finds little response among students, their parents or prospective employers. In effect, the Great Debate provided no more than an opportunity to display to educators that they and virtually they alone had (to paraphrase Bourdieu) a liberal relationship to liberal education.

The view of the MSC as the barbarians at the gates of the Celestial City of education is a symptomatic reflex of liberal-humanist educators. The major problem for this group is that it has never secured a broad social support for its values on their own terms. Rather, there has been (and still persists) a more diffused popular sentiment that knowledge naturally comes in the shape of 'subjects' and that the grammar school represented the ideal type of education. What we have is a sentimental loyalty to the grammar school model in association with a thoroughly instrumentalist definition of the 'aims' of education, i.e. to get a good job. This instrumentalism, without commitment to basic values, has made liberal education particularly vulnerable to the crisis in its 'purchasing power' which has come about as a result of credential inflation and mass unemployment.

Lacking a real popular mandate, liberal education persisted largely by virtue of the DES's lack of *capacity* to enforce change effectively. The Great Debate essentially attempted to use a liberal device to impress upon educationalists both the need and the demand for a compromising of their fundamental values – to acknowledge not only that the vast majority of people saw education as a means to an end rather than as a 'good thing' in its own right, but also that education had a duty to respond to the needs of the economy.

Behind this was the imperative from the international monetary community that a nation in Britain's economic plight had to help itself by planned investment in its own human capital rather than continuing to allow the self-indulgent cultivation of the cultural capital of a protected liberal elite. The secret garden of the curriculum should be given over to the rapid production of cash crops. The basic problem for British education in the late 1970s was that liberal education was sustained by a combination of popular, but ritualistic, sentimental attachment to one of its 'forms' (the grammar school) and a set of institutional arrangements (between the DES and the LEAs) which prevented the Centre from effectively imposing changes which were a precondition for continued support of a failing economy from international monetary organizations.

This demand that education should be more effectively harnessed to meet the nation's economic needs reflected the influence of Human Capital Theory upon policy makers. As Gareth Williams (1985) has pointed out, Human Capital Theory provided an apparent resolution to the tensions implicit in the demand that a liberal educational system such as that in Britain take account of the needs of the economy. It proposed that education is a major contributor to economic growth, but it focused upon the general level of education in a population rather than upon its content. This view effectively left education in the hands of academics and educationalists while providing a utilitarian justification for funding and expansion. Nevertheless, the logic of the argument still created serious problems for liberal education, simply because it *did* provide a strong economic rationale. These problems took three main forms:

1 The argument for expansion, and for increasing the numbers of more highly qualified people, called into question the received form of traditional, academic liberal education. In the British context, this form was seen as narrowly academic, exclusive and restricted. Major reports, such as those by Robbins, Crowther and Newsom, can all be seen as attempting to reconcile a liberal view of education with the need to expand numbers to meet economic needs. With Newsom, this took the form of an appeal to 'relevance' and vocationalism was a central aspect of this. Within this perspective, vocationalism was perceived as a way of making education more relevant to the needs of non-academic pupils rather than, in the first place, to the needs of industry. Vocationalism was essentially a pedagogic device for reconciling pupils to extended schooling.

   Hence, despite its formal indifference to content, Human Capital Theory nevertheless exerted pressure for expansion which led to a critical questioning of the received form of liberal education. Essentially, this was posed as an issue of motivating non-academic pupils (e.g. by using vocationalism as a way of increasing 'relevance'), rather than as a direct response to the skill requirements of industry.

2 Expansion also had effects beyond the educational system itself. Increasing numbers of people with higher levels of qualifications led to credential inflation in the labour market and an associated decline in the 'purchasing' power of the credentials they possessed. Ironically, the increasing emphasis upon vocationalism was associated with declining instrumental returns to education. The appeal to a more popular instrumental mandate, combined with declining returns, gave

impetus to a developing crisis of legitimation and credibility for the liberal credential.[6]

3 The 1970s in particular saw an increasing demand from policy makers and politicians that education should address the needs of industry *directly*. This involves, as Williams suggests, a fundamental shift in emphasis from Human Capital Theory. He defines this as a move towards a 'Manpower Planning' approach. In this case, the *content* of education is of primary significance.

The distinction between Human Capital Theory and Manpower Planning is associated with that between 'vocationalism' and 'occupationalism'. The latter can be seen as concerned directly with preparation for particular types of work rather than with the broader aims of vocationalism, e.g. 'understanding industry', awareness of 'the world of work'. This movement undoubtedly makes sense in terms of a popular instrumentalist mandate. But it also implies (and must effectively entail) a substantive reconstruction of institutional arrangements because it demands control over the content of education.

Human Capital Theory allowed educationalists to define what should count as educational knowledge. Its content could be derived from academic disciplines, forms of knowledge or the developmental requirements of children. The manner in which the expansion of liberal education raised issues concerning its form shifted the centre of gravity from the disciplines (controlling the forms of knowledge) to educationalists concerned with curriculum and pedagogic developments which could effectively accommodate new categories of entrants to the upper secondary school. Manpower occupationalism, however, more radically still relocates educational knowledge within the technical/social and life skill requirements of industry. Most significantly, this redefines those who should be seen as the authoritative source of what should count as 'educational knowledge'. People other than academics or educationalists (employers, but also MSC officials) now come to be those who should say what children should learn.

Callaghan's 'invitation' to a Great Debate on Education was expressive of the social democratic rhetoric of consensus. But it also reflected the fact that, in reality, the kinds of changes in education which were being urged by the DES, under pressure from organizations such as the Organization for Economic Cooperation and Development (OECD) and the International Monetary Fund (IMF), could not be secured within the existing decentralized structure of LEA control over education. Callaghan's Debate can be seen as a strategy to amplify a mandate which already existed in society, but which educationalists, strongly committed to liberal precepts, were able to ignore as a result of the Centre's lack of capacity to enforce change.

Although the Great Debate and the 1977 Green Paper could place the needs of industry at the top of the agenda, the entire approach was still predicated upon the view that the liberal educational establishment needed to be – indeed had a *right* to be – persuaded of the need for change. In much the same way that major industrial relations issues were settled over beer and sandwiches in smoke-filled rooms, so major educational issues were to be settled over strawberries and cream picnics in the secret garden.

However amorphously perceived in electoral terms, Thatcherism has consistently taken for itself a popular mandate to suspend what had previously been seen as a distinctive feature of British political life – namely, the requirement to secure at least the semblance of a popular and professional consensus around innovation or change.

Within the New Right's market economic perspective, such a consensus is redefined as no more than professional self-interest working against the interest of the 'consumer'. The 'consumer', in this case, is both the parent *and* the national interest. Both are seen as 'deserving' causes against which the interests of professional educators are, at best, self-indulgence (e.g. in 'fringe subjects' or 'trendy experiments') or, at worst, self-serving opportunism. Rather than the professional community, it is now 'the national interest' which comes to constitute the 'consensus' which educators must appease – a consensus which can be defined either through definitions of economic interest or the 'common sense' of the phantasmal community constructed by the popular press, outraged by 'loony' extravagancies such as anti-racist and anti-sexist education or gay rights.

TVEI is indicative of a radical change of approach and philosophy. The 'bid-contract' system fundamentally alters the way in which education participates in innovation. Education's ends, its aims and objectives, are now set by policy makers under political imperatives and educators bid to be the most effective "deliverers". Essentially, it is pedagogy that teachers are left with through which to define their professional expertise – the curriculum, and even the syllabus, is handed over to the 'consumer'.

Significantly, while the curriculum was a major issue in the Education Reform Bill and in the National Curriculum, *pedagogy* has received little direct attention (though it should be noted how assessment can be trusted to act back upon and constrain teaching methods). Where the question of *ends* has been taken out of professional educators' hands, determining the *means* (under the constraints of contract bidding, assessment and accountability) defines the new limits of teacher professionalism.

It can be suggested that in a particular sense TVEI marks not the continuation of the Debate but rather its termination. As Beryl Pratley has pointed out, in a Further Education Unit (FEU) review of vocational courses, the debate about vocationalism and the relationship between education and training has been settled *not* because philosophers of education have at last resolved the issues, but because policy makers and administrators have decided to ignore them:

> The fact that people working for the MSC have their roots in the Department of Employment rather than in education has constantly pushed the Education versus Training debate into prominence and although a resolution of the areas of potential conflict would seem to lie in the new emphasis being given to the unity of vocational preparation, there are recent signs that the resolution may be achieved by the application of cash rather than philosophy. Resources talk (Pratley, 1985: 25).

The apocryphal story of TVEI's genesis symbolically marks the distance travelled from the Great Debate. It is precisely 'debate'. so representative of both liberal education and consensus politics, which has been defined out of the frame.

Where teachers have adapted and modified TVEI, they have done so because of spaces in its original formulation and lacunae within the institutional contexts of its implementation rather than because it was ever taken that professionally they had a *right* to do so. It is the hybrid character of TVEI (reflecting an institutional compromise between DES and MSC) which has retained a space for educationalists.

The end of 'debate' has been brought about as much as anything by the contempt for the 'chattering classes' most characteristically associated with Norman Tebbit. At one level, what TVEI reflects is the emergence in power of a group which quite simply cares nothing for the approval of the liberal establishment. Indeed, government policy towards the universities has been almost as aggressive as towards the unions and precisely brackets together the radical and conservative ends of a spectrum which in earlier times had been seen as constituting the basic oppositions of British political and social life. For the New Right, the old liberal establishment (represented in different ways in the BBC, the Church of England, Oxbridge *and* Conservative Wets) was as much, if not *more*, 'the enemy within' as the organized working-class movement.

Linking schools and work

Although there is an obvious sense to the way in which cultural value arguments have been used to account for Britain's economic decline and to legitimate the current reforms of education, what is, in fact, most striking about the position of liberal education, is its limited and contradictory position within the wider social order. It was sustained not by the general acceptance of its values and cultural ethos, but by a peculiar set of institutional conditions which secured, under the post-war social-democratic settlement, the relative independence of its supporters within the educational establishment.

Popular support has reflected more an enthusiasm for the grammar school than any real understanding of, or commitment to, liberal values. Indeed, it was precisely the increasing divergence between popular instrumentalism and the progressive variants of liberal humanism in the 1970s which prepared the ground for the current dismantling of liberal education's institutional base. Contrary to the 'holistic' approach of the cultural value position, these institutional arrangements themselves can be seen as reflecting not so much the hegemony of a particular world view as the actual cleavages within British culture and society which have traditionally made governments reluctant to bequeath to their opponents a centralized, State education system.

The vocationalization of English education is meeting general acceptance because of the failure of liberal credentials to extend to the majority the advantages they traditionally bestowed upon the social elite. Liberal education was radically undermined in the 1970s by the fact that its high point in terms of the autonomy of educators coincided with the onset of a recession which reversed the material conditions which had supported the expansion of education throughout the 1960s. In the first half of the 1970s, teachers gained an unprecedented degree of control over education. The increased status of an all-graduate profession coincided with ROSLA and new capacities to control directly the curriculum and manage innovation through agencies such as the Schools Council and the CSE examination. The Great Debate was a direct response to these conditions. It reflected the combination of demands to relate education more directly to the economy and increasing public disquiet at progressive innovations inaugurated by professional educationalists.

For present purposes, the issue of the relationship between education and industry can be approached at two levels:

1 How do the educational and occupational *systems* relate to each other?
2 How do teaching *practices* mediate the relationship between the two systems?

The expressed intention of TVEI is to affect the latter in order to achieve a particular, desired version of the former, as represented by the MSC's model of the labour market. This model is associated with a behaviouristic approach to skill training, the skills in question being derived from the 'occupational training families' which are seen as underpinning the labour market. The starting point for this is the widespread view that the failure of education to adequately meet the needs of the economy is a major component of Britain's economic decline.

It is possible to see the vocationalist content or orientation of TVEI in terms of a spectrum ranging from a liberal 'vocational education', in the Newsom/ROSLA tradition, at one end, to a MSC labour market/skills training model at the other. As Peter Holly (1987: 19–22) has suggested, drawing upon an earlier argument by Brennan (1985), both of these approaches can take the concept of 'skill' as their starting point, but the former relates skills to *processes*, whereas the latter relates them to *objectives*. Brennan locates the 'processes' approach within the tradition of curriculum work associated with Stenhouse, which goes back to ROSLA and the Schools Council. The 'objectives' approach is associated in particular with the FEU's *A Basis for Choice* (often referred to as 'The Mansell Report' after Jack Mansell of the FEU or the ABC approach), which is clearly consanguine with the MSC's behavioural skills training model.

Ironically, it is often precisely these progressive pedagogic possibilities of TVEI which help reconcile teachers to its vocationalism. In many instances, teachers reject the idea that TVEI is a radical innovation and claim that it has simply provided an opportunity for them to develop things that they have been doing anyway or always wanted to do. Among older teachers of this type, TVEI is seen as relating back to the Newsom ideals of ROSLA and the CSE Mode 3. For many teachers supportive of TVEI, it is seen as a long awaited opportunity to actually realize the promise of ROSLA and to bring about a *real* and radical shift away from formal, academic, book-based schooling. In this sense, it becomes associated with precisely the kind of 'secondary progressivism' which in the early 1970s did much to fuel the developing concerns about education, which culminated in the Great Debate.

The hybrid character of TVEI provides a space within which teachers can successfully develop an *educationalist* version of the scheme which both broadens the narrowly *occupationalist* orientation of the MSC and translates its *behaviouristic* model of skills training into a more liberal educational learning approach which resonates with existing progressive currents in secondary education.

In terms of its own logic, this 'radical' aspect of TVEI is seen in terms of industry 'needing' people with an understanding of *process*, rather than simply an educationally approved *product*, i.e. people who can *do* things, rather than simply *know* things. Traditional, academic school knowledge and learning processes are seen as inappropriate to the needs of a modern economy.

Although it is undoubtedly the case that employers can be found who might put things in this way, it is probably fair to say that the most commonly encountered demands are of a much more educationally conservative kind. In this respect, the subject-based GCSE can be seen as closer to what employers say they 'need' than the more process-oriented TVEI approach.

The needs of industry?

The integration of school knowledge and 'the needs of industry' crucially requires some effective and authoritative source of information whereby schools can come to know *what* the needs of industry actually are. Schools might, perhaps, be excused the charge of ignoring industry given the ambiguous and contradictory messages they usually receive. On the one hand, they are being told how inadequate traditional education is in providing industry with what it needs, but on the other how progressive methods undermine 'standards'. While being urged to become more vocational, industrial recruitment consistently favours traditional humanists.[7] Teachers frequently report how when approaching local employers to offer collaboration in course planning they are told that that is their job and business is too busy to get involved. Where industry is prepared to talk, the demand is often for a narrowly defined set of basic skills served in a traditional form. Employers often seem to put a premium on consistency and familiarity (conventional GCE 'O' and 'A' levels) over and against innovation, however vocational in form.

There is, consequently, a basic problem of giving a substantive form to the 'vocationalism' of TVEI in terms of what the real 'needs of industry' actually are. While the shift from a Human Capital *vocationalist* perspective towards Manpower Planning *occupationalism* entails a move towards a much more precisely defined set of curricular objectives (entailing a commensurate reduction in teacher professional autonomy), precisely *how* to define those objectives remains unresolved.

As suggested earlier, the notion of 'skill' can lead in two directions – either through *process* to a progressive curriculum tradition which links back to ROSLA, the Schools Council and the influence of Stenhouse, or through *objectives* to a behavioural occupational skills training approach. The *objectives* approach tends to derive its set of skills from a specification of 'the needs of industry' as constructed through methodologies such as the occupational skills inventory or matrix. The MSC sponsored the development of this approach in this country, e.g. the Jobs Components Inventory (JCI). It is also associated with the notion of Occupational

Training Families (OTFs) and the concepts of 'generic' and 'transferable' skills. The approach provides a clear definition of 'the needs of industry' and elements of its vocabulary at least have passed into the current language of vocationalism.

The approach has an internal consistency which reflects its essentially theoretical character. Its methodology moves from a picture of the labour market in terms of OTFs and their constituent skill groupings into a set of learning objectives and through to a measure of competence in profiling. The approach has also elaborated an ideological rationale through the notion of 'skill ownership'. It is important to recognize, however, the extent to which it *is* a theoretical perspective firmly based in the methodological individualistic assumptions of a positivist behavioural psychology. Despite its formal claims to 'realism', it bears little relationship to actual labour market structures and processes or to the real-world features of skills acquisition through social network membership and on-the-job training. It does, however (as will be elaborated later), have a well-defined location within the MSC's broader ideological agenda.

In the absence of systematic local labour market links, the MSC 'objectives' model can come to be *the* source of definitions of 'the needs of industry' and the paradigm for the vocationalist dimension of TVEI. However, there are alternative sources of information. Agencies such as Project Trident and Understanding British Industry also provide information and links, and there are also the more direct associations between schools and local employers created by work experience schemes which, in some cases, predate TVEI but which TVEI has significantly expanded (see Chapter 8). Employment Compacts are another developing initiative through which schools can gain local labour market intelligence.

The actual experience of TVEI seems to suggest that 'the needs of industry' tend most often to come to schools through fairly *ad hoc* links between individual schools (even individual teachers) and firms: mainly those providing work experience placements. The character of these links is described in detail in Chapter 8. The significant point here is their relatively *ad hoc* character which limits the extent to which skills can be precisely defined or 'the needs of industry' more generally represented. This has important implications for the broader education/industry debate and especially for the rationales officially presented for the vocationalization of education.

Essentially, there is a basic division between a version of 'the needs of industry' as constructed by the MSC model and its associated method of behavioural objectives skill training, and one which might emerge from more or less systematic (at the moment predominently *ad hoc*) linkages between schools and firms in the local labour market. This division has significant implications. The MSC approach is based in a 'market' economic analysis of Britain's industrial problems. This perspective locates those problems in terms of supply-side deficiencies, i.e. as a failure to produce the skills that industry needs rather than, say, a failure to invest significantly in the modernization of manufacturing industry. It is labour rather than capital which has let the side down. Although the unions (through so-called 'restrictive practices') were held to be a major influence in this, Thatcherism's favourite scapegoat has been education. The major criticism of education has been its failure to provide the skilled workforce that industry needs. Hence the drive for occupationalist vocationalization.

This rationale is based in a number of assumptions. Most significantly it sees skills as attributes which workers possess *prior* to their entry into the labour market rather than things which they acquire on-the-job. The educational system is then defined as the major source of such skills. Although consistent with the assumptions of market economics, this view flies in the face of a massive body of evidence to the effect that skills are predominantly acquired on-the-job. This fact has two particularly embarrassing consequences for a government which has pursued the types of policy we have seen since 1979. First, the fact that workers become skilled by actually working is a difficulty for a 'regime' which consciously used unemployment as an instrument of policy. Secondly, it strongly suggests that training is the responsibility of industry and that industry should both provide training and bear the cost of doing so.

Discovering 'the world of work'

The MSC model promotes this supply-side deficiency analysis and, in doing so, both shifts the blame for Britain's economic decline away from capital on to education and, by defining education as the provider of skills, shifts the cost of training away from industry into the area of public expenditure. The major problem for this analysis which might develop out of direct schools–industry links is that they can reveal its intrinsic fallacies. Substantively, this is most clearly displayed through the use that industry in fact makes of education – as a means of simplifying the recruitment process through various types of screening mechanism rather than as a source of occupationally specific skills.[8] Only in very special cases, e.g. technicians or doctors, do employers treat education as *directly* providing skills.

The apparent ambiguities of industry's message to education reflect fundamental disparities between politically formulated accounts of education/economy linkage at a high level of generality and actual practices at the level of the labour market. TVEI, and current vocationalism more generally, embodies tensions which arise from the conflict between, on the one hand, *deducing* an educational programme from these essentially ideological analyses and then, on the other, orienting them *in practice* towards actual school–industry links.

There are a number of points at which school–industry links can reveal disparities between the official rationales and prescriptions for vocationalism and the reality of 'the world of work' at the level of the local labour market.

As has already been mentioned, industrial recruitment strategies do not treat qualifications as indices of *skills* in the first place. Predominantly, they play a secondary role as a screening device to rationalize the selection process alongside a further set of more important non-educational criteria. Employers (or, more precisely, *recruiters*) are, in reality, relatively indifferent to the '*content*' of courses. This is in sharp contrast to the official prescriptions of the skills objectives approach.

Employers' apparent educational conservatism reflects a desire for 'familiarity' and 'consistency' in school qualifications over and above any putative 'vocational' content. The major impetus behind GCSE was the simple fact that, despite everything, in the final analysis, employers never took CSE seriously. 'Old-fashioned' GCE 'O' and 'A' levels were sufficient for their needs.

A particularly significant area is that of equal opportunities. One of the most welcome and progressive aspects of TVEI has been MSC's formal insistence upon equal opportunity measures (see Chapter 9). Orthodox economic theory entails the (axiomatic) rationality assumption that workers are located in work on the basis of their productive capacities as reflected in their skills. In reality, location and distribution is strongly conditioned by non-economic and non-educational criteria such as gender, race and age.

The structure of discriminatory labour market segmentation effectively negates any progressive reductions in gender or 'racial' differentiation in education. There is a marked disparity between MSC's promotion of equal opportunity contract compliance in TVEI and elsewhere and the government's broader attack upon it in the public sector. Similarly, the government's enthusiasm for imposing central state control over education contrasts with its insistence that the private sector be free from government 'interference'. Industry's (and white, male trade-unionists') unfettered opportunities to carry on with customary discriminatory practices will both annul and discredit progressive developments in education.

A third problem area, which increasing involvement in the real labour market can bring to light, is the importance of 'informal recruitment networks'. The significance of 'grapevine recruitment' is well established by research. As the work of Margaret Grieco (1987) shows, the social networks which facilitate grapevine recruitment are strongly associated with kinship and are socially complex. By virtue of the extent to which pupils are, as family members, already network members, they already possess experience, competence and knowledge which stand in critical contrast to formal definitions of the technical and social skills demanded by 'the world of work'. These formal definitions of 'skill' not only misrepresent the true character of labour market processes, they systematically misrepresent pupils as incompetent in ways which are relatively insignificant while failing to acknowledge the 'really useful' experience they actually possess and which any truly 'relevant' education would want to address.[9] This kind of involvement with the real life of local labour markets not only questions the specific prescriptions of vocationalism, it further undermines the more general ideological propositions associated with the attack on education and accounts of Britain's economic and social problems.

Hence the ironic outcome of the experiential dimension of TVEI is that, through encouraging school–industry links at the local labour market level, it can create the possibility whereby teachers can come to construct a very different model of 'the world of work' from the official skills objectives model. In combination with the progressive educational links with the process curriculum tradition, TVEI contains at least the possibility of ressurrecting the kinds of radical educational alternatives which surfaced briefly after ROSLA. The major difference between then and today is the government's strong state/free market strategy which much more stringently controls the capacity of teachers to develop autonomous educational objectives.

Conclusion

At one level TVEI can be understood in terms of a particular type of diagnosis of Britain's economic and social decline. This stresses the inappropriate character of the liberal values (in both conservative and progressive forms) which have traditionally underpinned British education. These values have been sustained in education by the institutional arrangements which characterized the social-democratic, post-war era, i.e. the distribution of power between the DES, the LEAs and the teaching profession. These arrangements effectively insulated teachers from both the demands from the Centre for increasing economic relevance and popular instrumentalism. Hence the attempt to reconstruct values has to be accompanied by a restructuring of institutional arrangements and processes. TVEI represents such an attempt.

In its attempt to realign the relationship between education and industry, TVEI has addressed itself to the educational *process* as well as to the curriculum. In its promotion of an integrated, experiential pedagogy, it stood in contrast both to the subject-based GCSE and to the National Curriculum. In this respect, and in its demand for 'relevance', TVEI conflicts with the traditionalist, neo-conservative current of the New Right which has been so influential in shaping Thatcherite educational reforms. At the same time, the MSC, as a corporatist state agency, can be seen as conflicting with the consumerist, market model of the neo-liberal wing. Hence, TVEI occupies a difficult and anomolous position with the broader movement of New Right reformism. This is exacerbated by the way in which its pedagogy can be incorporated into an existing, educationalist tradition of progressive, process learning.

The hybrid character of TVEI delivery at LEA level constructs a further dimension of contradictory tendencies. Despite the rigours of contract bidding and compliance, the MSC has not been in a position simply to impose its own model of technical and vocational training. LEA and school autonomy have been sustained to an extent that teachers have been able to develop the progressive educational possibilities of process learning. Hence the 'pedagogy' of TVEI has provided the basis for the development of alternative models of its vocationalism: an *educationalist* model based on the concept of *process*, and an *occupationalist* model based on the concept of *behavioural skill objectives*.

Hence, TVEI vocationalism can be seen in terms of 'educationalist' or 'occupationalist' forms. The former tends to define 'skills' in terms of 'process' rather than 'objectives', as is the case with the latter. From the former point of view, TVEI is a way of bringing about curriculum innovation and change in a way which is consanguine with an established tradition of secondary innovation going back to Newsom (if not beyond).

Notes

[1] See Jones (1989) for an informative and interesting account of 'the conservative revolution in education', and especially Chapter 3 on the MSC.
[2] See Flude and Hammer (1990) for a wide-ranging set of essays on the ERA.
[3] See Dale *et al.* (1989) for a discussion of the idea of TVEI as a 'policy hybrid'.
[4] See Moore (1988) for a review and discussion of some research on employers' recruitment strategies and attitudes to young workers.
[5] For relevant comparative material, see Muller *et al.* (1987).
[6] For a more developed discussion, see Hickox and Moore (1990).
[7] See McGeever (1988) for the findings of the Council for National Academic Awards' 'Higher Education and the Labour Market' (HELM) project.
[8] See Ashton *et al.* (1983) for a discussion of employer recruitment strategies.
[9] See Moore (1990) on the construction of the concept of 'skill'.

CHAPTER 4

From national guidelines to local practice

It might either be optimistic or pessimistic, depending on one's stance, to expect that TVEI could be implemented exactly or even largely as originally conceived. It would, though, be quite unrealistic. This is because understanding TVEI is not so much a question of understanding the technical implementation of an educational innovation, as of understanding its construction and creation within definite but untested and contested limits. How the local practices that were TVEI were constructed and created from the set of national guidelines issued at the beginning of the Initiative is the subject of this chapter.

We can summarize the argument and prepare the ground for its amplification, by means of a diagram. This diagram (see Fig. 4.1) has acted as a kind of template for us in drawing together material for the substantive chapters of the book. It is based on the assumption that what TVEI was in any particular LEA was an outcome of the mandate negotiated for it between the MSC, LEAs and schools and their joint capacity to fulfil that mandate, mutual accommodations that led at each stage to further modification.

Some elaboration of this model will be useful, especially as it is so central to our thinking about TVEI. Figure 4.1 indicates chronologically that what was about to become TVEI in practice went through three broad phases – essentially at the national, local and school levels. These phases are further broken down into what we see as the seven key stages of the development of what was TVEI in any particular school. While Fig. 4.1 does have an overall chronological sequence, it should be noted that it necessarily simplifies what was a very complex process. In reality, while each stage was a more or less complex process in itself, contiguous stages could overlap. The stages were not all of equal importance, though their relative importance varied between the different schemes. 'Progression' through the stages was not necessarily even or smooth. There were successive series of 'loops' between stages in the process of continuing negotiation between the three main parties in

Figure 4.1 The phases and stages in the development of TVEI.

Phase	Stage	
Devising the scheme	1	*Sources* of TVEI
	2	Selective incorporation of these sources into *National Guidelines/Criteria*
	3	Selective incorporation/emphasis of these guidelines/criteria into LEA *submission*
Defining the themes	4	Specification of LEA *response* – selection of schools, programmes, etc.
	5	Thematization of submission into *expectations of schools*, delivery structures, etc – specifying the problem for the Pilot Scheme
Deciding the practice	6	*Locating TVEI in the schools* – structures, cohorts, departments, resources
	7	*The TVEI effect in school* – the outcome of the expectations of TVEI meeting the living traditions of the schools

TVEI, as particular solutions created new sets of 'problems'. It should be noted, however, that it is no accident that it is not represented either as a funnel (denoting a progressive narrowing of what TVEI represents as it moves from conception to implementation) or as a pyramid (denoting a progressive broadening of the concept), though either of these representations may be accurate in particular cases. Neither can it be assumed that progress through the stages can be represented as either a diamond (denoting that LEAs play the major role) or an egg timer, (which would depreciate the role of the LEA). No particular shape, denoting the relationship between the partners in the Initiative, can be pre-specified for the implementation of the TVEI guidelines. The reason for this is quite crucial to our general argument. It is that at every stage, selection and interpretation of the mandate handed down from the previous stage are involved, rather than an appropriately enlarged or scaled-down facsimile. And the basis of selection and interpretation is existing policy and practice. Thus the model provides an historical perspective. It indicates why, as well as how, decisions were taken; it provides access to causes as well as consequences. Most importantly, it shows that the forms that TVEI took were the result of a necessary series of political, and not just technical or professional, decisions.

This argument can be elaborated most effectively by illustrating what is involved at each stage of the model. Stage 1 predates the announcement and existence of TVEI. It is where TVEI came from. We have already gone into this in some detail in the last two chapters, tracing the provenance of TVEI both in the relatively short term (i.e. as a response to the Great Debate) and in the relatively long term i.e. as a culmination of the recurrent debate about the relationship between education and industry. To this we added our view that, in essence, it was a three-sided debate between the education and training traditions and industry, with TVEI a hybrid outcome of these short- and longer-term perspectives.

Two main factors characterize the way in which the TVEI guidelines and criteria were derived from the overall problem that confronted its creators, and the inherent instability deriving from its hybrid state. First, it was a consequence of the speed with which TVEI was set up. This was a key component of its success, but it did mean that TVEI was very 'underformulated' when it was originally promulgated. This is hardly surprising, given the little we know of its background, while the TVEI Unit within the MSC was staffed at a very low level for some time after the announcement of the Initiative, and the Director of the TVEI was not appointed until some time after bids from LEAs had been solicited. The reason why only 'guidelines' and broad 'criteria' for TVEI were issued, rather than a detailed request for submissions, may have been based on a view of the philosophy of the Initiative as an open and flexible affair, but it is hard to see that the timetable set out left a great deal of time for the detailed implementation of a sophisticated programme anyway. Though we attempted to trace the educational origins of TVEI in the last chapter, it is of some interest and value to consider briefly at this stage some of the more plausible candidates put forward as the *immediate* progenitors of TVEI. Possibly the best publicized, and the best warranted, as a source of TVEI is the Organization for Rehabilitation through Training (ORT) connection. ORT is an international organization in which David Young had played a major role, both in Britain and internationally. As its name implies, it seeks the rehabilitation of potentially deviant young people (mainly boys) through the provision of strictly vocationally oriented training programmes. Another clear contender was the restoration of a 'technical stream' for those in the middle to lower ability range. This was clearly in the minds of at least David Young and Norman Tebbit at the inception of TVEI. A close, if somewhat more consumer- rather than production-oriented variant of this was Sir Keith Joseph's well-known solicitude of the education welfare of lower attaining pupils, whose lack of benefit from (and poor attitude towards) schooling he felt could be mitigated by their exposure to more obviously vocationally relevant programmes of study and activity. A further contender for the educational source of TVEI is a conference held some months before the announcement of TVEI at the National Union of Teachers' (NUT) Conference Centre in Stoke Rochford. However, this is one contender whose claims it is relatively easy to dismiss. One of the key participants in that conference (a director of education) assumed that TVEI was indeed a direct outcome of it and submitted a first-round bid based on that assumption and the 'inside knowledge' that went with it. As he put it in an interview with one of us, 'we thought we'd written the script and so were sure to get the part', but his authority had to wait until the third round before its (radically reconstructed) bid was successful.

It may, then, never be possible to isolate the educational origins of TVEI, quite possibly because they did not exist in any coherent form. What is clear, though, is that both the possible origins that can be identified (from Young and Tebbit, and to a somewhat lesser extent, Joseph), and the existing MSC programmes and practices that provided the immediate inspiration and the funding for TVEI were located in a thorough instrumental, production-oriented, vocationally dominated conception of education. In the end, however, though there are some tensions discernible between the clear intentions of Young and Tebbit's emphasis on the linking of middle-range ability and technician level skills and knowledge, to create a distinct intermediate social stratum, Joseph's desire to ensure that the least able got a better deal from school that would enable them to contribute more economically (and cost less socially), and the DES's Great Debate-based attempt to expand the place of scientific, technical, vocational and entrepreneurial education, they do share common themes. Their lowest common denominator, and the dominant educational thread running through the original conception of TVEI, is the need and the desire to replace the academic/expressive/consumptionist view of education, and the curriculum, pedagogy and assessment processes it sponsored, with a technical/vocational/instrumental alternative.

So, while it may not have been a wholly zero-sum game between length and tightness of timetable and closeness of specification (i.e. if it's to be quick it won't be detailed, if it's to be detailed it won't be quick), it was certainly close to that in the early days of TVEI. (The TVEI Extension criteria were much tighter; 5 years experience of the pilot scheme enabled much closer specification of what was required.)

If this condition underlying the selective incorporation of the sources of TVEI into a set of guidelines and criteria seems, to say the least, to have been less than rigorously planned and thought through, the second appears to owe rather more to calculation. TVEI was launched in a blaze of publicity as a key component of the government's programme to reform education, improve industrial efficiency and reduce youth unemployment. It showed the government was 'doing something'. It thus had a very high public profile. That public profile was immediately the target of the bitter and almost universal hostility from the rest of the education world, none of whom (including the Minister of State at the DES, the director of the MSC and the chairman of the ACC, let alone the secretary of the NUT) had been consulted or even informed beforehand. The need for success in a hostile environment had three major consequences for the shape and the rigour of the TVEI mandate. First, it led to an emphasis on its pilot status; hostile and critical questions about the Initiative were typically deflected by reference to its experimental nature. The second and third consequences derive from the fact that success could be neither radical nor rapid without some measure of cooperation from the LEAs. While it would have been possible, as David Young pointed out at the time, to implement TVEI by means of an entirely new category of schools, that could certainly not have been done quickly and cleanly (as witness the protracted negotiations over the introduction of the CTCs). This meant that it was necessary to work through LEAs, and given that, that success could be either radical but restricted – through close specification and monitoring of a few narrowly technical and vocational schemes – or less profound but more extensive – through the encouragement of the planting of a thousand loosely defined plants, in the hope that a good proportion of them might turn out to be flowers that bloomed. The latter course was adopted, perhaps as much in reaction to the large number of LEAs making submissions for the pilot scheme (around 80% of which were sure to fail and to leave many LEAs disappointed, even angry) as from any major commitment to variety.

The sources of TVEI, and their specification in the form of guidelines and criteria rather than close prescription, represent the bedrock of what TVEI can be. They provide guidance for the formulation of LEA submissions that within broad instrumentalist/vocationalist outlines was flexible and loosely defined. This permitted considerable further interpretation rather than merely consultation, and negotiation about the content and not only the implementation of the programme. It also provided the basis of the contract (though it should be noted that some schemes ran for over a year before any contract was agreed and signed by the MSC and LEA). The submission and the contract together we shall call *the scheme*, the pilot TVEI project within each authority.

The LEAs' mandate for TVEI – what they took TVEI to be in their submissions, and what the MSC accepted as meeting the aims of TVEI – was then again a matter of the uneven and not entirely predictable hybridization of two alternative but, since the Great Debate, increasingly overlapping traditions. Getting the TVEI contract and the resources it would bring that mandate as set out in the LEAs' submissions represented merely its freezing at one point in time with a particular purpose in mind. We discussed the substance of the mandate in Chapter 3 and will return to it again later, but formally if it did not leave all to play for – for these were clear limits to the direction, degree and dimension of change possible – at least it left open the possibility of interpretation and modification. And when we recognize that there were likely to be within any LEA, or school, individual groups with different interests in interpreting and modifying that mandate in different ways, it is clear that the TVEI mandate was broad and dynamic rather than narrow and set.

However, recognizing the flexibility, unpredictability and instability of the mandate takes us only a little further to understanding what TVEI is in any particular case. It is not only a matter of there being different interpretations of TVEI and different individual group agendas raised by it. Neither is it a matter only of there being different levels of commitment to TVEI, though we should note at this stage that a whole-hearted commitment to the project on the part of everyone involved could certainly not be assumed. At the outset of TVEI, very few people at any level were prepared to stake their careers on it. (The timing and strength of Chief Officer supports, for instance, was an intriguing feature of all the schemes we looked at, and an important indicator of their local acceptability and success.) Though the number doing so snowballed as the career potentialities of TVEI became more clear (e.g. see Chapter 6), the only groups dedicated to the success of TVEI were those directly and wholly involved in it, employed by it at every level. This created a shared interest directed towards demonstrating that TVEI was a success, which included those whose careers were committed to it at every level from the TVEI Unit to school co-ordinator. And, as we shall argue below, the existence of this shared interest is very important to understanding TVEI as a whole and in individual cases. It cut across divisions between and loyalties to the partners to the Initiative (MSC, LEAs, schools) and led to the construction and formulation of TVEI programmes and processes acceptable to all three partners, yet promising justifiable and identifiable 'success' for TVEI and for those with direct and sponsoring interests in it.

In addition to recognizing the dynamic nature of the LEAs' TVEI mandate, we must also bear in mind their different capacities to put it into practice. There are three issues involved here: conditions, capacity and political will. The conditions for introducing an initiative like TVEI could scarcely have been more propitious than they were in the early 1980s. Cuts in educational spending, the almost total absence of any professional developments in the curriculum, and low teacher morale created very fertile ground. However, even allowing for those LEAs most desperate for resources and funding, there were many (well over a third) whose political opposition to TVEI as they originally perceived it, was strong enough to prevent them even bidding to be included. The same was, and remains, true at the level of the schools, where very many teachers were strongly opposed to the idea of outside political intervention in schools and refused to have anything to do with TVEI; in some cases, this led to their schools as a whole not being included, in others to continuing pockets of resistance to the scheme and its implementation.

It is, though, in the area of capacity that LEAs most significantly, if least consciously and intentionally, influenced the shape and nature of TVEI. For one thing, as we have suggested above, certainly at the outset of TVEI, no LEA was likely to place its full capacity at the disposal of the Initiative. More importantly, the LEAs' capacity to implement TVEI was both inherently limited and inherently biased. What LEAs and schools are capable of doing at any given time is the result of what they have prepared and equipped themselves to do over several generations. It represents the residues of past and continuing professional commitments to certain kinds of both educational philosophy and forms of organization. Thus LEAs and schools have reputations for greater or lesser efficiency, for relative levels of devolution of authority, for particular subject strengths or professional initiatives. A particular example of this is the LEAs' experience in, and preparedness for, setting up policy to extend the opportunities available to girls. As Chapter 9 shows, this varied enormously and set distinct limits to what was possible over the pilot phase of TVEI. While these strengths and weaknesses cover a wide range, the crucial point is, of course, that the professional residues and commitments that they represent almost exclusively draw on liberal, educationalist, expressive, consumptionist views of education. And this kind of capacity cannot easily or quickly be turned to purposes different in many ways from those it has grown to execute.

Practically, the basis of the selection of issues to be raised, and the claims and offers to be made which made up each LEA submission, drew on the best guess that could be made of what the MSC would be looking for combined with that LEA's existing strengths and potential provision. The original submissions differed considerably from each other in style, approach, length and content. This is hardly surprising, because the LEAs had no experience of this kind of thing in 1983, and it is by no means certain that the MSC knew what to expect, or what exactly they were looking for. It is a significant achievement of TVEI that submissions for later phases of the pilot scheme, and especially for the Extension, were on the whole much 'tighter' and more similar in format than those in the original round. One possibly significant feature of the first 14 successful submissions is that several of the LEAs had been involved in Schools Curriculum Industry Project (SCIP), which may have provided them with a more appropriate conceptual and linguistic apparatus. Certainly, this seems to have been the view of a number of LEAs who put in first-round bids, and made strenuous efforts to contact SCIP personnel for advice in preparing those bids.

Exactly how the MSC selected the successful 14 submissions to make up the first round of TVEI from the 66 submitted is not clear. A number of criteria seem to have been operating. A desire for a good geographical and urban/rural spread can be inferred, for instance, as can a keenness to include both Labour- and Conservative-controlled LEAs. It is possible, too, to guess that educational criteria were also in operation, in the inclusion of authorities with good reputations for secondary education, or for having already invested heavily in technological education. A reading of both successful and unsuccessful first-round bids does not reveal any obvious features of either the quality or the content of the successful submissions which would accout for their success.

Defining the themes

The next stage overlaps somewhat with the submission stage, as submissions did contain – at least in outline – indications of how the claims and commitments they contained would be implemented. The evidence from all the schemes we have been involved with, however, suggests that they contained a good deal of 'window dressing' in the form of claims and commitments that could not be met. This was not just a case of finagling on the part of the LEAs. It was at least equally the result of the process of drawing up the submission. In the first round, this typically contained little if any input from those who were to be directly involved in the scheme, often because of the very limited time available. In many cases, responsibility for drawing up the submission was given over to officers responsible for further education (because they handled the other MSC initiatives), and this widened still further the likely gap between what was claimed in the submissions and what it was realistic to believe could be achieved. The submissions, then, are best seen as formal statements of TVEI schemes (we doubt if many of those even most closely involved can recall the contents of, or have even seen, the original submissions).

This does not, of course, mean that the submissions can be reduced to simple opportunism. All of them were informed by more noble and more appropriate considerations than merely obtaining large amounts of extra funding at a time when LEA and school budgets were stretched to the utmost. While none of the schemes we examined displayed the extremes of evangelism for the extension of technical and vocational education that were found among some early practitioners of TVEI, they all had more or less clear visions of what kind of technical and vocational education they wished to introduce and why. The clearest part of this vision was typically founded on a desire to do something to improve the employment prospects of the young people in the area. How this could be done varied with local labour market conditions and the precise extent of youth unemployment, but in every case it was a paramount feature of an LEA's submission.

The process in the second and subsequent rounds was rather different. There was at least some element of 'case law' to be inferred from those unsuccessful in the first round. Most of those bidding in the second round had bid in the first round and had some indication of where they had 'gone wrong'; indeed, they frequently received extensive coaching from TVEI Unit personnel on preparing their submission. Furthermore, the more widely canvassed political and educational fears about TVEI had not been realized, convincing some waverers that TVEI might be a bandwagon worth joining rather than an expensive and embarrassing failure. Thus not only was there time to include more groups within LEA submissions in drawing up the second-round bids, but more groups were willing to be included. The level of funding was both lower and much more precisely defined than it had been in the first round. However, while all this made for better targeted and less speculative bids, in our view it did not necessarily make for bids that were clearly more realistic or 'deliverable'. Often second-round bids like first-round bids were 'over-bids', and offered more than could be delivered. Necessarily, then, the submissions went through a process we call 'thematization'. This refers to the process of selective interpretation and identification of what were to be the key themes and targets of the scheme in practice. It was carried out within and between the schools and the authorities. In a sense, the process we are calling thematization, highlighting problems and drawing boundaries, began much earlier in the development of TVEI when the institutions to be included in the scheme were chosen; this automatically ruled out certain possibilities and facilitated others. Sometimes, there was an element of self-selection of institutions and programmes, where LEAs invited separate consortia (and the forming of schools into consortia became increasingly common as the pilot phase of TVEI progressed, as a means of overcoming a range of practical problems both for LEAs and schools) of schools to prepare bids, and then put one of these forward, possibly in a modified form, as their own bid. Another model of selecting the participating schools, however, saw the consequence for the success of TVEI of their selection as almost incidental. In these cases, for example, TVEI was used to hasten, delay or modify a restructuring of secondary education, or to reward heads who had been loyal to the authority; in one case we have heard of, TVEI was put into the schools in the districts of the most powerful councillors. In other cases, the school's TVEI potential as judged by the LEA was paramount, and this investment was thought likely to yield most in the form of desired outcomes. But even in the cases where this was so, it was never in our experience the only criterion; we know of no case where the LEA picked out the 'best' (in the sense of 'most likely to succeed') 4–5 schools in the authority to take on TVEI. That selection was always influenced by other factors: geographical distribution within the authority, urban–rural balance, the political need to represent schools with a range of different catchment areas. The importance of this selection of schools (and colleges) to take part in the scheme cannot be overestimated, and not just because it was in the schools that much of (though not the whole of) the impact of TVEI was generated and delivered.

It is also important because it represents the high point of LEA power and influence in the scheme. While the MSC could lay down guidelines for what would be acceptable in TVEI, and while they could specify the number of institutions to be included in each scheme (there was a preference for 5 – 6 schools and colleges, and a reluctance to take on schemes proposing 8 or more participating institutions), they could not control which schools were chosen. They did not have the requisite intimate knowledge of the schools that would have enabled them to intervene, even if they had wanted to. Certainly, we know of no cases where the MSC either vetoed or suggested particular schools, at the point of selection. And though things were different once the schemes were under way, when the MSC did acquire through its team of regional TVEI advisers at least sufficient knowledge of the participating schools to permit some judgement of their effectiveness and efficiency as deliverers of TVEI, we know of no cases of individual schools being 'thrown out' of the scheme – notwithstanding a number of hints and threats that this might happen. Indeed, the fact that no participating authority left the pilot scheme for any reason is a very important feature of the Initiative that is very easy to take for granted.

After this selection stage, which as we have mentioned in some cases had only indirect and incidental influence on the shape of TVEI, the LEAs autonomy with respect to further thematization was somewhat more limited. It became very much more a matter of their capacity to deliver the promises of their submission, in negotiation with the MSC. As we said, the submissions were prepared with a particular audience and a particular purpose in mind. Most importantly, no LEA could hope to offer equally high performance across the whole spectrum of TVEI guidelines and criteria, and while this may have been reflected to some extent in their submissions, their can be few successful submissions which did not contain promises it would have been exceptionally difficult to deliver (one example of this would be a commitment to ensuring equality of opportunity to boys and girls from LEAs and schools with no policy or record of achievement in the area at all). From the start, then, there was often a more or less closely defined 'real' programme in the minds of most LEA officers who prepared the submission – and this was based on what it was hoped TVEI could achieve, and what is felt the authority and the schools could deliver. If they wanted to change the schools – as they undoubtedly did – they also wanted to ensure that it was 'change in continuity', and it was this which determined the particular themes emphasized in the different schemes.

Another, less direct, aspect of the selection/thematization process was the management structure adopted. This was not merely an administrative device, but provided limits and possibilities for TVEI. The formal management structure of the schemes differed from each other and will be discussed below. However, for the purpose of this chapter, it should be noted that the structure stipulated by the MSC called for a local steering committee, to be representative of local organizations and industry, and a full-time co-ordinator (also known as the 'director' in some cases) for the scheme. There is considerable variation in the composition of the steering committees in the schemes we looked at. In some cases, very 'high-powered' steering committees were recruited, made up of major figures in local industry and commerce, and leaders of the local community, such as the leaders of the major political parties represented on the council. In other cases, membership was made up of the nominees of bodies like the chamber of commerce and (much less often) the local Trades Council.

In practice, however, local politicians, in particular members of the authority's Education Committee, were the most influential figures on the steering committees. The steering committees were often chaired by the chair of the Education Committee (or his or her nominee); in one case, the TVEI steering committee was a sub-committee of the authority's education committee. The representation of the education interest overall was increased in most cases by representatives of teacher unions. This paralleled their representation on other LEA bodies, but it represents a distinct difference from the union representation on the National Steering Committee, where teacher union members are present as representatives of the TUC (and hence potentially replaceable by any union representative) and not of the teacher unions themselves. (This created some intriguing occasions, as education management and employees on TVEI steering committees simultaneously sought to defend their common interest, and use the forum for the continuation and development of debates and issues raised between them elsewhere.)

There are two main reasons for what frequently became the effective incorporation of TVEI into local education decision-making channels rather than it representing a broadening of community, and especially industrial and commercial, influence and control over what goes on in schools (as it might be inferred from subsequent legislation that the DES as well as the MSC were keen to achieve). The first is a matter of existing capacity and expertise. There were no effective alternatives to the LEA, and within the LEA there was no major, irresistible or enforceable alternative to 'running' TVEI in rather similar ways to those used to run any other of the authority's interests. The LEAs had to be represented on steering committees, but they both set them up and serviced them, and did so in ways compatible with their existing practices.

The second main reason for the incorporation of the steering committee by the LEA was the seemingly permanent difficulty of finding effective and continuing representation of industrial and commercial interests. In part, of course, this is a chronic problem. 'Industry' and 'commerce' are by no means homogeneous and are almost as difficult to 'represent' as parents. In addition, only larger firms are able to release employees to participate in such public duties and, even among these firms, there tends to be a division between the interested and knowledgeable but effectively powerless representative of the personnel or training departments, and the influential senior manager who knows little about education or even training. Industry and commerce, then, are almost inevitably less than effectively represented on such bodies. This may also be the case at the level of the National Steering Committee, though their remit is rather different from that of the local steering committees.

The consequences of this incorporation of the steering committees by local education politicians were not immediately apparent, as the whole steering committee system operated in a rather low key way. One reason for this was that the steering committees were never precisely clear as to what it was they were intended, or had the authority, to do. They were hardly policy makers; the policy was laid down in the contract. They had no executive role; that was the duty of the co-ordinator, Chief Officer and the MSC. They had no monitoring role; MSC's regional advisers, and the national evaluations of the scheme, carried out this function. They did not control the budget; that too was part of the contract.

The ways this near vacuum was filled had two major, and one relatively minor but piquant, consequences. First, the steering committees provided political legitimation for local schemes. They were corporatist rather than pluralist in their operation, i.e. their members represented interests which were bound by the decisions of the committee. (In this way, they paralleled other MSC-created bodies, even the Commission itself, whose actions were assumed to have, for instance, the support of all trade unionists once they had been agreed by the TUC representatives.) Secondly, and at least equally important, the dominance of the education interest ensured that the effective agenda of the steering committees was not confined to how far local schemes were conforming to the contract, but took in also the effect of accepting the contract on the schools involved and on the work of the authority as a whole. There was often a sense at meetings we attended, that the steering committees were seeking to defend and preserve the interests of *all* the pupils and all the schools in the authority against potential unwelcome change. In particular, they often sought to minimize the differences that TVEI would create within, and especially between, participating and non-participating schools. This had been a major fear at the outset of TVEI and represents one of the major 'meta-struggles' between its contributing traditions, the one stressing universalism; the other the need for functional differentiation, hierarchy and competition.

The third consequence had little direct effect on the story we have to tell, but a considerable effect on us as individual evaluators. It is that, because local evaluation was almost the only activity over which the steering committees had any direct influence or control, it tended to take on what seemed to us an inordinate importance in steering committee meetings: it was frequently the longest item, for instance, receiving far more attention than matters of much greater substance. It was also invested with considerably greater influence than it merited. Because it was 'there' and had no independent power, it frequently became seen almost as either panacea or scapegoat. The local evaluator was often seen as the '1% solution' to the scheme's difficulties (all authorities had to set aside a minimum of 1% of their funding for local evaluation, and few exceeded that amount) or sometimes as being somehow responsible for any bad news she or he brought to the steering committee.

The appointment of the local TVEI co-ordinator and the matching of him or her (one woman was appointed as co-ordinator of the schemes we looked at) to the local definition of the role, were of absolutely critical importance in both the success and the shape of the scheme. The most significant point in the choice of a co-ordinator was whether they came from inside or outside the authority. Both types of co-ordinators had a case to make. The 'insiders' pointed to their knowledge of how the local system worked, and of the key personnel within it. The 'outsiders' pointed to their clean sheet, the lack of preconceptions about them, and the confidence that comes from having been brought in to do a specific job. In the event, both were likely to find their assumptions proved faulty, and this was due not so much to their inside/outside status, but to a less than perfect matching of qualifications, attributes, experience and ambition with the way the post was both conceived and with the way it was shaped by the existing power system within the authority. This raises some broader and even more significant issues. We observed a range of interpretations of the TVEI project co-ordinator's role (interestingly, the post was often described as 'director' rather than co-ordinator, and at least for some of those involved the different label was seen as having important connotations for their authority and influence. However, we observed no correlation between title and authority; a 'director' was no more likely, *ipso facto*, to carry more weight in the LEA or with the schools than a 'cordinator'). At one end, we observed a co-ordinator who could be for lengthy periods a virtual satrap; at the other, one who was little more than a highly paid clerk. These interpretations of the role were not static, however; they all changed in the course of the TVEI pilot. Nor were the different interpretations the result of different formal job descriptions. In each case, the definitions of the co-ordinator's role and the nature of his or her integration into the project was a complex matter involving the LEA, the MSC and the schools, and the relationship between them.

Specifically, considering how the TVEI co-ordinator 'fitted in' with existing LEA structures and how well he or she 'got on' with the heads and teachers of the schools involved, required us to address the question of the 'real' management structure of local TVEI schemes. For however much LEAs may have wished it otherwise, TVEI was different. It could not be *fully* incorporated or wholly assimilated into existing processes and practices. The same was true for schools. However invisible they may have wanted TVEI to become, at the very least participation in the scheme involved different systems of monitoring, and accountability to different bodies.

At the level of the LEA, the 'difference' of TVEI and the difficulty of assimilating it easily into existing practices, were probably most evident first in the relationships between TVEI and the local inspectorate/advisory service. In almost every case we looked at, there was at least initially considerable tension between TVEI and the advisory service, for whom it often appeared to represent a rather troublesome cuckoo in the nest, ideologically as well as organizationally. Ideologically, the local inspectorate/advisory service frequently conceived of themselves as the guardians of the educationist tradition. They were above all, concerned with the quality of the education received by the pupils in their local authority. It was, too, among the local advisers/inspectors, perhaps, that the criticism of the quality and direction of education of the kind stimulated by the Great Debate and culminating in TVEI was most strongly felt, and TVEI provided a ready focus for the resentment created by that criticism. This resentment was quite widely felt. Those in the humanities felt it because it represented a further attempt to erode their contribution to education; those in technical and vocational areas often saw it as a direct criticism of what they were doing. Certainly in the early stages of TVEI, then, indifference and even obstruction often characterized local inspectors'/advisers' reactions to TVEI.

Organizationally, TVEI, with its separate budget, specific targets and dedicated personnel, could not easily be fitted into existing arrangements. It was, for instance, in all but two of the authorities we looked at, housed separately from other LEA officers (and one of the two exceptions had been given its own separate offices by the end of the pilot). This was doubtless due in part to its short-term nature, the sharing of accommodation and its relatively localized area of operation. It did, though, have the effect of emphasizing any distinctiveness it may have acquired, and of facilitating the autonomy of the TVEI scheme within the authority. All the factors listed above meant that TVEI had to be managed by the local authority more or less separately from the way it managed the bulk of its services. This did not, however, in itself entail any particular form of management, closeness of supervision, weight of intervention, etc., and each of these aspects differed from scheme to scheme.

They did not, however, differ only on the basis of existing LEA and school practice. For there was, of course, a third party involved in the management of TVEI, the MSC. One form of MSC intervention in local schemes that became increasingly prominent as the pilot phase developed was to provide support from the centre targeted on particular features of the scheme. A number of issues (including local evaluation) were treated in this way. Especially taxing or novel issues like progression post-16 or profiling were among those where the TVEI Unit attempted to clarify the issues and indicate the way forward. However, the most prominent was the issue of gender equality (MSC efforts in this area are described at greater length in Chapter 9). The pattern these central initiatives took was rather familiar; almost an oral, face-to-face version of what was contained in the TVEI Unit publications. The MSC sponsored national and local conferences and workshops addressed by experts and personnel from TVEI schemes with some experience, if not success, to report in the area. In some cases, an official was appointed to the TVEI Unit to take particular responsibility for an area; a former president of the NUT took up the post in the area of equal opportunities.

The MSC also appointed regional TVEI advisers responsible for particular schemes. The regional advisers were each responsible for a number of TVEI schemes; this varied with the number of schemes and the number of advisers, but was typically between six and ten. In essence, the advisers policed the contract from the point of view of the MSC. Their job was to ensure its continuing adherence to the principles of TVEI as conceived by the TVEI Unit. Though they also carried out forms of audit monitoring – such as asking to see the timetable for the use of equipment or facilities provided by TVEI funds, in order to ensure that the TVEI cohort in the school were at least given priority in its use – they were most importantly involved in negotiating the implementation of TVEI. In effect, this meant that they represented the MSC on the ground, and became the immediate arbiters and definers of what counted as TVEI. A considerable part of this work involved negotiation over how the TVEI budget could be used. While some of these negotiations concerned 'cohort disputes' (there was a running problem over how far TVEI benefits had to be confined to the nominated pupils in each school), others necessarily involved definitions of what counted as TVEI. The regional advisers were not merely responsive, however, nor did they act only as bureaucratic monitors checking the degree of adherence to the contract. They also (to a greater or lesser degree) took the initiative in interpreting TVEI and in suggesting its major implications for schools. They might, then, be seen as HMI with sanctions. They certainly became the key definers of TVEI, articulating and rearticulating what it was really about, and how that could best be achieved in the prevailing conditions. It is important to note, however, that the regional advisers were not a homogeneous group. They differed not only in the amount of discretion/intervention they exercised, but also quite crucially – for they were the most important reality definers for TVEI participants – they interpreted what counted as TVEI in different ways. There is one account, for instance, of two TVEI schemes in adjacent LEAs, but with different regional advisers, being given diametrically different guidance on the validity of the same innovation that they both wished to introduce under the auspices of TVEI; one LEA was told it did meet TVEI criteria, the other that it did not. This variation in 'official' interpretation of TVEI obviously increased the range of what counted as TVEI overall, though it did not necessarily enhance the flexibility of local interpretations – far from it in some cases. However, this variation in interpretation of the regional adviser's role decreased somewhat over the course of the pilot phase. Not only did the central TVEI Unit expand and its work become more routinized over the course of the Initiative, but increasingly the regional advisers, who were always very largely recruited from the world of education, were recruited from within TVEI itself as existing TVEI co-ordinators, heads and teachers were seconded to the TVEI Unit (which may also have contributed to their increasing homogeneity and consistency).

In a situation where on the one hand the LEAs and the schools had little or no experience in dealing with a project like TVEI, and where on the other the management structure laid down for the project contained within it two potentially powerful reality defining figures in the shape of the project co-ordinators and the regional advisers, it might be expected that the TVEI projects would have led lives relatively isolated from, but also relatively automous from, the continuing work and the influence of the LEAs and the schools. This did not happen very often, or for very long, for a number of reasons. First, it was the LEA that had at least a contractual responsibility towards TVEI. Secondly, as we pointed out above, most LEAs took much more interest in TVEI than the basic contractual responsibility would require, and tended to exercise this interest in ways that tended to curtail the autonomy and the isolation of TVEI. There was one interesting exception to this in the authorities we looked at which demonstrates the importance attached to the LEA role. In that authority, TVEI was located in an area geographically remote and socially distinct from the rest of the LEA, including its headquarters. The scheme proceeded rather uneasily, and it was many months before the contract was signed, with the relationships between the LEA and the MSC, and the project and the MSC, both being rather acrimonious and unproductive, with the result that little progress was made with the project. Matters came to a head when a group from HMI who had looked at the project after it had been running for about a year, told the LEA that it (the LEA) 'had abandoned responsibility for the project'. This confirmed that for TVEI to operate effectively, active rather than passive involvement was required from LEAs.

This does not, of course, mean that a formal line management structure for TVEI within the LEA was either possible or desirable. On the one hand, the strength of the

LEA's political commitment was variable and could not be guaranteed at a particular level. On the other, and most importantly, schools could no more be required or guaranteed to deliver TVEI than anything else. That is to say, neither the mandate nor the capacity of TVEI were sufficiently determined or predictable to enable the installation of orthodox line management. Futhermore, we might even have expected major political tensions to arise between the various parties to the project which would inhibit development or even lead to stalemate and stasis. This did indeed occur in a number of instances, typically fairly early in the scheme's history and for relatively short periods before the logjam was broken.

However, even if the objective conditions under which TVEI operated were not such as to require or necessarily favour the creation of a separate, distinctive and autonomous TVEI cadre, such cadres did frequently develop, and were most influential in the shaping of TVEI. Organizationally, these took the form of central advisory teams. These teams usually grew from the creation of curriculum advisers with responsibilities for fostering and encouraging 'TVEI relevant' subject areas that had been relatively underdeveloped previously. In almost every case we studied, such advisers were to be found in the areas of Craft, Design and Technology (CDT), Information Technology (IT), Business Studies and the creation of systems of pupil profiling. Such central advisory teams were strengthened, and indeed frequently became formalized as a result of the introduction of the TVEI-Related In-Service Education for Teachers (TRIST) scheme. TRIST placed further large sums of money at the disposal of local authorities (again on a bid/contract basis), essentially for the spreading of the TVEI word, and for extending the input of TVEI, by means of training cohorts of teachers in what was expected of, and what had been learned from, TVEI. Authorities had to appoint TRIST directors. Their relationships with the existing TVEI team varied considerably. In some cases, they effectively became an extension of the existing TVEI team in an authority, and this strongly reinforced the move towards the establishment and dominant influence of central advisory teams. In other cases, TRIST seemed almost to be set up in opposition to, or at least as an alternative to, the existing TVEI scheme. This occurred in cases where the original TVEI scheme was proving less successful than the authority had hoped, but where both the substance of TVEI and the way it was funded had proved sufficiently attractive for the authority to wish to maintain and extend it. Indeed, one incidental but very significant outcome of TVEI was the way that LEAs reacted to the proliferation of schemes funded on the same bid/contract basis as TVEI by creating as part of or in parallel with or as a spin-off from the TVEI central advisory teams, high-powered task forces whose job it was to prepare the authority's bids for the increasing number of centrally funded schemes. Certainly, TVEI increased LEA flexibility and speed of response to a point where the initial response to its introduction seemed within a relatively short time laboured and amateurish.

It was not only organizational factors that fostered the development of TVEI cadres, however. A crucial additional factor was the *commitment to the success of what went on as TVEI shared by all those directly involved in it*. This included those directly employed in the service of TVEI, such as co-ordinators and regional advisers. It also included those most directly involved in the LEAs and the schools.

Whatever their initial feelings, once they were participating in TVEI, there was little mileage for LEA officers, heads or teachers in sabotaging it or in doing less than they could to make it a success. However, this common interest in achieving and demonstrating the success of TVEI was not only the cement that bound the TVEI cadres together or indeed that enabled them to come into being. It also influenced the way that the executive cadres used their discretionary power, i.e. it gave local TVEI schemes their distinctive shape and character. The TVEI cadres did not alter their boundaries of discretion; they could no more guarantee implementation than could orthodox LEA management.

But while the shared need for TVEI to be successful did bind together representatives of the different partners in TVEI, it did not extinguish the different interests they had in the project, or even the different criteria of success held by those interests. This created an atmosphere of both compromise and complicity. There was even compromise over setting the criteria of success which might fit well with a particular position, but be unacceptable or unacheivable for other interested parties. Regional advisers could no more insist on adherence to the letter of the contract than heads could insist on treating TVEI funds merely as additional capitation, because for either to have done so would have threatened the success and viability of the whole scheme. And while each particular participant could possibly have denied responsibility for such a collapse, they would inevitably be implicated in it. Indeed, far from insisting on separate success, the cadres operated on a basis of complicity in disguising the failures of any of their members. Failure was typically ignored or denied, for the failure of one part could have led to failure for the whole scheme. (And it has to be admitted that those of us who were external evaluators were sometimes equally complicit, remaining silent when drawing attention to an issue might have rent the whole scheme asunder.)

The second major series of stages in the development of TVEI, i.e. defining the themes, was then a continuing success of negotiation, but one which took place in particular histories and constrained by particular conditions and interests, and in a context where being able to demonstrate that something called TVEI was successful was the dominant criterion. The processes described in this chapter are so far essentially the development of, within and between the MSC and the LEAs, mandates and capacities for TVEI. We can summarize and embed them more thoroughly in the arguments we have put forward so far by relating them in particular to the issues we considered in Chapter 3. The MSC presented itself as representing to education 'the needs of industry'. As such, it provided for teachers a particular version of those needs and, derived from this, a model of vocationalism. There are, however, additional sources of such information which do not necessarily conform to the MSC prescription. Apart from agencies such as Understanding British Industry and Project Trident, schools have also developed their own local industry links through work experience schemes or Compacts. These alternative sources can often diverge quite radically from the MSC version of 'the needs of industry'. Educationalists need to keep in mind that as far as industry is concerned, the MSC is the Civil Service. Consequently, the occupationalist version of TVEI vocationalism can assume different forms depending upon how far it takes on the MSC model or develops around a more diffuse set of local school/industry links.

A similar distinction can be made in relation to the educationalist version. In this case, the basic tension was between TVEI as a project under the control of a project director with a team of school-based co-ordinators and TVEI limited to school-based initiatives. This tension reflected the threat that TVEI was often seen as presenting to the traditional power and autonomy of headteachers to run their own schools. The project can be seen as introducing a centralizing tendency into TVEI schemes at authority level. Project directors had the power to intervene directly in the running of individual schools, influencing the direction of funds, timetable organization and the distribution of TVEI-sponsored resources. Inevitably, this aroused considerable opposition from heads and often from other staff not directly involved with TVEI. At the same time, a strong project director could establish among TVEI teachers within an authority's scheme an alternative sense of professional identity which involved loyalty to the project and identification with it rather than with the school. In this way, TVEI teachers coud become a kind of cadre of curriculum innovators within an authority. TVEI teachers could often encounter a conflict of loyalties when attempting to reconcile TVEI project objectives with the policies of their individual schools.

At the other extreme, where the power of the project and its director was effectively curtailed, either as an authority policy or because of concerted opposition from heads, TVEI became more fully integrated into existing school practices and, correspondingly, less coherent at consortium or authority level. In many respects, this situation can be seen as the ideal form for TVEI as far as headteachers were concerned. Indeed, it was quite common to encounter the admission that schools tried to 'take the money and run'. Hence, in much the same way that a diffuse form of occupationalism could be constructed through *ad hoc* school/industry links at the local level, so a diffuse form of the educationalist model of TVEI could be established where projects failed to establish a strong, coherent form within an authority.

In addition to the educationalist/occupationalist dimension, we can distinguish between centralized/diffuse forms of TVEI – the latter reflecting the degree of power realized by the project director and of coherence achieved by TVEI between the schools within the scheme. Movement along this dimension towards the centralized or 'strong' project end of the spectrum entails changes in the professional identity of TVEI teachers, realized through the particular ideological form the project assumed along the educationalist/occupationalist dimension. The general hybrid form of TVEI delivery created a space within which these possibilities were worked out in terms of various structural/ideological combinations.

Hence, there are two fundamental sets of questions which can be asked: what was the source of a TVEI scheme's model of vocationalism – educationalist or occupationalist – and how far was the scheme centralized or diffuse? Putting the two together (Fig. 4.2) it becomes possible to define four basic ideal types:

1 *Centralized educationalist*. This can be termed 'the project model' and was centred around TVEI as an agent for progressive curriculum innovation based in experiential, process learning.

Figure 4.2 The structural and ideological dimensions of TVEI.

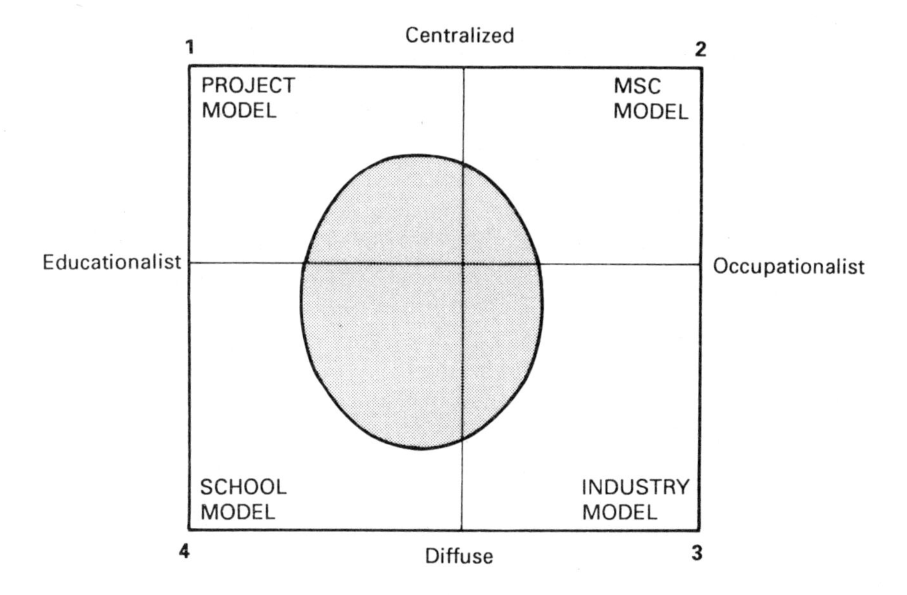

2 *Centralized occupationalist.* 'The MSC model', centred around manpower planning requirements and based in skills training objectives.
3 *Diffuse occupationalist.* 'The industry model', grounded in local school/industry links and concerned with developing 'industrial awareness', etc.
4 *Diffuse educationalist.* 'The school model', which prioritized school autonomy and independence within the framework of the TVEI project within an authority – the 'take the money and run' approach.

Experience suggests that 1 and 2, and 3 and 4 tended to be complementary, in that strong project directors invoked the authority of the MSC to back up contractual requirements where authorities or individual schools were seen to be falling out of line. At the same time, the MSC could call upon the director to ensure that the contract was being delivered. Developing independent links with local employers could be an effective strategy, whereby individual schools (and even individual teachers) could retain a sense of ownership over 'their' TVEI, and employers often preferred to make their own arrangements with schools rather than be involved with MSC 'bureaucracy'. Indeed, on the basis of personal experience, quite strong hostility towards the MSC can be encountered from industry training officers who resented what they saw as 'a bunch of civil servants' trying to tell them how to do their jobs.

In reality, these 'ideal types' were not to be found in pure form. As the shaded area of Fig. 4.2 illustrates, actual projects displayed features of each in a provisional form depending upon the changing balance of power and interests in any local situation.

Hence, TVEI is not a clearly defined 'thing', but a negotiated and dynamically evolving configuration of elements structured within the basic ideological and structural parameters of its local context. It was essentially a matter of identifying emphases and creating structures that enabled the TVEI submission to be accommodated by the authority and its schools, and the resources TVEI brought to have maximum incidental effects.

It is in the form of these themes, emphases and structures that TVEI effectively confronted the participating institutions. However, these themes, etc., were not imprinted on a *tabula rasa* when they were taken into the schools. Their reception and implementation in the schools represented the final, and in many ways the most crucial, stage of the progressive selection, interpretation and formulation of what became TVEI in practice. The schools that took on TVEI had histories, traditions, interests and conventions that could not be changed overnight, even if there had existed a willingness or a requirement for them to do so. Just as the version of TVEI that came to the schools was shaped by the LEAs' existing priorities and by their variable capacity to deliver different parts of the submission, so what became TVEI in schools similarly had to be accommodated to what existed – in terms both of mandate and capacity. This does not mean that the movement was all in one direction. It was certainly not a case of schools absorbing TVEI and its resources gratefully and carrying on just as they had before, except that these were somewhat better resources. This was known in the TVEI world as the 'take the money and run' approach, but it did not, to our knowledge, exist anywhere in anything like a *completely* pure form. It was, and is, very difficult for schools not to have to make a series of changes in what they do and how they do it as a result of taking on TVEI.

While the nature of these changes varied greatly, it is possible to indicate some broad dimensions of difference. The first set of differences came from how TVEI was managed within the schools. Some aspects of the management problem were laid down for schools by the nature of the contract. There had to be, for instance, a school co-ordinator, and a cohort of pupils identified as following TVEI. Cohorts varied in size, though 50–60 per school was the model size. Both features had direct and unavoidable consequences. The need to appoint a school co-ordinator added a new element to the school's management structure. School co-ordinators were appointed to all levels, from deputy head to scale 2 teachers, reflecting the status of TVEI in the school. The cohort acted as one basis for the school's accountability for the performance of its TVEI contract to the LEA and the MSC. In addition to this, TVEI represented a quite novel kind of problem for schools in the requirement to allocate and spend unprecedented high levels of resources, in a very short time, under a particular set of accountability conditions (e.g. the cohort, the contract), but with relatively little guidance as to how this should be done – apart from a set of guidelines and criteria that were rather unspecific when it came to school and classroom practice.

This latter problem, knowing how to spend the money, was paradoxically, the biggest problem for many TVEI schools in the early days of the pilot project. It was all very well to have new management and accountability structures, but that certainly did not, *ipso facto*, indicate how the money should be spent. The extent of this dilemma naturally varied from authority to authority depending on how tightly specified was the authority's remit to the schools. This varied in the authorities we looked at, but nowhere were schools left with no latitude or autonomy in deciding how to allocate their TVEI resources.

Across the TVEI authorities, two distinct models of reaction to this problem can be identified. One, identified by Murray Saunders on the basis of his evaluation of TVEI in several local authorities, is known as the 'enclave' model. The features of this model, as may be inferred from its label, are that the idea of this cohort is taken very seriously (it exists *de facto* as well as *de jure*), the resources are concentrated in a relatively narrow range of identifiable activities (especially the development of unequivocally technical and vocational subjects) and the TVEI has a distinct identity within the school. The other model might most appropriately be labelled the 'universalism' model. Here the potential benefit of TVEI to the whole school is the key criterion and, consequently, as resources are seen as enabling a technical and vocational advancement of the whole curriculum, the cohort tends to become a paper exercise, and TVEI as such has a very low – or even non-existent – profile within the school.

There are two crucial points to be noted about these models. First, they seem to be very much school-determined. Examples of each can be found in all our authorities. For instance, in one authority, two schools consistently refused to identify any cohort at all, the work of the TVEI co-ordinator was largely confined to completing returns to the MSC and national evaluation bodies, and most teachers as well as most pupils were unaware that for instance the computer network that enhanced work in all areas of the school had been funded by TVEI. In another school in the same authority, knowledge of TVEI was largely confined to the head and the school co-ordinator, who was also head of CDT. Resources were concentrated in a narrow range of areas for the benefit of pupils who followed a distinct curriculum. When the original head left the school as the end of the pilot phase approached, he was succeeded by his senior deputy, who knew nothing at all about TVEI. The second point is equally important and it brings us to the final stage of the template. It is that schools are not bound or confined to their original model. In the course of the pilot phase, TVEI in most schools that we know moved to a greater or lesser degree out of the enclave, and began to penetrate ever wider areas of the schools' offerings; the example given at the end of the last paragraph represents a limit case, where practically no movement at all took place in the pilot phase. The movement was also, in our collective experience, all in the same direction, i.e. towards universalism. We know of no cases where the definition and practice of TVEI became narrower over the course of the pilot phase.

Our broad explanation of why this shift took place and what its consequence for what TVEI was in the schools has two components. First, it registers that over the course of the project TVEI 'improved on acquaintance', and this had significant effects on both LEAs' and schools' perceptions of, and practices in, TVEI. Secondly, it draws on the notion of TVEI effect. This idea tries to capture the essence of the negotiation/accommodation between the pre-TVEI school and the changing emphases requirements of TVEI.

Given that TVEI came to the education world like a bolt from the blue and that it had to be up and running in such a very short time, it is not surprising that there was considerable ignorance about what it was, what it was intended to achieve and how. Neither was it surprising that this near vacuum of information was filled by speculation in the education world that was almost uniformly hostile. However, as information about how TVEI would actually operate gradually became available, and the first 14 pilot schemes got under way, it became apparent that the more that was known about TVEI the less threatening it seemed. And this process continued, until TVEI had become very widely accepted by the end of the first pilot phase, with even the NUT – who had been very strongly opposed to the idea – accepting its superiority as a means of curriculum development over the National Curriculum. What made this possible was not just the absence of substantiation of the original opponents' worst fears, but the gradual development of the idea that TVEI could form the basis for a new approach to secondary education, and bring about educational change in ways that were not threatening to the school's existing priorities (commitment to liberal education and a high level of exam passes). One vehicle for this change was the changing response of the LEAs. One of the criteria for TVEI was that its pilot programmes be 'readily replicable' in non-TVEI schools, and the need to spread the findings of TVEI pilots was necessarily on the LEAs' agenda. This, together with their formal role in the management of the projects, created the possibility of TVEI being used as the core, or the stimulus, for broader developments across the authorities. This possibility was brought closer to realization by two other factors. The first was the increasing 'acceptability' of TVEI. It came to connote not so much 'barbarism' as 'sensible responsiveness', to be a matter of a maximizing the pay off from the MSC's investment rather than limiting its damage. It became something to be associated with rather than to be avoided – and thus had the effect of putting much more LEA muscle at the disposal of TVEI (e.g. increasing contributions from Inspectors). There were two aspects to this. One was that the increasing 'acceptability' of TVEI was not merely a matter of LEAs and schools recognizing the inevitable and changing their attitudes. Real changes took place in what was officially sanctioned as part of TVEI. Over time there was less emphasis on such MSC-derived features as Occupational Training Families, and more recognition of the value of the development of personal qualities as well as technical and vocational skills (which is one major reason why, as we said at the start of this book, the goals seen by the director of the Extension of TVEI – as yet to be attained – were very similar to those that had informed the pilot scheme). The other aspects of this changing response to TVEI was the enthusiasm teachers in the pilot schools had shown for the more 'educational' versions of it. As is shown in Chapter 6, many teachers felt liberated and enabled by TVEI to teach topics they had always wanted to teach in ways they had wanted to teach them. The other factor was the announcement and installation of TRIST. As we have suggested, this had the effect of forcing the LEAs to strengthen and extend the role of their central TVEI teams, which were the source of both the greatest substantive and the greatest procedural expertise on bidding for and delivering external funding earmarked for the technical and vocational areas.

All this meant an expanded role – and a greater share of the resources – for the local TVEI Units, and concomitantly less resources for individual schools. It meant too an emphasis on programmes that could be replicated without great expense, which tended to mean a decreased emphasis on equipment and a greater emphasis on new tests of human resources, which in turn meant a broad shift from subject enhancement to curriculum initiatives. The way that TVEI became to a greater or lesser degree embedded in the practices and policies of the schools involved may be registered through what we call the TVEI effect. The separate features of the TVEI effect are discussed in detail in subsequent chapters, but it will be useful to bring this account of the installation of TVEI in practice to a close with a brief account of how they interacted with each other and especially with the existing characteristics of TVEI schools.

Critical differences between TVEI schemes come not only from their emphasizing different aspects of the guidelines – such as subject development, profiling or work experience – but from the particular combination of these aspects in each school. This combination is a key component of the 'TVEI effect', and its precise formulation was shaped by the reaction to, and interpretation of, the TVEI guidelines, and the resources available in the changing context of each school.

The TVEI effect – what TVEI meant within any school – was not produced only by each school's interpretation and combination of the set guidelines, however. It was also a function of the salience of the scheme within the school. This was made up of a number of factors, which will be discussed below. Like the combination of TVEI guidelines adopted within a school, the salience of TVEI results from the reaction of the headteacher and staff to the introduction of the scheme in the context of a particular school at a particular point in its history. The combination of TVEI guidelines and the scheme's salience within a school were mutually influential (whether mutually supportive or mutually hostile), and their relationship together with the effect on the scheme of any changes in the major part of the school, gave the TVEI effect its internal dynamic and determined the nature of the school's response to external factors.

Most obviously, introducing TVEI into a school might be expected to involve some change in what is taught, either through the introduction of new subjects to the curriculum or in the modification of existing subjects. There was, however, considerable variation in the extent of change in what was taught, from the introduction of a whole new slate of 'TVEI subjects' that did not previously exist in the school, to the use of TVEI resources to teach existing and unmodified syllabuses more effectively. It is important to recognize that the degree of subject change brought about by TVEI is not the only nor necessarily the most important index of its effect on schools. Though we would be right in assuming that it was typically a central component of the TVEI effect, it is possible to conceive of a potent TVEI effect being achieved in a school with little modification of pre-TVEI syllabuses.

A key 'non-subject' aspect of the TVEI was profiling. Though the guidelines speak only of 'records of achievement', in the great majority of TVEI schemes that requirement was met by something called 'profiling'. The possible variations of practice under that heading are very wide. Some schemes adapted 'off the shelf' existing forms of profiling, while others devised their own, often at great cost in terms of teachers' time and effort. A variety of possible uses for pupils' profiles exists. They can be summative or formative, for teacher use only or available to parents and student too, and so on; but the major distinction in their contribution to the TVEI effect was between those (relatively few) schemes where that contribution was substantive, with profiling a key organizing axis of the whole scheme, and the majority that limited it to a more or less important service function.

The contribution of work experience to the TVEI effect can be appreciated in a rather similar way, in that its extent and nature varied with the way students' periods of work experience were integrated into the scheme as a whole. The curriculum as a whole and the period of work experience could be organized in full recognition of the mutual benefit they could provide; or the organization of work experience could be seen as just another chore entailing taking the TVEI money and using it for things that were really important. The reaction to, and integration of, work experience can, indeed, stand for the perceived place and importance of 'links with industry' as a whole within TVEI schemes.

Residential education's contribution to the TVEI effect also varied with the nature and extent of its integration into the scheme as a whole. This applied to both of the two main forms it appears to have taken: the 'outward-bound' form, with the 'adventure and self-reliance' medium as a more central part of the message than the actual context in which it took place; and the 'curriculum enrichment' form, where students were brought into contact with aspects of their subjects that lay outside the ability of the school to provide. Besides the guidelines contained in the contract, there were some other necessary accompaniments of bringing TVEI into a school, which contributed to the TVEI effect. One of these was the prominence of the scheme in the school. Another very important one, already alluded to, was the need for schools to spend in a relatively short time relatively large sums of money (though the precise amount of money available for spending by schools and the precise degree of control they had over that spending varied). This presented both technical and political difficulties. The technical difficulties arose as much as anything from the schools' sheer inexperience of disposing of large sums of money in a short time in the most appropriate way. This inexperience, together with the short time-scale, did indeed lead to a conservatism in spending the money, i.e. a tendency to spend it on somewhat more advanced equipment for teaching essentially the same content. More time for deliberation and the consideration of alternatives may have led in some cases to rather more 'radical' uses of the money.

The political problems associated with the distribution of the extra funds may also have tended to push it into a similarly conservative direction. Any distribution, whether it is of equipment or additional salary points, is likely to be perceived as threatening by one or other subject departments or groups of staff within a school, and again there was some pressure towards changing as little as possible, 'doing more of the same', or introducing initiatives that crossed the whole curriculum.

The magnification of the TVEI impact in the school through monitoring and marginality clearly enhanced its prominence. This related to the 'salience' of TVEI in the school. It was made up of three components: identity, integration and compass. Identity refers both to the amount and to the nature of what was known about the scheme within the school. The public identity of a school's TVEI scheme could be found in the way the scheme was publicized to the staff, pupils and parents. It appeared perhaps most clearly in the way TVEI was 'marketed' to pupils and parents.

The nature and explicitness of references to TVEI in schools' 'option booklets' varied. A preferred target audience could also sometimes be inferred from these booklets by examination of subjects it was and was not possible to combine with TVEI options. The marketing of TVEI in different schools and schemes also placed varying emphases on its technical and vocational nature, and on how helpful it might be in obtaining a job. The clarity, popularity and divisiveness of the TVEI identity within a school were rooted in part in the kind of public face presented. They were also rooted in the less public aspect of TVEI in practice, which itself derived from the kind of changes entailed by the way the school interpreted and combined the guidelines.

Together with its identity, the extent of its integration into the school as a whole determined the TVEI 'people' in the school. It was possible, for instance, for TVEI pupils, their parents and teachers not to be aware of their TVEI status. The degree of integration of TVEI into the school was associated with the degree of separateness of the TVEI group(s). This was a function of the number of hours they spent being taught as a separate group, the number of teachers teaching them, whether or not they were a group for non-TVEI purposes – especially whether they were a distinct registration group – and whether or not they had their own accommodation. The extent of TVEI's integration into a school was also determined by the spread of information about it among those teachers not directly involved, whether they were made aware only of what they 'needed to know for the smooth operation of the scheme' – which in many cases was nothing – or of the broader details and ramifications of the scheme as a whole as it developed.

Its 'compass', the degree to which it penetrated and affected the workings of the rest of the school, was another part of its salience. The compass of TVEI in a school came about through a combination of articulation and infection. Articulation refers to the changes necessarily implied for the rest of the school by TVEI; for instance, in the timetable, or the need to construct viable classes in particular subjects. Infection refers to the 'voluntary' reactions in the rest of the school to TVEI. These could be positive, as might occur, for instance, in a decision to profile whole year groups and not just the TVEI/pupils, or negative, as might occur in the refusal of departments teaching 'core' subjects to accommodate any changes in approach implied by the introduction of TVEI; such as, for instance, a shift from English to 'communications', or Mathematics to 'numeracy'.

It is crucial to realize that the form taken by both components of the TVEI effect, the combination of the guidelines and its salience, emerged – and continued to change – through a complex process of negotiation between what was before TVEI and what might emerge as a result of it. These negotiations, explicit and implicit, between head and staff, co-ordinator and departments, members of the same department and so on, did not take place in a neutral arena. That arena was defined and marked by the history of previous negotiations unique to each school. TVEI both heightened the importance of some facets of that history, and brought new aspects of it into play, as well as filtering the effect of external events into and on the negotiations. Among the especially prominent conditions of negotiation over TVEI were:

1 The generally low level of morale within the teaching profession, following some years of declining funds, falling rolls and apparent decreasing public esteem. This meant a warm welcome for almost anything that promised extra funding and the possibility of professional development.
2 Considerable resistance among both the leadership and the rank and file of the teaching profession to a narrowly defined 'vocational education' – the preparation of factory fodder – and to anything that threatened the principles of comprehensive education.
3 The heightening of this resistance through the apparent attribution to teachers of blame for national decline in the debates that prefigured TVEI, where teachers appeared as scapegoats, as part of the problem rather than part of the solution.
4 The existence of a growing pressure towards some kind of differential reward for different performance in the payment of teachers.
5 The possibility that some subjects might disappear from the curriculum with declining staffing levels.
6 Apprehension over the effects of the entry of the MSC into the area of further education.
7 A heightened awareness of competition between secondary schools, possibly involving their very survival, as a result of falling rolls.

Not all these factors applied in all cases. More importantly, they did not all carry equal weight. For instance, the need for extra funds may have sometimes outweighed reservations about TVEI. It did not remove those reservations, though, and a common pattern of acceptance of TVEI into a school was to attempt to do it with minimum infringement of those reservations. But that was only one form of response, albeit fairly typical. The main point is that whatever the orientation towards TVEI, however significant the various conditions of negotiation may be, TVEI was never merely imposed on schools. It was always accepted on certain implicit or explicit conditions based largely on the existing history, ideology, structure and location of the school, to produce a TVEI effect unique to that school (see Dale, 1990; McCulloch, 1989).

PART 2

TOPIC STUDIES

CHAPTER 5

Records of Achievement and profiling in TVEI

Introduction

While this chapter aims to explore Records of Achievement (ROA) and profiling as aspects of the TVEI, it is recognized that both have broader histories and, in recent years, have received direct and discrete government attention and finance. Consequently, we face the difficulty of separating out the 'TVEI effect' on ROA from that of other developments. Indeed, the interim report of the Pilot Records of Achievement in Schools Evaluation (PRAISE) team makes much the same point about the ROA initiatives.

> Such changes are clearly not the product of the records of achievement initiative alone but are part of a concerted thrust brought about by GCSE, TVEI, CPVE and other initiatives; the respective contribution of each of these is impossible to separate out (Broadfoot, 1987: 85).

Records of Achievement, profiling and the TVEI agenda

The insertion of ROA and profiling into TVEI partly reflected the MSC's concern to tackle very similar problems to those the government had identified, and partly came from the spread of profiling in the New Vocationalist movement associated with the Further Education Unit (FEU) and the validation boards (e.g. City and Guilds of London Institute (CGLI) and Business and Technician Education Council [BTEC]); namely, the desire to record the personal development of students, the belief that non-academic achievement should be recorded and thus rewarded (linked to questions of motivation), and the suggestion that the information provided by examinations is insufficient for employers to use as a basis for selection. However, at this stage, profiling and ROA were seen in a slightly different light by the

DES, 1984 and the MSC (1984a); this was a question of emphasis, not a major difference of opinion. Where the MSC stressed the benefits to student motivation and assistance in gaining employment, the DES retained a concern for the broader educational benefits, such as helping schools to cater more effectively for individual students' needs and motivating students to learn a whole range of skills, not just those relevant to the world of work. This difference between what might be termed an 'occupationalist' and an 'educationalist' view has been present throughout the TVEI pilot projects (see Chapter 3).

In addition, the different 'messages' from the MSC and the DES were further complicated by the shifts of emphasis from the government on ROA and TVEI, over the period of the pilot schemes. The proposals for National Criteria, for GCSE, for a National Curriculum and, finally, the Education Reform Act in 1988, all had implications for ROA and TVEI. As the PRAISE team pointed out, reflecting on the 'climate' for the development of ROAs:

> Recent policy developments in terms of the national curriculum and testing initiatives have substantially added to these worries since it would appear that the philosophy behind these moves is at odds with that of records of achievement in emphasising pass/fail assessment, testing which is not integral to the curriculum and a subject rather than a skill based curriculum (Broadfoot, 1987: 93).

We believe this confusion arose from the commitment of the government to the ideology of the 'free market' and the difficulty they have found in translating this into social policy and, in particular, into educational policy.

Conservative social policy and the 'free market'

For the free marketeers within the government, the ideal labour market would be based on a relationship between education and the economy in which the wage nexus determined the long-term levels of supply and demand for labour (Moore, 1986). It would be characterized by an educational system that was responsible for ensuring the supply of labour to an economy which generated the demand for labour. The market would operate in the same manner as other commodity markets with educational credentials indicating the potential 'value' of labour to employers. In the modern economy, with labour in a differentiated and hierarchical form to meet the needs of the division of labour (the latter being considered, by free marketeers, to be the outcome of the most technically efficient and profitable method of distributing the workforce), the output of the educational system would mirror the division of labour and the subjects taught would serve the needs of the economy (Dale and Pires, 1984).

However, translating the long-term economic aims into social policy proved to be far from straightforward for the government. To begin with, the very existence of a state-financed education sector which had been permitted 'licensed autonomy' (Dale, 1979), and was thus detached from direct state control, provided a problem for those in the government committed to a free market economy. Simply maintaining such a sector allowed the possibility of a 'disconnected' system to continue, i.e. an educational system neither regulated by the State on behalf of the market nor dependent upon market forces to decide the quantity and the 'quality' of the different types of labour supplied. This situation was made all the more difficult when the free market economy was not the only 'consumer' of the educational system's 'products'. In addition to employers, parents and students, the further and higher educational systems and the public sector were also viewed as consumers. Thus any free market economy would find itself in direct competition with the interests of other social groupings. The difficulty for the Conservative government was constructing a mixture of educational and assessment policies that would provide the sort of allocative and regulative mechanisms that could make education part of a free market economy.

In terms of assessment, the 'ideal' social system for the free marketeers might look something like the social extension of the free market philosophy that is to be found in technical function theory (Dale and Pires, 1984). This suggests that qualifications should come to act as an entitlement to jobs, with employers simply allocating the appropriately qualified people to the 'correct' slot within their firm (the apotheosis of a demand-led meritocracy!). At the same time, the educational system would become rapidly aware of changes in demand and would adjust its distribution of different skill levels and the content of courses in response. Thus qualifications would stand in a dual relation to the educational system and the economy: first, as a means of differentiating labour for allocation, in conjunction with the wage nexus, to the appropriate position in the labour market; secondly, as a mechanism for ensuring the educational system produces the variety of human skills necessary for production, i.e. as a means of quality control. Put rather more succinctly, they would operate in conjunction with wages as an allocative and regulative mechanism, servicing the economy.

TVEI, ROA and profiling were all initial attempts to refine the supply side of the problem, i.e. inserting a technical and vocational element into the curriculum, making it more relevant to the world of work, and through a refinement and expansion of the data gathered on students, helping to ensure the products of the educational system were more effectively allocated.

	Supply (education system)	*Demand (employers' 'needs')*
Allocation	Profiling, ROAs	Recruitment policies
Regulation	TVEI 'content'	'Market forces'

Thus, while it is quite possible to see above how the underlying aims of TVEI and the ROA, on the supply side of the matrix, might be 'accommodated' within a free market framework, it is rather more difficult to see how the strategy of state 'interference' relates to 'market forces'. Indeed, it is possible to suggest the two are in direct contradiction. Free market economics privileges the demand side, and in particular the regulative side of the matrix. This requires the government to withdraw from intervening on the supply side. However, whatever the long-term plans of the free marketeers in the government, the complete dismantling of state educational provision and its replacement with a private or 'privatized' system, was never a political option. Consequently, there was a tension within the government between the maintenance of state provision and the creation of a free market position for education. As others have observed, this tension was politically evident in the split between the neo-liberal and neo-conservative elements within the New Right (Gamble, 1985).

The announcement of the proposals for a National Curriculum and the further contents of the 1988 Education Reform Act, have shown up this tension and created further uncertainties over the climate for TVEI and ROA. On the one hand, the National Curriculum is highly state-interventionist; on the other, the plans for Open Enrolment and Local Management of Schools seek to open education up to market forces (Ball, 1988). In the latter case, we can now see how the government intends to create an 'educational market', to produce a mechanism within education that will match the markets of the economy, as well as opening education up to wider 'market forces'. In an information pamphlet for the National Union of Teachers (NUT), Ted Wragg (1988) clearly shows how the elements of the 1988 Act add up to an attempt to employ market principles to the field of education. If this analysis is right, then it suggests the government is now less concerned with the old policy of intervening on the supply side to 'connect' education to the world of employment and far more with applying the market mechanism within and around the educational setting.

This provides a role for the State not unlike that of the 'head office' of a national commercial or industrial concern, i.e. the checking of standards and quality control. The interest of the State in testing and assessment now becomes more concerned with the external measurement of the effectiveness of institutions in maintaining standards. The question of how students are hierarchically differentiated for their placement in the workforce is no longer an issue for the State; it is to be resolved at the interface between education and employment. Neither is pedagogy a central source of worry; that is the responsibility of the teaching profession. The concern of the State is to ensure that educational institutions are held accountable to market forces via 'measurable' criteria, i.e. performance indicators. Such indicators place a stress upon quantifiable, summative documentation about student achievement on specifiable courses of study, at present the National Curriculum. This stands in direct contradiction to the principles many institutions have developed for their ROA, where formative processes and qualitative information are highlighted.

While this contradiction between the summative and the quantifiable on the one hand and the formative and the qualitative on the other is now emerging as an overtly political issue, the recognition of such a tension within the ROA and profiling 'movement' has been longstanding. A great deal of the debate within the LEAs, TVEI Units and educational institutions revolved around this tension. The 'messages' from the government, the DES and the MSC were keenly watched for evidence of how the ROA and the profiling lobby were 'faring' at a policy-making level. If we are right in suggesting that in the long term the balance has been tipping towards quality control and institutional effectiveness, then the mandate for the sorts of ROA and profiling favoured in the developments we have seen may well be under threat.

The role of Records of Achievement and profiling in the local authority projects

The first section indicates that there were a variety of 'agendas', apart from that of the MSC, providing LEAs, educational institutions and individuals within these settings, with varying and sometimes contradictory views of ROA and profiling. Furthermore, our evidence indicates that the LEAs and the schools embraced ROA as part of their *own* agendas for changing education. Agendas that contained differing aspects of those identified above, but tended to lean, perhaps not surprisingly, towards questions of motivation and more progressive forms of pedagogy. In this section, we want to explore how the differing agendas, histories and capacities of the MSC and the LEAs have produced a diverse picture of developments in ROA and profiling.

The original submissions to the MSC vary greatly in the stress they lay upon either profiling or ROA. Although the criteria for the TVEI contained the following:

> On completing their studies, students should be issued by the LEA with a record of achievement describing qualifications gained and recording significant elements and attainments which are not readily deducible from the qualification, e.g. work experience and personal success (MSC, 1985a),

it would appear that the MSC did not insist on a detailed plan for implementing such records as a central criteria for accepting LEA submissions.

There is clear evidence that some authorities none the less chose to make it a vital part of their submission, and have used it as a vehicle for curriculum development (Training Agency, 1988). Others have only begun to develop ROAs as the implications of the government's Statement of Policy, 1984, began to filter through, i.e. that LEAs would need to begin a developmental process that aimed to establish '. . . agreed principles and a framework of national policy which can provide a basis for introducing records of achievement throughout England and Wales' (DES, 1984).

Authorities varied in the aims they set out for developing either profiles or a system of ROA. These appear to have been split along two axes; based, on the one hand, upon a continuum running from an interest in a more effective method of recording student achievement to a concern with curriculum development, and, on the other, from the commitment to an 'educationalist' view to the belief in an 'occupationalist' view (see Fig. 5.1). It is important to note here that we are not suggesting that 'educationalist' equals teachers and 'occupationalist' equals employers. However, for the most part this division of concern between teachers and employers was evident.

Figure 5.1 Reasons for introducing Records of Achievement or profiling

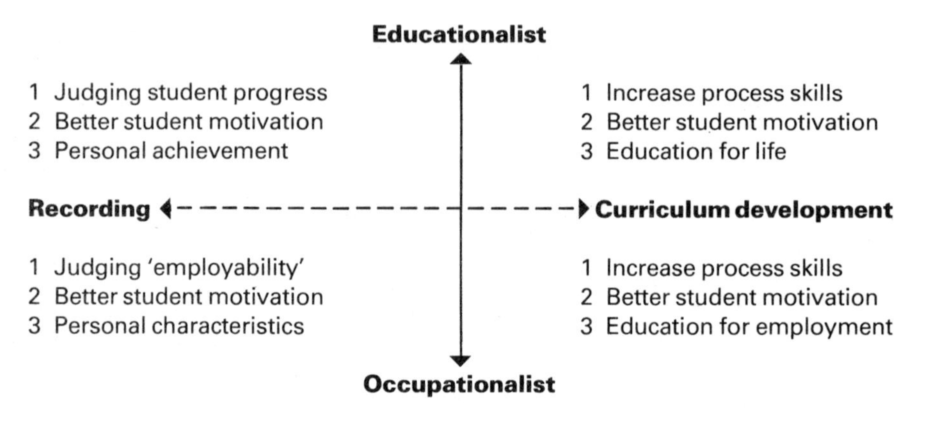

Interestingly, in the case of the horizontal axis, the PRAISE team found precisely the same split in their sample:

> While some schools welcome the potential of records of achievement to galvanise or legitimate curriculum development, and build curriculum development and staff development objectives into their development models, other schools have the less ambitious objective to establish a more effective recording and reporting procedure which requires no curriculum development (Broadfoot, 1987: 58).

We believe it is necessary to add the second axis to indicate the split between those who believed any system should be educationally rooted and seek to enhance educational processes, and those who showed a greater concern for preparing students for the world of work and employment and therefore looked towards the requirements of outside agencies as a starting point. The sectors show the different motivations of those involved in developing ROA and the interesting 'constant' is student motivation. On the latter, the crucial difference was that some saw employment as the key motivator, whereas others considered student involvement in the learning process as central. This variety of concerns appears to have informed the processes that TVEI projects developed for producing ROA or a system of profiling. The precise outcome reflected the particular approaches taken by the LEAs and the local TVEI Units. Who they chose to involve, when and how they chose to involve them, and the capacities of those involved to insert their own concerns above or alongside others' concerns.

We were very aware that consultation with employers varied in both its quality and extent and in the purposes it was intended to serve. Some authorities involved employers from the outset and even began by trying to set up a summative profile with their help. However, this was an exception rather than a rule. Far more common was a period of consultation, following the development of a profiling system within the school (often, but not always, involving the TVEI cohort only), that came out of a recognition that the summative document was to serve different purposes to the formative documents. Thus one authority 'briefed' employers about its development of a formative system and only drew them into a period of consultation once this was well established. Interestingly, the response of employers to such an approach was extremely positive, accepting the need for a phased style of consultation and appreciating the order of events. For some authorities, the consultation only involved requests for comments on alternative pro-formas for the summative profile, while others involved employers in the whole process of design and the principles that would operate in compiling the summative document.

Throughout the pilot projects, the commitment of individuals and organizations was highly variable as the 'messages' from the key bodies appeared to change. The considerable amount of work required multiplied any sense of discouragement and it is an indication of the commitment of those involved that so many ROA and profiling schemes were in an advanced state of development by the time projects moved into Extension. Furthermore, many of the Extension proposals lay a far greater stress on ROA than the original pilot submissions.

One very important decision by local TVEI Units was the appointment of development officers or advisers to oversee ROA and profiling within all the TVEI schools. (Some authorities and TVEI Units negotiated dually funded secondments from the schools; others were seconded from the advisory service and there were some external appointments.) These people made a considerable difference to the speed with which things moved forward, although their activities were generally circumscribed by the overall approach of the authority and the TVEI Unit. For the most part, they worked closely with the TVEI project director/co-ordinator and with a team of school co-ordinators, either appointed to oversee TVEI in the school or with a more specific ROA/profiling brief. In view of the impact of development officers and advisers, an impact that was equally evident in the case of individuals who were appointed for aspects of curriculum development, the timing of the appointment became a significant factor. Most appointments were made in the later years of the pilot schemes, which was partly an indication of the priority given to ROA and profiling and partly a measure of the perceived need to respond to the government's Statement of Intent in 1984.

What remains difficult to assess is the extent to which TVEI actually affected the approach and the content of the emerging ROA and profiling. We have indicated that many of the findings in the PRAISE document strongly resonate with our experiences in TVEI. With respect to the LEAs and the TVEI Units and their relations with the central TVEI Unit, it seems that the original submission allowed a great deal of freedom for local developments to move at their own pace and pick up their own inflections. Although the MSC agenda for ROA and profiling may well have differed from the concerns of educationalists, their capacity to impose such an agenda was rarely, if ever, in evidence. Far more important were the local responses of the LEAs, the TVEI Units and the educational institutions. Thus, as the policy 'slipped down' towards the schools it developed in different ways as key individuals and groups brought their own educational agendas and interpretations of the limits and possibilities inherent in the policy to bear upon the implementation process.

The educational institutions

The developmental process

Whatever strategies or principles for ROA and profiling were negotiated between the MSC, the LEAs and the local TVEI Units, the major developmental work was always going to rest with the 'grassroot' teachers and lecturers. The fact that introducing a system of ROA or profiling went far beyond simply requiring teachers and lecturers to adopt new reporting procedures, resulted in a developmental process in which the relations between the LEAs, the local TVEI Units and the educational institutions were far from 'top-down'.

All of the schemes with which we are familiar included a commitment to formative assessment (using assessment as a means of helping students' progress) and showed a concern to value students' 'non-academic' achievements. Such commitments and concerns had considerable implications for teaching and learning styles and for the level of administration that needed to be undertaken by the 'grassroots' teachers and lecturers. Thus while it was often the case that the local TVEI Unit, the LEA and the senior people in the educational institutions wished to take a key *strategic* role, it was often the concerns and issues of classroom teachers that played a central role in the processes and momentum of developments. Consequently, the strategists, requiring the cooperation of the teachers and lecturers, were forced to take 'winning consent' very seriously and had to include teacher and lecturer cooperation as an element in their strategy.

Setting up ROA and profiling tended to become bound up with the issue of institutional autonomy *vs* central direction, an issue that retained a constant place upon the schools' and colleges' agendas. To begin with, any process of change required work that would be cut across by the demands of subject departments for profiles that reflected their own subject area. In many cases, the local TVEI Unit and the LEA were forced to accept that subject-specific profiles would have to be a starting point before a more general development of ROA could take place. This in turn had a tendency to undermine the capacity of the local TVEI Unit and the LEA to secure coherence in the profiling and ROA schemes, at least at the outset.

Furthermore, the ill-defined specification of the desired outcome in the original submission, coupled with this sheer organizational complexity, tended to make it even more difficult for TVEI Units, at a central or local level, or indeed LEAs, to control the developmental process tightly as it continued to unwind. This was exacerbated by the initial recognition within the TVEI bodies and the LEAs, that educational institutions were at very different stages of development, both as institutions and with respect to departments, and this added to the difficulty of imposing an approach or a timetable of change that was uniform across the authority or indeed authorities. Again, the experiences of the PRAISE team implies there were interesting parallels in their sample of schools and colleges:

> Schools need flexibility to use resources in the way that best meets their needs and their existing funding procedures, echoing the balance between institutional autonomy and

scheme coherence that must now be regarded as the key issue in the development of records of achievement (Broadfoot, 1987: 88).

The outcome in many authorities was an institutionally based growth, with co-ordination across institutions, and even within institutions, emerging rather slowly. Not surprisingly, this led, in some cases, to a neglect of the issues of validation and accreditation and a concentration upon what was to be recorded and how. While some authorities and local TVEI Units attempted to solve the former problem by linking up with the examination board initiatives (Oxford Certificate for Educational Achievement [OCEA], South East Records of Achievement [SERA], etc.), the sense that the summative document might not have a 'national' status did not help 'grassroots' confidence. We can therefore detect a tension between the external acceptability of the final ROA and the desire to retain levels of autonomy in the developmental process (or 'delivery' *vs* creating 'a sense of ownership', in the language of TVEI).

In Fig. 5.2, an attempt has been made to show some of the concerns and issues that were generated within the institutions by the tensions implicit in the developmental process. It is important to recognize that the manifestation of such tensions has both historical and micropolitical dimensions. Thus for many projects, the early discussions were dominated by the upper quadrants of the figure, with concern over the lower quadrants an ever present worry. As projects continued, so the discussions moved increasingly towards the bottom of the figure. However, this was not the picture in every case and the varying involvement of local employers, examination boards, the LEA and the local TVEI Unit, and at different times in the process, produced varied developmental histories.

Consequently, although the majority of the evidence we have suggests that educational aims featured far more prominently than selection aims, this may be an artefact of the period in which our data was gathered. That is to say, the formative aspect of profiling and ROAs were given greater prominence at LEA and school level, particularly where the Inspectorate were drawn in, because the developmental

Figure 5.2 Institutional concerns about the development process

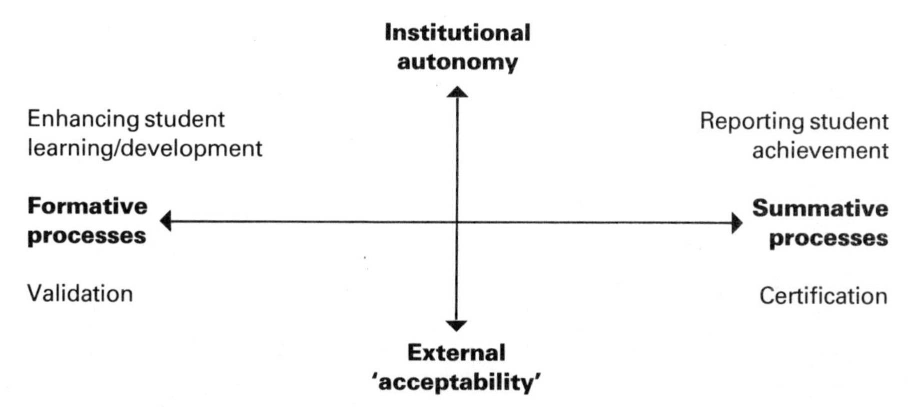

process was still in its early stages and required a specific relationship between the educational institutions and the LEA level. It is perhaps illustrative that where profiling or ROA development officers were appointed, often with advisory status, to focus developments across the whole authority (some of these being jointly financed by the LEA and TVEI), many reported that their major task was 'negotiating' between departments in schools, and between schools themselves and the LEA and local TVEI Unit to secure some level of agreement over the principles that were to underlie ROA.

Such tensions, of course, correspond closely to those noted by other authors (e.g. see Hargreaves, 1985) between the formative and summative aspects of profiling and ROA. The extent to which the former is allowed 'space' to develop depends a great deal upon decisions taken at a national level and the capacity of teachers and others to make an impact here as well as the local 'climate' and the acceptability of ROA among external users.

Virtually all the evidence we have points to considerable enthusiasm among those employers who have been consulted. However, getting a representative sample of local employers was far from straightforward. Small and medium-sized firms had great difficulty providing people who could attend all the developmental meetings and participate in the growth of ROA. While many were sympathethic to the general aim of supplying more information about students, it is not altogether clear what use the majority of employers will make of profiles. There was a suspicion among the personnel and public relations officers of the large firms (very often the people who 'represented' employers) that the page containing examination results would be considered first, thus excluding the other achievements of students. They felt this would be compounded where there were a large number of applications, leading to people feeling unable to take the time to read the whole of a profile. The difficulty of involving employers in the developmental work could, therefore, lead to a misuse by them of the final document, possibly undermining the value of the summative document and, in particular, the non-examination achievements of the students.

Institutional processes of change

It is within the institutional processes of change that the hopes and fears of educational policy makers at the national and LEA levels are realized. The powerful histories of institutions, transcribed within their managerial structures, practices and ethos may well have either complementary or contradictory impacts upon the processes of change set in motion to develop ROA and profiling.

In general terms, teachers have reacted positively to the development of profiling, however unsure and reticent they may have initially been. This concurs with the evidence from the PRAISE report:

> The reports are almost united in reporting improved teacher–pupil relationships and of teachers being delighted with the impact of new teacher strategies in creating better learning climates (Broadfoot, 1987: 90).

In our particular sample, this of course applied far more to those with a TVEI 'brief', who had already had the opportunity to consider the benefits that new teaching and learning styles could bring in terms of better teacher–student relations and student motivation. There remained difficulties for TVEI staff in convincing their colleagues that change was necessary. Ultimately, that will be crucial to providing a system of profiling or a ROA that gains credence in the eyes of the staff, students, parents and other users.

For many teachers, profiling and ROA contain within them contradictory elements. Thus, while the process of profiling may well appeal to teachers committed to more liberal forms of educational provision, the connection of this to the needs of employers sits rather uneasily with their views of education as a 'good thing in itself'. For the more traditional teachers, who take a far more content-based view of the curriculum, the shift towards a skills-based curriculum is seen as a weakening of both educational standards and the formal teacher-student relationships that ensure 'discipline'.

We were interested to note the impact of the local labour market and levels of employment/unemployment upon teachers' commitment to ROA and profiling. There were certainly some staff who viewed high unemployment as a factor in deciding to pursue profiling, the logic being that students needed all the help they could get in securing jobs and ROA provided a more positive account of achievement than the stark recording of examination results. In areas where there was little unemployment, great efforts were required to convince teachers of the merits of any change. This was especially the case where a good examination success rate raised the question in teachers' minds, why change?

Set against this generally positive view of ROA and profiling were longer-term processes that began to make an increasing impact upon the schools during the period under consideration. Some of these processes have been expanded and deepened with the announcement of the Education Reform Act in 1988. To begin with, Michael Apple's notion of 'innovation overload' became increasingly evident. This has brought with it what he has termed 'intensification', whereby workloads have tended to reduce the opportunity for constructive and reflective interaction between teachers: 'Getting done becomes more important than what was done or how one got there' (Apple, 1983: 59). This has had important effects upon the institutional processes of change in many of the schools, tending to concentrate the activities of teachers upon what Apple refers to as the technical and administrative tasks, i.e. 'delivering' a profile has become more important than considering the educational and philosophical issues it raises.

Futhermore, there is a sense in which some schools have turned to 'management' as at least one panacea for dealing with the overload. The latter has been clearly encouraged by TVEI (see Chapter 10) and also reflects other aspects of government policy (Ball, 1988). This process of increasing the managerial work of senior staff has been a steady development as external initiatives have been placed upon schools' agendas.

Decision making, planning and setting priorities has not only been a new feature of the curriculum, it has become a far more prominent activity of heads and deputies as well. Dealing with the increasing requests for information and for responses to a whole mass of initiatives from both central and local government has required a much greater level of managerial skill from senior staff. The cost to many classroom teachers has often been a sense of exclusion from developments. However, as we have noted, many teachers have shown a dogged commitment to the 'educational' aspects of ROA which may well reflect a desire, in the words of a number of teachers and LEA officials, we spoke to, '. . . to get something going before it is imposed upon us'. In other words, the early indecisiveness evident in the developmental process was seen to present an opportunity to 'make policy' and control their destinies in a way that was being denied in other areas. Equally, however, teachers' responses to ROA were sometimes negative, the considerable amount of change in teaching and learning styles required and the consequent demands upon teachers' time and overall commitment being set against the erosion of teacher morale and their feelings of exclusion from the processes of consultation over educational change and in respect of their pay and conditions of service.

Student reactions have been mixed, and in some areas the initial enthusiasm has waned as the reviewing and counselling processes have become a routinized aspect of school life. There was evidence of difficulties, ironically among low-ability students who found the self-motivation, decision-making and problem-solving elements of profiling especially difficult to accommodate. However, teachers regularly pointed to the fact they felt they were having to learn new skills and that the different approaches to teaching and learning with students would take time before they became really effective.

Discussion

Quite apart from TVEI, LEAs are certainly having to develop strategies for ensuring that the mechanisms necessary for the awarding of ROAs, in 1995, will be in place (DES, 1984). Many LEAs have undertaken massive amounts of work with teachers to fulfil this edict. However, more recently, the Education Minister, Angela Rumbold, announcing the bringing in of regulations on reporting individual pupils' achievements, stated:

> We intend, however, that the requirements of the regulations, particularly as they apply to years between the ends of Key Stages, should be kept to a minimum, so that they do not add overall to the volume of work already undertaken by schools in recording and reporting pupils' achievements (DES, 1989).

This has been interpreted by many teachers and educational observers as a nail in the ROA coffin. It appears to effectively rule out non-academic achievements and to thus stultify aspects of the formative process.

This leaves us with a very unclear picture of future developments. It may be that the government's commitment to the National Curriculum, the pressure on LEAs to 'deliver' both this and the local management of schools (LMS), and the involvement of schools in preparing for LMS could squeeze out or restrict the scope of ROA; in particular, producing a neglect of attainments outside the National Curriculum. A great deal will depend upon the extent to which the institutional processes of change already begun actually produce a cultural shift in the schools' and colleges' attitudes to ROA that override the new pressures they will face under the Education Reform Act of 1988.

CHAPTER 6

Teachers in TVEI

Introduction

Implicit in the stated aims of TVEI was the overriding intention to change the nature of state-funded secondary education and, thereby, to change the role and nature of teaching and teachers. Fundamental changes are, perhaps, more likely to be 'successful' if they proceed from the basis of a fresh start, with totally committed staff working in a purpose-built or 'dedicated' environment. For example, John Watts (1980) commented that the Countesthorpe experiment could not even have got off the ground if it had been attempted with an existing, rather than a selected staff. The TVEI did not have this luxury. Quite a number of people were recruited to posts created by TVEI but the majority have found themselves involved just because they happened to teach in a particular institution. Furthermore, classroom teachers themselves had very little to do with the initial design of TVEI schemes, because those writing the submissions tended to be advisers and, occasionally, headteachers. Partly due to lack of time, wider consultation was frequently, at most, perfunctory and limited. TVEI was, therefore, an 'imposed change' (Sikes, 1989).

Those delivering TVEI were teachers who were trained and experienced in particular approaches. They worked in institutions and with colleagues who, like themselves, had certain aims and values predating, and different from, those of the initiative. In some respects, TVEI could be seen to carry an implicit criticism of these approaches, aims and values and of what had gone on before. This obviously coloured teachers' attitudes towards the change. Fullan (1982: 24–6) suggests that the crux of change is how individuals come to terms with it in the context of their own reality. This means that the same change can be experienced as positive or negative on what the teacher perceives and experiences it to mean for them, and the extent to which it is compatible with their aims and values.

Whatever form it took, the TVEI was a social construction, realized through peoples' ideas, interpretations and understandings in the context of the organization in which they worked. If, following Ball (1987) and Barr-Greenfield (1975), an organization is defined as 'the varied perceptions by individuals of what they can, should, or must do in dealing with others within the circumstances in which they find themselves' (Barr-Greenfield, 1975: 65), any investigation and attempt to begin to (a) understand and explain the processes and events associated with the TVEI and (b) to develop a basis from which to assess the nature and extent of TVEI outcomes and achievements, must go back to individual perceptions, motivations and experiences. Taking such an approach links the macro and the micro, for by studying individuals it is possible to discern the general (cf. Goodson, 1980; see also Thomas and Znaniecki, 1919–20).

Innovations and changes in existing practices have widespread implications. As Ball (1987: 32) notes, they

> tend to advance or enhance the position of certain groups and disadvantage or damage the position of others. Innovations can threaten the self-interests of participants by undermining established identities, by de-skilling and therefore reducing job satisfaction. By introducing new working practices which replace established and cherished ways of working, they threaten individual self concepts. Vested interests may also be under threat: innovations not infrequently involve the redistribution of resources, the restructuring of job allocations and redirection of lines of information flow. The career prospects of individuals or groups may be curtailed or fundamentally diverted.

Our aim in this chapter is to look at what the introduction of TVEI meant to some teachers and lecturers with a view to illustrating the ways in, and the extent to, which the scheme 'succeeded' in changing their perceptions and experiences of their role. We have chosen to focus on experiences and perceptions relating to:

- TVEI and promotion/job prospects;
- TVEI and job content, divided into 'servicing the scheme' and 'classroom/subject content'; and
- pedagogy.

While these divisions are artificial, they do serve as a useful framework for ordering the information.

We have adopted, as an analytical tool, a two-dimensional career-based model (see Hughes, 1937; Sikes, 1986a) and have asked:

1. What implications TVEI had for *objective* careers, i.e. what *actually* happened to people because of TVEI? For instance: Were they promoted? Did their working conditions or the content of their job change in any way?
2. What TVEI meant for their *subjective* career, i.e. how they felt about and interpreted their 'objective' TVEI career and what part they thought TVEI played in making their life what it is?

Inevitably, circumstances, including objective career structures, constrain and influence subjective careers, but this does not make them any the less unique experiences and constructions of the individual. In other words, people give their own meanings to their careers. This means that two people in practically identical jobs can have quite different subjective experiences of that job because their other careers and life-experiences are different and take place in different social and cultural contexts.

A two-dimensional model is also a helpful device for indicating the reflexive relationship between teachers' careers and the shape of TVEI itself. For example, there is evidence to suggest that in the early days of the initiative, some teachers believed that they could improve their prospects of promotion by developing conspicuous and elaborate innovatory schemes. Consequently, for a time and in some LEAs, TVEI came to be identified and characterized in terms of such schemes.

TVEI and promotion/job prospects

During the 1960s, a growing population meant that the educational system was constantly expanding. Teachers were in short supply and jobs were plentiful. People could pick and choose, promotions were often bestowed without being actively sought and there were many accelerated careers. Falling rolls and the consequent contraction of the 1970s resulted in a dramatic reduction in the number of promotional posts available and an increase in the number of teachers whose career expectations and aspirations were disappointed (see Dennison, 1981; Sikes, 1986a). Morale was low.

Then into the scenario came the TVEI, bringing with it money for promotion points. It also created new jobs, and hence a new career structure, within schools, at LEA level and nationally with the MSC. Although in actual numbers these job opportunities were limited, some teachers *did* benefit, and the very fact that there were new jobs did perhaps help to begin to raise optimism in some quarters.

Because the TVEI was innovative, many of the jobs associated with it were new and characteristically different from existing posts. For example, they included MSC regional advisers who were each responsible for advising and guiding a number of TVEI projects; scheme co-ordinators/directors and assistant co-ordinators/directors who administered, co-ordinated and developed LEA TVEI projects; and school co-ordinators who co-ordinated projects within schools.

In addition, across the various projects, there were specific and idiosyncratic TVEI-sponsored or -initiated jobs at all levels from 'main grade' through to advisory positions. In general, the majority of school-based TVEI staff were internally recruited (Pole, 1986), and central team members tended to come from within the authority where much use was made of secondments.

Within schools, many subject-related TVEI posts of responsibility were in 'practical' areas which previously carried 'low status' and few and limited opportunities for advancement (see Bennet, 1985; Hilsum and Start, 1974; Lyons, 1981). Similarly, because of the TVEI emphasis on practical, technical and vocational subjects, scheme co-ordinators (who were generally paid on the same scales as headteachers or advisers), were often recruited from these areas. Traditional status hierarchies (and the expectations associated with them) were, therefore, challenged (cf. Harland, 1987: 48). As the teacher quoted below pointed out:

> All of a sudden the boot's on the other foot. We're the ones with the money for a change and they don't like it, or its given them a shock. Craft subjects have always been the Cinderella subjects but money makes a difference. They might still see us as being primarily for the duggies, I think there is some feeling along those lines with some of the staff, not all, but TVEI has given us a bit of a leg up. And of course, as you know, there aren't many senior posts in the area, right so there may be a head of department on a (scale) four, but there aren't many headteachers from woodwork or metal work or the practical subjects in general. You tend to have to go out of school into advisory posts, and practical teachers, they quite often have their own extra business if you know what I mean. But the TVEI director down the road in [. . .] was metalwork and he's not the only one so its improved job prospects, not a lot but it's made a difference, psychologically if nothing else (design and technology teacher).

Also, because some TVEI jobs were new and different, very few people had previous direct experience and therefore no particular group of teachers were obvious candidates. This opened up opportunities for those whose career prospects via the 'traditional' routes were poor or not as good as they had hoped, and for those who were looking for a change of direction in the hopes that it would speed their progress. For instance:

> I suppose my prospects were relatively good anyway, I mean, I'm 27, I went to Oxbridge, I've got a PhD, and I'm a physics teacher, that sounds awful doesn't it? But I thought that there might be a better future within education, and I must say I'm committed to education 'cos I could obviously be earning much more in industry, if I got involved in TVEI, I felt a change of direction might not be altogether a bad thing (TVEI teacher).

The most obvious example of the 'new' jobs was that of the school co-ordinator (see McCabe, 1986a). While these posts carried salaries ranging from incentives B to E (previously, scale 2 to senior teacher) and, in a few cases, deputy head, incentive D (scale 4) seemed to be the norm (see Pole, 1986: 42). Our evidence suggests that when the job of co-ordinator was open to application rather than 'bestowed', the people who applied often did so for instrumental, entrepreneurial reasons, because they saw it as a positive career move which might prove a stepping stone to higher things. No-one talked of taking the post *primarily* because they saw it as interesting or as offering potentially intrinsically satisfying opportunities (see Pole, 1986: 42); though a small number of people did remark that becoming a co-ordinator was a natural 'progression', or even a ratification of what they had been doing prior to TVEI. In one scheme, for example, four out of six school co-ordinators were male PE or ex-PE teachers. Promotion prospects for male PE teachers are particularly poor, largely because of the relatively low status of the subject but also because, compared with those working in other subjects, PE teachers tend to reach their career ceiling at a relatively early age (see Hilsum and Start, 1974; McNair and MacDonald, 1976). The 'problem' for these teachers is compounded by the fact that as they get older it often becomes physically more difficult to continue full-time PE work and a change of job becomes a necessity. Traditionally, PE teachers moved into pastoral work, but falling rolls meant increased competition with people who frequently had 'better' or more 'respectable' academic qualifications (see Sikes, 1988). TVEI posts offered a valuable alternative and it may be that the, albeit small, boost they provided in terms of job prospects played an important part in the 'success' of the Initiative.

Moving into new, previously uncharted territory carries risks, and not the least of those faced by many TVEI appointees involved in the pilot projects was that of their position at the end of the 5-year scheme. Some LEAs made a commitment to maintaining TVEI salaries, others were unspecific, and some offered short-term contracts. Especially before the Extension was announced, some people, like the female school co-ordinator quoted below, were uncertain as to what they could do to justify their position post-TVEI (see also McCabe, 1986):

> If it all collapses, and it probably will without the money, what do we do? I mean there won't be anything to co-ordinate from the pupil point of view because I know the consortium won't continue, it causes enough problems as it is and it's basically my job to sort them out.

Some were apprehensive about their possible future careers:

> I want to know where I stand. I'll have been seconded out for 5 years on a scale 4 as assistant [scheme] co-ordinator and I strongly suspect that they'll [the LEA] try and put me back into school on scale 3. And, my school is closing, I've only got a few years before I retire so what's my position going to be? Not very good I suspect (assistant scheme co-ordinator).

Others just needed to get a new job:

> It's quite simple. My contract expires at the end of the pilot and I need another job. I knew this when I came in and it's not something that I can't cope with or I shouldn't have taken the job (scheme director).

The way in which some pilot schemes were staffed, with people on short-term contracts, indicates that some LEAs were not readily prepared to take on long-term commitments and put their own money in. However, the evidence does suggest that the MSC became less supportive of such arrangements, perhaps because their aim was that LEAs should integrate TVEI into their basic provision beyond the lifetime of the funding. In the event, this does appear to have happened, with TVEI staff at all levels being absorbed within the LEA.

One thing that people accepting TVEI responsibilities sometimes had to risk and take on trust was that they would actually get a promotion for their work. On occasion, finance committees took months or even a year or more to ratify posts for which the money was available.

There appeared to be a common belief among teachers that TVEI experience was a positive qualification for further career advancement (beyond their initial involvement in the scheme), mainly within education but also, in some cases, in other occupations. Through TVEI-engendered links with industry, some teachers had the opportunity to become aware of alternative possibilities and some gave serious thought to switching careers, with some actually doing so.

As yet, it is perhaps too early to suggest that TVEI teachers are beginning to be significantly represented in senior posts, but our own impressions do indicate that they are being appointed to deputy headships, headships and advisory posts, and that those who were involved in first- and second-round projects are using their experience as a marketable commodity that employers are happy to buy.

The corollary is that non-TVEI teachers have sometimes felt themselves to be unfairly disadvantaged through no fault of their own. Thus promotions and career prospects were among the 'enclave' effects of TVEI (Saunders, 1986a, b).

We noted at the beginning of this chapter that one of the aims of TVEI was to change the role and nature of teachers and teaching. It is, therefore, perhaps no accident that the teachers whose careers developed as a result of TVEI often made use of the same sorts of enterprise skills that the Initiative sought to encourage in young people. These skills, and associated ideas to do with education as a competitive, open market service (if not commodity), have been increasingly emphasized and called upon – the bid system of funding for in-service training (LEAGTS) is an example of the shift.

TVEI and job content

The responsibilities of TVEI personnel varied considerably from scheme to scheme. This was partly because the MSC did not lay down compulsory role specifications, but largely because jobs involve what their incumbents understand them to involve. Even where specifications did exist, individuals were able to meet them while interpreting them differently (see Bell, 1986). We have, therefore, aimed at a generalized description.

Servicing the scheme

In this section, we look at the administrative, organizational and day-to-day running requirements of TVEI within an institution with particular emphasis on the implications for individuals.

Being involved in TVEI meant being involved in organizational and administrative structures additional to those (already meeting the needs) of the DES, the LEA and the institution. Thus the arrangements that individual institutions made in order to accommodate the TVEI, depended upon their existing organizational framework and the overall structure of the scheme.

The MSC increasingly emphasized that TVEI should become and be seen as an integral part of an LEA's and institution's educational provision. To some extent, this was made difficult (and was actually contradicted) by the way in which institutions and individuals involved in the Initiative were answerable (for at least part of what they did) to the scheme's director/co-ordinator and the MSC. This was most unusual, though with the increased power of school governors under the 1988 Reform Act it is now less so. As Bell (1986: 79) notes, 'it is rare for a teacher within a school to be responsible to someone operating outside the school'. The significant point is that the scope of headteachers' jurisdiction was curtailed in that they did not have the same kind of authority over the TVEI as they do over other things going on in their school. Some heads explicitly acknowledged this. For example (see also Sikes, 1986b):

> Things have changed and it's no longer the autocratic patriarchal head whose got total control over the school. TVEI is, in my experience, the first real initiative to come into a school and blatantly, if you like, claim a share of teachers' allegiance and be able to direct and take responsibility for teachers and kids as it does. Some of my colleagues, fellow heads, can't accept that but they'll have to because things are changing (headteacher, TVEI school).

An additional element tends to mean additional work and the TVEI was no exception. Furthermore, because the pilot was closely evaluated and because the MSC wanted to monitor developments and keep account of how money was being spent, there were numerous forms, returns and questionnaires to complete. The burden on the school co-ordinator was especially heavy. The following quotes are representative of the rule rather than the exception:

> I'm drowning under the sea of paper that I'm sent. I could quite easily spend all my time filling in forms. They're always wanting information. They want so much I seriously doubt that they can process it all (school co-ordinator).

> It's ridiculous and it gets me down. I'm always getting things sent to be completed by tomorrow. They're [the central team] always wanting information but I know that most of the time they're only collecting what the MSC are asking for (school teacher).

> Who's going to bet me that he [the scheme Director] doesn't come in this afternoon with over 29 pieces of paper for us to read, fill in and return? The record stands at 28 but I'm sure he can beat that easy (school co-ordinator in a co-ordinators' meeting).

While teachers have always informally evaluated their work, they had rarely been involved in a systematic multi-level and multi-strategied evaluation of the type set up to monitor the TVEI. This evaluation involved the collection of different types of data by various branches of the MSC's TVEI Evaluation Unit, by teams from the NFER and Leeds University undertaking a national evaluation, by researchers pursuing special studies of particular aspects of the Initiative, and by local scheme evaluators. The aim was to learn as much as possible about the implementation of TVEI and feed back the information gained in a formative on-going manner as well as to produce 'summative' reports. (Whether or not this aim was achieved is open to question.)

Much of the burden of providing information fell on scheme directors and school co-ordinators, but all teachers in TVEI schools, particularly those teaching TVEI students, were likely to be involved at some stage. Their involvement took various forms, including completing questionnaires, being interviewed or being observed working with students. Not only did this take time, it could also be threatening to teachers used to working relatively privately within their own rooms (see Simons, 1987). On the whole, evaluators stressed the formative nature of their work, presenting it as being positive, an aid to development and improvement and process-based, rather than negative, judgemental and mainly concerned with outcomes. Some schemes explicitly involved their staff in the evaluation and also provided training. Teachers, as might be expected, perceived and experienced evaluation differently. The following represent a range of views:

> [On seeing the local evaluator enter the staffroom] . . . Watch out, it's the MSC spy (teacher in a TVEI school). (A similar comment has been overheard in all our schemes.)
>
> There is such a lot of evaluation. TVEI must be the most evaluated project ever. You get tired with it all. They're always wanting something or other (TVEI co-ordinator).
>
> We had one of those NFER questionnaires for the pupils. My God! It was so long and complicated and it took a lot of organising, and time (TVEI teacher).
>
> I think it's good because someone like you [local evaluator] coming and asking questions, it forces you to think about what you're doing, to get things clear in your own mind (TVEI teacher).
>
> I think the attitude has changed. At first they were apprehensive but now they have had some experience of the way in which evaluation can provide them with useful feedback I think the general feeling is very positive (TVEI director).
>
> I think evaluation should be an integral part of every teacher's approach and by formalising it as it were it's becoming so. I think the staff in my school are interested to see what they can learn (TVEI co-ordinator).
>
> I think it's been very good to have an external evaluator within the authority and I don't think it should be confined to TVEI either. I know that evaluation is part of the advisers' job but they don't have the time (headteacher).

Co-ordinating a scheme across its participating institutions generally required meetings, and TVEI staff reported that they spent a considerable amount of time out of school. Pole (1986: 41) found that attendance at meetings was one of the six most common tasks mentioned by co-ordinators, but headteachers and subject specialists also have co-ordination, dissemination and development sessions to go to. In addition, subject specialists were often involved in negotiating course accreditation with examination.

As well as these meetings, there was in-service training which affected large numbers of teachers and generally took place within school time. Inset had considerable importance because it was invested with much of the responsibility for changing teachers. Its accommodation was, therefore, seen as a priority. While TVEI usually provided supply cover, teachers were often concerned about leaving their students and this was particularly the case when they did not believe that the meetings were necessary or that the training was appropriate or useful. For instance:

> I come to these meetings and I sit here listening to people talking about their problems and while I sympathise and feel sorry for them if they aren't my problems too I'm all the time thinking about what I could be doing if I was back in school. I'm fed up with what seems like meetings for the sake of meetings (school co-ordinator).
>
> There seem to have been a number of courses just lately that when you get there it's 'What do you want to do?' Now that annoys me intensely because I'm going on the

course in the first place to find out how to do something, or for suggestions. I don't know what I want to do, I want to be told (school teacher).

Of course, not all meetings or courses were felt to be a waste of time, but when time is at a premium, as it generally is in school, it is jealously guarded.

TVEI staff themselves were sometimes involved in providing in-service training in their own institutions, within the LEA and even nationally, and this became more frequent with the introduction of GCSE and the National Curriculum. In some cases, training and dissemination were part of job specifications, but in others it was an aspect that developed as people gained experience and expertise. Sometimes individuals put themselves forward as disseminators, others were approached:

Well, I feel that we do have something worthwhile sharing. We've had the benefits of the TVEI money that've allowed us to go forward with profiling. We've had the chances to make the mistakes and without sounding too big headed I think we can help people by warning them of the potential pitfalls and by giving them the benefit of our experience and the training we were fortunate enough to have through TVEI (TVEI teacher).

I was asked to go and talk at this conference for over 100 teachers. I'd never done anything like that before and I must say I was nervous. And I took the coward's way, I took some kids with me. I gave the introduction and talked about the course, then they gave prepared speeches on their mini-enterprise work. They were nervous and that helped me. Awful aren't I? But I think it was good experience for them as much as for me. They didn't think they could do it but they could, and so could I (TVEI teacher).

When the TVEI was organized on a consortia basis and particularly if students moved between institutions, considerable changes and arrangements often had to be made. Frequently, the timing of the school day had to be altered to bring it in line with the other participating institutions and to accommodate student travelling time. When this happened, it affected everyone, not just the minority involved in TVEI. Actually ensuring that travel arrangements worked could also be disruptive, especially to the co-ordinator and the staff working with peripatetic students. Rarely did everything run smoothly. The beginning of terms were particularly bad, and a not inconsiderable amount of time was typically spent 'phoning bus companies' and sometimes ferrying groups who were left behind or not even collected. The following quotes are typical:

I'm bloody fed up. I don't think a week has gone by with something going wrong with the transport. I must have spent hours trying to sort it out. In fact I'd go as far as to say that it's the worst thing about the whole of TVEI (TVEI co-ordinator).

Come half past eleven you don't get much work done because they're starting to worry about catching the bus. You see, there have been quite a lot of occasions when they've not been picked up, either it's come and gone or it doesn't come at all. So they're wanting to go, they can't concentrate, it affects any group work, it affects visiting speakers and it means that our kids [those in their home school] get affected. It has got better but I would say that we lose around 40 minutes a week because of it. Our own kids, they can

> get on for an extra quarter of an hour when the others have gone but I don't really think the others miss out that much because I know they do extra homework in order to keep up. I think it's because they are keen but also it's because they do a lot of group work and they don't want to hold the group up (TVEI teacher).
>
> It does have some effect on what you can do. It means your timing has to be excellent because if you spend too long on the demonstration or discussion or if you don't leave enough time for them to make mistakes and be slow then their dish is still going to be in the oven when they've got to go. Actually it's not bad training because you do have to work to deadlines in the trade but I do find it a bit much sometimes (TVEI lecturer).

Arranging work experience and/or making links with industry were other major administrative and organizational tasks. Some schemes made use of other agencies such as Project Trident, Schools Curriculum Industry Project (SCIP) and the careers service. In some cases, provision already existed and TVEI was able to just key in. Even when it was not necessary to start from scratch there was liaison and co-ordination work to do. Some teachers found that they spent quite a bit of time working with people from industry, commerce and business, both in school and in the workplaces. As we have noted, this opened up new opportunities for some people.

Looking after, maintaining and being responsible for equipment purchased for TVEI courses was, for some TVEI staff, a major task. In more than one scheme, TVEI schools had considerable amounts of equipment stolen. Computers were particularly prone to theft, but life-like models for child care and first aid, stationery and machinery also went despite elaborate security systems. Teachers sometimes felt, or were given to understand, that they were personally responsible for security, and this was a major headache for those who had already lost TVEI resources.

Co-ordinating and monitoring the use of TVEI equipment and resources within an institution was another area of responsibility. In some cases, where there were TVEI ancillary staff and/or specialist TVEI accommodation, this involved a considerable amount of work and time, particularly when problems arose. The following account is typical of incidents occurring when structural changes were made as a result of TVEI:

> When we got back to school in September the business studies course couldn't start in its proper rooms because they hadn't finished converting them. Two weeks into the term they'd got all the decorating finished but they'd not done the wiring, this wasn't completed until October half term. What this meant was that we couldn't teach the course because we had no way of fixing all the word processors and computers up. It was ridiculous. The teachers kept coming to me and I kept getting on to the TVEI director who said he kept phoning the building department and they kept putting him off. At one time we got a lecture on priorities. They said there are only a limited number of council workmen and if they get a call to go out and fix an old lady's roof or something because she's living in dangerous conditions then they have to leave us because our health and safety doesn't depend on electrical plugs. Well, that's true but the kids aren't getting the course they've been promised, they're losing out and I don't think I should be made to feel guilty about something that should have been finished during the summer (TVEI school co-ordinator).

Management, administration and organization tend to be noticed when things go wrong. As one male teacher commented:

> If the administrative and managerial systems are efficient then you shouldn't be aware of their existence. There wouldn't be any hiccups or problems, everything would just appear to happen. It's not often like that though I'm afraid (teacher, TVEI school).

Those who were responsible for managing TVEI had to try and ensure that everything did work smoothly. They had to attend to day-to-day administration, respond to needs and requests and cope with crises, often at the same time as they were teaching. Time is limited and people worried that they were not able to give of their best. For instance:

> I'm afraid that my teaching has suffered this term because I've just not had the time to attend to it properly, all my time seems to be spent on sorting things out. People come with a problem, it's got to be put right before they can teach and so you have to deal with it and this happens all the time (TVEI school co-ordinator).

> The cost of my involvement [in TVEI] is borne by my exam classes and the impact will be seen in their results (TVEI school co-ordinator).

> I've got a pile of papers on my desk that's a mile high. I don't seem to have any time to deal with it. I get in at a quarter past eight in the morning and I leave around five, five-thirty and I'm on the go all the day (TVEI teacher).

Any teacher, regardless of whether or not they were involved in TVEI, could justifiably put the same case of too much to do and too little time. TVEI did make additional demands which, as we have tried to show, had implications for the way in which teachers perceive and experience their work and for the management and organization of the institution as a whole. Managing schools is an increasingly complex task for which many teachers feel they have been inadequately prepared. Contrary to 'deskilling' teachers in every respect, it seems to us that, overall, TVEI gave some people the chance to gain experience which could stand them in good stead – in career terms – in the future. (Of course, the corollary is that those who lack this experience are disadvantaged.)

Classroom

In this section, we will consider teachers' perceptions and experiences of the *content* of TVEI courses.

The MSC interprets 'Vocational Education as education in which the students are concerned to acquire generic or specific skills with a view to employment.' TVEI courses were supposed to embody 'initiative problem solving abilities', include work experience as an integral part, and 'be capable of being linked effectively with subsequent training/educational opportunities.' These requirements had implications for the content of the courses, as they placed the emphasis on the practical, applied and experiential, rather than the academic and theoretical.

The extent to which teachers identified TVEI courses as different from other courses in the same 'subject' area varied. These areas do, in any case, tend to be more practical than others in the curriculum, and they also often involve a vocational, applied element, and links with industry, business and commerce have frequently been well established for some time. When this is the case, teachers generally said that the main difference was that they had better equipment, improved resources, technical and administrative assistance, and more money to spend on getting students out of school on visits and bringing outside speakers in. From their comments, teachers saw this as expanding their scope, rather than as an attack upon their competence and knowledge:

> What we're doing in the classroom hasn't substantially changed. We've been doing this sort of thing for years. Where there is the difference is in the resourcing. We can do it properly now (TVEI teacher).

> TVEI lets me do what I've always wanted to do. It's the money (TVEI teacher).

In many cases, the teachers themselves were involved in creating the syllabuses and the courses and so had considerable control over the content and pedagogy. When this happened, they often used their existing work as a basis for development rather than doing something completely different.

An important difference could often be discerned in the orientation, emphasis, nature and scale of the content. This difference can be characterized as a shift from the personal and amateur to the public and professional. It could clearly be seen in the catering and services areas where, traditionally, schools have concentrated on 'home' economics or 'domestic' science, focusing on the small-scale 'family' or private unit, whereas colleges of further education dealt with the large-scale institutional and public sector. Under TVEI, schools had to start to deliver courses on 'public' catering. They were usually provided with the equipment to enable them to do this, but a shift in approach and thinking was also necessary. Some teachers had to learn to cope with a substantially and substantively different content. Similarly, in the craft, design and technology areas, there was a move from the production of individual and idiosyncratic artefacts and domestic maintenance to industrial and commercial applications. Thus:

> In home ec. we teach how to make a batch of a dozen scones for example, whereas in TVEI it's about how to produce 50 or a 100 for sale. I s'pose you could say it's the difference between 'making' and 'producing'. I've had to learn quite a lot because it's not just a matter of increasing quantities, there are other considerations about time and costing and things like that (TVEI teacher).

> We've always done plumbing, how to fix pipes and suchlike but now we put in central heating and toilets. We've converted this old cloakroom into a plumbing workshop and we've got about 10 toilets which they can put in – then we take 'em out and start again (TVEI teacher).

Further education (FE) lecturers were sometimes sceptical about the way in which teachers taught on the large scale. For example (admittedly personal views):

> They teach cookery for the home in school. I'll give you an example they always teach them to use wooden spoons for mixing, that's disgusting, it's filthy, you've got to use your hands. You can wash and scrub hands and get them much cleaner than a mucky old spoon that's been rolling around in a drawer picking up germs and what have you. The

> kids come in and there's all sorts of things. 'We don't do it like that at school. Mrs so and so said to do it this way.' I tell you, it takes you at least a term to get them into a commercial attitude (TVEI FE lecturer).

> If they've done drama at school we have quite a battle with them at the beginning because what they do in school drama isn't the same as what they do here. There it's all self-expression, here it's that as well but you've got to have a professional attitude and that means bloody hard work and practice, practice, practice. The temperamental *prima donna* attitude is no good, you've got to be one hundred and one percent committed if you're going to be any good in this business. That's why we tell them they're on probation when they come here and if they aren't up to scratch, or if we don't think they're going to succeed in any way we ask them to leave. In many cases by the end of the first term they've self-selected themselves (TVEI FE lecturer).

Students usually spent approximately 1 day a week on the substantive part of their TVEI course as opposed to the more normal 2 hours given to GCSE options. This gave more time for in-depth work and also meant that teachers did not feel under as much pressure from examination syllabuses.

There was more time for students to do and experience activities and the emphasis tended to be on skills and problem solving rather than on learning a body of knowledge. The task of the teacher was often, therefore, to present an assignment (which can range from a specific piece of work to be completed within one session, to setting up and running a mini-enterprise project over a term or longer) and ensure that the students had access to everything they needed to get on with it. (Following GCSE this is now a much more common approach.) Teaching of this kind includes providing knowledge through 'traditional teaching', but it can also involve considerable organization and management of equipment and resources:

> There are 101 things to think about. If you haven't got everything they're likely to want you can waste a lot of time. I think you get better at knowing what's likely to crop up as time goes on (TVEI teacher).

Teachers who were not used to this way of working could find it very strange:

> When we first started TVEI I was rather worried because if the students are doing it all what do you do? I mean the first session, when they were working on their own I stood there like a lemon. You'd done all the preparation and so on, lots of work but what then? I soon realized that I'd not been made redundant though! I'd say you do more this way than in the conventional style of teaching. It can be exhausting. But I enjoy it (TVEI teacher).

The management of resources is not, of course, only an issue for TVEI teachers, but it may be that because there was an official requirement to link content with 'real world' activity and to account to external bodies, teachers experienced it as being more significant. (This is borne out to some extent by the way in which teachers who were compelled by the new GCSE syllabuses to take a similar approach often sought the advice of those with TVEI experience.) Thus those teaching courses which relied more heavily on academic, book-based work, such as Law and Accounts, which can involve considerably less student 'activity' than business studies, sometimes justified and even apologized for what they were doing under a TVEI heading. For instance:

> We are doing Law and Accounts with the fifth year but we've scrapped it for the fourth year, no-one's starting that course now. . . . We scrapped it because it was so heavily academic and book-based, it didn't seem right that it should be TVEI because apart from visits to courts there wasn't much else to do to fit in with the syllabus (TVEI teacher).

Another requirement was that TVEI courses should, at some point, involve Information Technology (IT). In the early days of the pilot, IT was frequently taught as a separate subject, but as teachers became more confident and aware of the possible applications of the resources and equipment, the emphasis shifted to integrating IT into other aspects of TVEI courses. This shift gave the lead to what is now seen as desired practice across the curriculum:

> There isn't an IT slot on the timetable any more, we don't teach it as a separate entity. It comes into all aspects of the course, for instance they use word processors for writing up their assignments and for compiling their profiles and they're quite likely to use spreadsheets and computer graphics at some stage (TVEI teacher).

Just as many TVEI teachers had to learn how to use computers, word-processors and electronic information networks and mailing, they also had to become familiar with profiling. Because legislation required that by 1990 all students must leave school with a profile, TVEI teachers in some schools were able to gain prior experience, both of the mechanics of profiling and of the type of relationships that can develop as a result between teacher and student.

None of the TVEI teachers we met expressed concern about the nature of the content of the courses they were teaching. They were positive about directly relating the curriculum to the 'real world' and mimicking what they believed happens in the workplace. They did not see what they were doing as inimical to a 'good' education, nor did they see themselves as 'trainers' who were reducing young peoples' options through too early vocational specialization. Teachers in non-TVEI areas sometimes voiced these reservations and criticisms, but then both sides did have vested interests and, despite continuing convergence, to some extent still represent different traditions and strands of education, the theoretical and academic on one side and the practical and applied on the other.

In the view of the students, the content of TVEI courses often differed from anything else they had experienced. However, this is true of many subject areas which are not encountered until the fourth year and, in any case, the general trend is towards more subjects having a greater active and applied element.

Pedagogy

LEAs, schools and individuals were primarily attracted to the TVEI because of the money. After years of deprivation, some relief was offered, albeit to only a significant few (cf. Harland, 1987: 46–7), and it was readily grasped. At least initially, and especially in the case of first-round projects, TVEI was largely seen in terms of resources.

Vast numbers of computers were bought and so were expensive pieces of equipment, such as the ubiquitous CNC lathe. Hardware alone could not, however, meet the criteria that TVEI projects be characterized by 'clear and specific objectives, including the objectives of encouraging initiative, problem-solving abilities, and other aspects of personal development' (TVEI aims and criteria). This required particular teaching approaches; approaches which relatively few secondary school teachers used. Consequently, the emphasis had to be on changing teaching styles and in-service training.

Rather than being the expert purveyor of a body of knowledge to an ideally, passive audience of pupils, TVEI teachers were expected to take the role of 'facilitator', providing relevant experience and assisting students who are actively learning by doing. Furthermore, the students themselves are to be made explicitly responsible for that learning.

This is obviously a simplistic description. By definition, all learning is active, though not necessarily experiential, and ultimately much of the responsibility for whether or not the pupil 'learns' always lies with them. Nor is this shift in the teacher's role confined to TVEI. For some years, the rhetorical trend has been away from 'traditional', didactic teaching towards an active experiential approach and GCSE has to some degree institutionalized this.

Experiential and active learning, group work, adults other than teachers in the classroom (AOTs), and greater student responsibility have implications for the nature of the relationship between students and teachers and between teachers and their superiors within the TVEI hierarchy. Control is a central issue. When the teacher becomes the facilitator and students are given responsibility to go and get on with their own work, there has to be some trust that this will occur. Discipline has to become internalized (cf. Harland, 1987: 41–2), and there therefore has to be some convincing rationale for why it should be. Continuous assessment, monitoring, being identified as a 'special' privileged group, the chance to do interesting work which is relevant to the 'real world', and the possibility that the experience might help in getting a job, are all strategies we saw being used. The same rhetoric can be seen to apply to teachers working in TVEI themselves.

Shifting the balance of control was perceived and experienced as threatening by some teachers who were afraid that standards would fall, that students would fail and that they would be held responsible. Some found it difficult to let students see that they did not know all the answers, while others were more worried about indiscipline and riots, and about how their noisy classrooms appeared to outsiders. Teaching has tended to be a private activity, but many TVEI courses involved team teaching, either with colleagues, staff from other institutions or AOTs, and so teachers had more experience of and became more used to being watched and watching others at work. Indeed, observing 'good practice' was recognized as a valuable form of in-service training and visits to other TVEI classrooms and schemes were popular and relatively common. Even so, perhaps because we were 'evaluators' and associated with assessment, before going in to observe sessions, we were often taken aside by the teacher and pre-briefed. The following quotes are typical:

> It might seem to be noisy in there but they're all working, they're all on-task. If you listen in you'll see they're talking about their work (TVEI teacher).

> They're moving about the room and coming in and out and it's a bit noisy but it's because of the way we work in here. They're all getting on, they work incredibly hard but they don't sit still behind desks and do it (TVEI teacher).

Despite these worries and fears, many TVEI teachers did attempt to adopt active, experiential approaches, and the general belief seemed to be that they can be more effective than traditional methods.

> I believe in this sort of approach. I think the children do learn more when they're doing it. I've always tried to work in this way (TVEI teacher).

> I'd much rather teach like this. It's harder work, you have to be on the alert all the time, ready to deal with whatever they bring to you but it's much more worthwhile in terms of benefits to the pupils (TVEI teacher).

In the majority of the schemes we have worked in, teachers claimed to have altered their approach and students frequently said they were given more responsibility than in other lessons. Relatively, and in terms of their perceptions and experiences, this was no doubt 'true'. There were, however, instances when teachers complained that students did not recognize changes. This raises interesting questions about teachers' intentions and perceptions and it also suggests that, to the students, some changes are insignificant. As Barnes *et al.* (1987: 24) point out, teachers may 'fear endangering their hard-won mastery' of tried and tested methods and any change is likely to be slow as 'teachers gradually try out new methods with the support of others similarly engaged'.

In practice, teachers rarely use one distinct and identifiable approach all the time, but rather use what they deem appropriate given their previous experience, their preferred and ideal styles, the students they are working with and the content of a particular session. What is significant is that many of them felt that through TVEI they had the opportunity allowed by smaller classes and generous resources to experiment and adopt different teaching styles. We must point out that these teachers were involved in pilot rather than extension schemes and that they themselves did stress the uniqueness of their situation and, in particular, the small groups, the motivated students, and the in-service support which made risk-taking less dangerous. This last is crucial. One thing that TVEI did do is bring teachers together to talk about what they did and how they did it, to work on joint enterprises, to develop a modular curriculum, to supervise students on work experience, to plan residentials, to co-ordinate the scheme, and so on. Such opportunities for sharing are perhaps the most effective way of giving teachers the confidence to experiment.

Finally

Ultimately, the teachers were the people who interpreted and realized TVEI as it was translated to them by regional advisers and scheme and school co-ordinators. They made it what it was. The situational context was important, as was the historical context into which the Initiative was introduced. As Harland (1987: 47–8) notes, TVEI came at a time when morale was low, resources were poor and there seemed little to look forward to, and she likens TVEI teachers to the released prisoners in *Fidelio* who emerged from the darkness of the dungeon to the free air and light of the world above. But rarely are all the prisoners freed or freed without obligation and the teachers were, to some extent, bound by the parameters of the MSC's criteria.

TVEI has had significant effects on the objective and subjective careers of many teachers. In this chapter, the focus has been on the positive, but there is also the negative side. Those teachers who were not closely involved with the pilot projects may have perceived themselves to have been disadvantaged as a result, although others felt that they were not. And yet, the fact that TVEI happened means that it had personal and general implications for all secondary school teachers. This is not least because as a pilot project TVEI was the basis for an extension which was eventually to touch all secondary schools.

It is not possible to say that TVEI alone has in any way 'changed' teacher approaches. There are far too many other influences, such as the changes necessitated by the GCSE, CPVE, ERA and the National Curriculum. In any case, any changes in education do take place very slowly. As we pointed out at the beginning of the chapter, the teachers working in TVEI had many years of experience and they are unlikely to give this up quickly, particularly if they did not see any need or benefit. Having said that, many teachers do identify TVEI as having had important consequences for their careers, the content of their job and for the teaching methods they use. One wonders whether these consequences were the ones the MSC were hoping for.

CHAPTER 7

Curriculum issues in TVEI

We have already referred to the diversity that characterized TVEI practice several times so far. Much of that discussion implicitly concerned curriculum issues; after all, changing the curriculum was the major, most visible and most 'natural' single aim of the whole initiative. However, we also stated at the very beginning of this book that TVEI had not achieved major success in the curriculum area. In this chapter, we will attempt to delve further into the reasons for this and try to identify particular curriculum-relevant sets of problems that inhibited a more profound change in the secondary school curriculum.

Three sets of problems seem to have been especially important: conceptual problems, what might be called 'education-political' problems and organizational problems. We will look at each of these in turn, exemplifying them from our collective experiences.

The fundamental problem that TVEI inherited, of course, was what constituted technical and (especially) vocational education. As we suggested in the first part of this book, TVEI in one sense represented only one more in a series of efforts to make the curriculum more relevant to the nation's economic needs that has continued throughout most of the century. We stated then that TVEI was not successful in achieving that greater relevance, though it was much more successful in demonstrating ways of how educational changes might be brought about.

The point was that there existed no curricular ambitions for TVEI at its outset that were either more original or more closely specified than those that had been put forward in dozens of other schemes of technical and vocational education. Indeed, they were characterized by considerable vagueness and if, as we have argued, TVEI was effectively constructed 'on the hoof', those constructions were based on a range of interpretations of what TVEI was really about. In the early days of the pilot schemes, the most common question to be heard in discussions of how schools should adjust to TVEI, what curriculum changes they would seek to install, was 'Is it TVEI?' – a question to which no-one had the answer because no answer existed.

The official guidelines and criteria provided few effective pointers to practice. Indeed, when taken seriously, they could deepen rather than relieve schools' dilemmas over what curriculum and pedagogic changes might be most appropriate. It is worth expanding on this point, which was also taken up in the research conducted by the University of Leeds School of Education into 'The TVEI Curriculum 14–16' (Barnes, *et al.* 1987), and based upon the report of case studies in 12 schools in 1985–6. The Leeds team provided a powerful conceptual framework for evaluating the curriculum content of TVEI courses. Starting with broad TVEI aims of developing courses which reflect 'real-world problems' and developing 'initiative, motivation and enterprise', they operationalized these into what they term the 'Realism Dimension'. This was refined into the three following aspects:

1 A distinction between decontextualized exercises on the one hand, and learning activities which are a close reflection of the world outside school on the other.
2 A distinction between those learning activities where the tasks and issues are supplied by the teacher and those where the teacher accepts problems from the students and encourages students to find problems themselves.
3 A distinction between those learning activities where the tasks have been pre-analysed and have right answers, and those which reflect the complexity of problem solving in the real world.

We have found this to be a particularly useful framework with which to evaluate the curriculum content of TVEI, as it captures one of the essential features of the TVEI project. We can develop this concept of realism further by drawing on Bernstein's concept of boundary maintenance. What we assume TVEI was intended broadly to do was not only to challenge and question but also to erode many of the boundaries which exist within the educational system. We refer here to the boundaries of male/female, teacher/pupil, school/work, school/community, able/less able, and of particular importance in this chapter between subject areas, between academic and practical knowledge, and subject-based learning activities/experiences.

The link with the Realism Dimension is established by the TVEI imperative of enhancing the conventional school curriculum by introducing new curricular experiences which are relevant to the changing needs of British society and the economy in the late twentieth century. Following Bernstein, the conventional categories and boundaries can be seen as being incompatible with the kinds of individuals, workers and citizens required by a society based increasingly upon flexibility and interdependence. For Bernstein, this change is complexly related to the maintenance of social order, cohesion and stability. The changes in the categories and boundaries which inform and are transmitted by the education system, change the way individuals see themselves in the world they inhabit. TVEI in this framework can be seen as part of an adaptive response to the requirements of the economy and society.

However, there is an alternative conception of those requirements. For writers like Braverman, the main requirements of a capitalist economy are for a workforce increasingly characterized by separation of conception and execution (of mental and manual work), in order to further the long-term interests of capital in its long-term quests for increasing profit and control. The labour process is becoming more fragmented, routinized and deskilled, not only for manual workers but for white-collar workers too, who are also being divided into those who are 'conceivers' and 'executors'.

In short, new boundaries and categories are being established. If TVEI is essentially involved in boundary reduction, it may be contradicting one of the imperatives of a capitalist economy which is establishing new boundaries in the labour process. The implications of this for TVEI may be quite significant. In attempting to produce an educational system seen as valid for all pupils, one based upon experience, participation, negotiation, problem solving, and reduction of boundary, it may be diametrically opposed to the specific requirements of capital for a cheap, docile, uncritical labour force whether on the shop floor or at the work station.

As long as capital requires such labour, the TVEI curriculum may not only be inappropriate to these individuals but it also may be developing characteristics that are most certainly not required by many employers for some sections of their workforce. We see here a whole set of contradictory forces and realities. On the one hand, TVEI is supposed to be for all abilities. However, if a particular school/pilot scheme rigorously translates TVEI aims into practice, the ensuing educational experience may be more appropriate for those areas of employment requiring more problem-solving, creative and enterprising characteristics. We may have here the beginnings of an explanation as to the problems frequently encountered in trying to 'sell' TVEI to parents, employers and teachers.

The 'conceptual' problem cannot, though, be reduced entirely to an intrinsic lack of clarity of TVEI curricular aims to those who were to implement them in the classroom. The teachers' perspectives on those aims were neither neutral nor infinitely flexible. Their views of the scope of education – what it was preferable and possible for schools to achieve – had been formed in an era of liberal expansion marked by the very values that made it possible – even necessary – for the guardians of those values, HMI, to speak of the MSC as 'the barbarians at the gate'. (The debate over the compatibility of these 'liberal' values and TVEI ran throughout the life of the pilot scheme: (see e.g. Pring, 1985). This produced a full spectrum of reactions from 'suspicion' at one end to 'opportunism' at the other. The crucial point is, though, that there was at best a restricted place on that spectrum for what might be called 'authentic' TVEI curriculum development. This changed in the second half of the pilot phase as both the scope of TVEI became more closely defined and schools became more comfortable with a role that was changing but under their control. However, the initial lack of conceptual clarity produced by the difficulties intrinsic to the idea of vocational education, together with what was not so much teachers' hostility as their professionally socialized indifference to, or lack of purchase on, the kind of issues involved in creating 'TVEI' curricula, set parameters that circumscribed the construction of curricula throughout the pilot phase.

On the basis of our observations, we can identify three ideal typical responses to these curriculum problems in TVEI. The first we refer to as *enhancement*. It involved identifying what were unequivocally technical and vocational areas, such as Craft, Design and Technology (CDT) and Business Studies. These would then be 'beefed up' in various ways, and have a TVEI package 'bolted on', but would remain essentially recognizable as subjects that might have predated TVEI had the resources been available. Examples of beefing up abound in the projects we looked at. New lathes proliferated. Model offices flourished up in all sorts of odd corners. One school bought an industrial robot (whose running costs rapidly reached a level that made its continued operation impossible). Electronic typewriters replaced manual typewriters only to be supplanted in many cases by word processors. Computers sprang up everywhere and seemed to become the emblems of TVEI in many places. Their mere presence registered modernity and relevance, however appropriately or inappropriately they were used.

The TVEI requirements most commonly bolted on to these courses were profiling and attempts to mitigate gender stereotyping. As Chapter 5 shows, profiling was often a complicated and major process in itself, but in the enhancement mode of response to TVEI, it was typically used as an additional form of assessment. It did not replace existing forms of assessment (not least because public examinations depended on these), but was typically presented as a means of making pupils' learning more active and self-aware. In the early days of the pilot schemes in some schools, such commitment to profiling was as likely to be gestural or cosmetic as it was their substance. However, this changed as the initiative developed, as those involved became more acquainted with both the substantive possibilities of profiling and with the degree to which it was necessary to continue using it for 'window dressing'.

The situation was similar but not identical in respect of attempts to mitigate gender stereotyping. As Chapter 9 shows, such attempts immediately attained, and retained, a very high profile. Not unassociated with this, the extent of the implementation of such attempts could be relatively accurately measured. This, in turn, often turned the gender issue into a numbers game and little else. Content was rarely changed to reflect the different gender composition of classes. The curriculum and pedagogy for girls in overalls or boys in aprons seldom varied from what had been offered to single sex classes. Nevertheless, as Chapter 9 demonstrates, even in the enhancement mode at the very least consciousness of the existence and consequences of gender stereotyping of subjects was raised as a result of having to play the numbers game.

One common and significant form of enhancement that employed the mode to its limit involved combining 'beefing up' resources and 'bolted on' TVEI requirements to create courses that were recognizably similar in content to those they supplanted, but somewhat divergent in their philosophy and purpose. The best example of this is the conversion of Home Economics courses into Catering or Food Studies courses. Extra resources were used not so much to update existing equipment as to provide a further range of equipment and to subsidize (where necessary) a level of consumables/raw materials sufficient to permit batch production rather than the domestic production that traditionally characterized Home Economics. However, when augmented by such TVEI requirements as 'relevance to work' and 'how industry works', this quantitative change led in some cases to distinctively different programmes that could be seen as an authentic TVEI curriculum. The kind of pragmatic response, represented by the effective conversion of Home Economics into Catering (or Food Studies), represents the best example of how a recognizable and authentic TVEI curriculum could be constructed on the hoof from the hybrid traditions that underlay the initiative and its guidelines and criteria.

The second mode of response we noted is best described as the *extension* of the curriculum possibilities of TVEI. Essentially, what it involved was a demonstration that the requirements of TVEI could be met by subjects that had traditionally little or no 'technical' content and few, if any, claims to vocational relevance. Typically, certainly in the early stages of TVEI, it tended to be a defensive strategy on the part of departments that saw their student numbers, if not their whole futures, threatened by the entry of TVEI into the school. However, one of the most marked shifts brought about by TVEI in the curriculum area came about as traditional teachers of humanities subjects moved beyond that initial defensive, even defiant stance ('deny us if you dare' would have been accepted as a rallying call in several cases we observed) to one that celebrates the positive virtues of adapting 'liberal' subject matter to demonstrate its practical vocational relevance. Perhaps the most common – and most predictable – examples were those where the vocational relevance of foreign languages were emphasized, as in the regular 'French for Business Studies' courses. Less frequent but perhaps more imaginative were courses that emphasized the skills base rather than the content base of a subject. Thus Geography or History would be adapted to place their unique methods of investigation (frequently as augmented by various forms of Information Technology) at the centre of their appeal, rather than the content of the subject. Therefore, developing the ability to interrogate historical or geographical databases became at least as important as being able to reproduce the findings of the disciplines, or the theories underpinning them. In at least one early case, the case for a TVEI Humanities programme was argued on the basis that the skills it provided were precisely those required by the Occupational Training Family in which most of its students were likely to find themselves employed.

The other main area to make use of the extension mode was Personal and Social Education. Unlike the traditional humanities subjects, this was an area with little coherence or prestige within most schools, and TVEI was recognized as a means of redressing at least the former of those shortcomings. One of the effective requirements of TVEI schools was that they assist the personal as well as the academic development of their pupils. While most schools reacted to this requirement through the enhancement mode, it did provide outstanding opportunities for the defence of apparently threatened subjects as well as for entrepreneurship on the part of individual teachers. Almost anything could be – and was – justified as part of a programme of Personal and Social Education (PSE). One of us remembers with particular pleasure an Annual Review meeting where it was revealed that in one pilot school TVEI funds were being used to support classes in yoga. This caused great consternation to the MSC regional adviser responsible for the scheme, but when it was justified as contributing to pupils' personal growth, he was very rapidly mollified.

As so often, the nature of a situation can be illuminated by what was not said or done, or what did not happen. In the case of the impact of TVEI on the curricula, the most revealing absences are to be found in science and Computer Studies. On the face of it, one might have imagined that these two subject areas would be among those with most to gain from a technical and vocational education initiative. And yet on the whole what we found was very little change in science curricula as a result of TVEI, and a serious decline, even in some cases the demise, of Computer Studies. Computer Studies as an academic subject with an emphasis on understanding how computers work, and writing programs rather than using commercial software, seems never to have met the expectations of most pupils – or teachers – and the opportunity to replace it by very much more applied courses in Information Technology (IT) was taken up eagerly.

With one or two notable exceptions, for instance some individual initiatives by Physics teachers, the science subjects stayed relatively distant from TVEI; the same is true to some degree of Mathematics, though here a number of programmes stressing basic numeracy were introduced in response to TVEI. Two allied explanations suggest themselves. First, science and Mathematics were both high-status areas and, unlike the high-status humanities subjects, had little if anything to fear from TVEI. However, they also had little to gain. Their high status inhered in their academic strength rather than in their vocational relevance, and moves to strengthen the latter might have to be introduced at the expense of the former. This links directly to the second explanation, which we adumbrated briefly in the first part of the book. That is, that technical education has always two faces; the one looking to increase the instrumental relevance of what is offered to the 'brightest' students, the other to using the apparent relevance and interest of technically and vocationally oriented curricula to solve problems of motivation and control in the lower streams. We suggested earlier that while there were few clues that would locate TVEI initially on one or other of the sides of that divide, TVEI in practice had leant very much in the control direction. The place of science is a good test of this, and it does seem to confirm the view that whether or not it was intended to, TVEI, like many other attempts before (see McCulloch *et al.*, 1985, and Shilling, 1989a) did very little to forward the application of science rather than its 'pure' study.

The third and most radical mode of response to this curriculum dilemma by TVEI was what we will call the *'expansion'* mode. This involved creating and setting up programmes of study that responded to the TVEI guidelines but that had few, if any, precedents in the schools. Though they necessarily relied on instigation and promotion within the school, such programmes might involve bringing in outside expertise and/or pupils pursuing their studies outside the school. A rather more detailed example than we have provided so far will be useful to illustrate this mode of response, as there is, by definition, little referential experience that readers can draw on. To do this we shall focus on one particular example, namely the introduction of a Creative Arts course for 14- to 16-year-old pupils in a four-form entry comprehensive school, serving a council estate in a northern industrial town. This modular-based course replaces the more conventional Music, Art and Drama subject-based courses previously available.

We have chosen this particular example because it exemplifies many of the strengths, problems and issues raised by TVEI curriculum developments. It provides a good illustration of an attempt to offer educational experience which exerts a higher degree of realism as defined earlier. It also exemplifies a course which has eroded several of the boundaries that prevail in and between conventional Music, Art and Drama courses. The inclusion of this Creative Arts course within TVEI shows the breadth of its (TVEI's) curricular parameters. However, this particular course also highlights a number of key problems facing new curricular developments in TVEI, not least of which is the resistance of many educational categories and boundaries to change, and the difficulties of introducing a higher degree of realism into the pupils' learning experiences.

CREATIVE ARTS YEAR 1

Course outline

In order to give common purpose to all the elements of the course and to facilitate interaction through performance, there will be a thematic structure which will be referred to in all study modules.

Module 1 options			*Subject area*
A	Sound Workshop		Music
	Drama (Movement)		Drama
	Film Making		Art
B	3D Design	8 weeks	CDT
	Graphics		Art/CDT
	Textiles		Home Economics
Module 2 options			
A	Sound Workshop		Music
	Drama (Acting)		Drama
	Film Making		Art
B	3D Design	8 weeks	CDT
	Textiles		Home Economics
	Graphics		Art/CDT
Module 3 options			
A	Sound Workshop		Music
	Drama (Animation B/L)		Drama
	Film Making		Art
B	3D Design	8 weeks	CDT
	Textiles		Home Economics
	Graphics		Art/CDT
Module 4			
Final Commission		12 weeks	
(Specialization or Group Performance)			All

N.B. Not permitted: 3 'A' options or 3 'B' options.

The following brief notes give some insight into the curriculum content in this particular Creative Arts course. In Creative Sound Workshop, students have the opportunity to use and experiment with electronic music synthesizers, portable electronic keyboards, percussion and self-made instruments, sound recording and mixing equipment. The skills learned include programming an electronic music synthesizer and structuring synthesizer sounds into a real-time track to suit one of the set themes and to recognize the pre-set voices and rhythms of a portable electronic keyboard. Students experience the sound-making potential of pitched/unpitched percussion instruments, everyday objects, self-made instruments, and play and create simple melodic figures at the keyboard. The students also demonstrate the ability to use a range of technical equipment, recording and mixing techniques and working as part of a group to produce a sound track and/or music to suit one of the set themes.

In the Drama Workshop (including Dance/Movement/Mime), the students are involved in a series of induction exercises that include group dynamics and interaction, and practising techniques in improvisation and simple choreography. The students experiment in individual and group themes and are expected to demonstrate freedom of expression, confidence in performance, the ability to make critical judgements, creativity in scripting and developing a performance.

In Technical Graphics, the students learn how to produce a graphically clear design work folio, and study graphic techniques through practical work which are based on one of the set themes.

In the Design Workshop (3D Design), students work in a variety of media to explore the possibilities of performance-related design. They learn how to use a variety of materials in two and three dimensions, to design and plan their work, and to make critical judgements about its quality and effectiveness.

In the Basic Design procedure (3D Design), students learn how to recognize a situation or problem which is suitable for development, e.g. a stage set, a theatre programme, a design brief. The students analyse, compile and display researched data leading to solutions to the design problems and the production of a model of the design artefact.

In Textiles, the students learn about different materials and techniques for joining and decorating them. These techniques may relate to theatrical costume design and are skills which complement methods of stiffening, shaping, decorating a fabric and also simple block printing on to fabric.

All of the students produce a Final Commission which is a compulsory module within the programme, and which is based on one of the set themes. The students work to a schedule and gain knowledge of planning, management and structure of a performance project. They are encouraged to use their personal skills for the benefit of the group, to show imagination and creativity in production and/or performance, and to perform or exhibit their work as part of a team for an appropriate audience. In Year 2, the course is divided into two elements. In Part 1, the student is required to make an individual contribution to a group project in the form of a public performance, live or recorded. In Part 2, the student is required to undertake a personal project based on one of the previous year's modules or a theme chosen with teacher approval. The project may take the form of written work, a sound or video-recording, a two- or three-dimensional design, a performance or a combination of these.

Modes of Assessment include personal diaries/notebooks, video-recorded material, sketches, 2- and 3-D designs, models, constructions, tape-recordings, performance, a folio of work and teacher-written records of assessment. GCSE Mode 3 accreditation was sought from the outset.

The main conditions for the successful introduction of this course were the highly motivated, imaginative and creative staff, and a TVEI director who recognized at the outset that courses like Creative Arts fitted perfectly with the philosophy and aims of TVEI. This was not always the case. Many authorities, schools, teachers and regional advisers were at best very hesitant about including such programmes in a technical and vocational initiative. At worst we observed in some authorities and schools outright opposition to the inclusion of such courses on the grounds that they were not technical, technological or vocational.

Another form of resistance was observed in the particular scheme being discussed here. The attempt to extend/replicate the Creative Arts course met with some resistance, particularly from the more traditional subject-centred Music teachers, several of whom embody the philosophies of the traditional/liberal educator. These teachers saw Creative Art (and indeed TVEI) as being a low-status course for low-ability pupils. Ironically, this is what actually happened at the school in question, where the students for the Creative Arts programme were identified as coming from the lower ability range. The more able pupils appeared to be opting for the conventional Music, Art and Drama courses, leading to GCSE accreditation. The role of the advisory service was particularly interesting. The Art adviser has proved to be a keen and sympathetic supporter. The Music adviser displayed no direct involvement with, or support for, the course and appeared to view modern contemporary popular music in all its forms as an inferior art form and unworthy of serious study.

The clear strengths of this particular Creative Arts course are most clearly exemplified using the Dimension of Realism discussed earlier. The first aspect of the dimension makes the distinction between contextualized and decontextualized learning. The curriculum content and learning experiences of this Creative Arts course reflected the activities of the world outside school, and the teaching continually showed the use and importance of the particular skills and knowledge being acquired, particularly in the production of the pupils' Final Commission. The second aspect of the Realism Dimension ascertains the extent to which the tasks are set by the teacher or derived from the pupils. On this particular course, the pupils were actively encouraged to identify particular problems and devise strategies for their solution. The third dimension of realism asks whether the tasks undertaken by the pupils have been pre-analysed and have 'right answers', or whether they reflect the complexity of problem solving in the real world. The Creative Arts pupils were continually involved in complex tasks again exemplified in the Final Commission, where pupils came together to produce a live or recorded performance and got first-hand experience of the complex nature of the problems involved in putting on a production. Not only did this course exhibit a degree of realism as defined above, it also involved extensive use of the new technology in music, recording techniques, lighting, photography/editing, etc.

However, the staff on this particular course soon became aware of the need to make the content more relevant to and reflect more realistically the world outside school, particularly in terms of the entertainment industry. There is a tendency for courses in the Arts to become insular and dominated by 'artistic' concerns and 'creative' processes. There was a realization among the staff that this Creative Arts course was to some extent insulated from (a) other subject areas, (b) the world of work, future careers and further study in the fields of art and entertainment, and (c) the local community.

So while boundaries have been reduced between Music, Art and Drama, and between teachers and pupils, others still exist. There was no cross-curricular work for example between Creative Arts and other TVEI courses such as Business Studies and Community Studies. In Business Studies, Creative Arts students could have undertaken such projects as working out the financial and organizational aspects of setting up a band, putting on a function or production, etc. In Community Studies, pupils could have conducted a survey of Arts and entertainment provision in the local area. Similarly, the Careers Service was not involved with this course. Very few staff concerned with the course appeared to be aware of the wide range of employment opportunities that exist in the entertainment industries; indeed, none of the pupils interviewed had thought of either working in this area or continuing with further education in the Arts. This weakness was compounded by the failure to develop links with residential and work experience. No work placements were found in the entertainment industry and very little information existed about these possibilities. An equally important absence in terms of the aims of TVEI was the failure to involve professionals in the Arts and entertainment industry in the design and delivery of this course. We are referring here to those involved in the several sound and video-recording studios in the area, local radio and television stations, sound and lighting equipment manufacturers, graphic designers, local theatres, dance halls and clubs, local photographers, music and record shops, local costume suppliers, as well as the many musicians, actors, artists, agents and promoters. None of these appear to have been involved in the 'secret garden' of curriculum development.

The key point about this example in our view is that it illustrates the political rather than the technical nature of the problems associated with the curriculum as with every other area of TVEI. Even where, as in the Creative Arts example, a coherent philosophy had been extracted from the available guidelines and criteria, the limits to its implementation were not only, or mainly, technical – all the shortcomings noted towards the end of the account could have been relatively easily overcome, especially with the level of resources TVEI made available. However, what the example demonstrates, is that the entry of TVEI on to the educational scene had no fundamental effect on the politics of the curriculum at school level. It did not abolish the distinction between high- and low-status subjects, or place on ice questions about the professional status and responsibilities of teachers, or absolve schools from deciding between the competing claims for the education of groups of pupils with quite different expectations and needs.

That is to say, TVEI heightens, rather than reduces, the importance of 'educational-political' problems. These problems fall into two categories: those wholly internal to the school and associated with the distribution of TVEI resources across departments, and its implications and a set of wider problems generated for schools and LEAs by taking on TVEI. This latter category is of particular interest because it is so easy to overlook the fact that throughout the pilot phase TVEI involved proportionately very few of the pupils in any school. Even where, as in one of the LEAs we studied, the TVEI cohort comprised 150 pupils per year (out of around 250), they were still in a minority in the school. In the typical case, the TVEI cohort (including sixth form) numbered no more than 200 pupils in a school, i.e. rarely were more than one-quarter of the pupils in a school involved, and then for only a minority of their time (and this was very much more the case in the colleges of further education in TVEI). And even though, as we have argued above, the TVEI's impact on most schools involved was disproportionately much greater than might be inferred from the nature and level of pupil involvement in it, it was only for a minority, and there were other things going on in the school that had to be maintained.

One quite crucial aspect of this discussion is that the period when the TVEI pilot was running was dominated by falling rolls in secondary schools. Many of them lived under the threat of closure or amalgamation, and for at least a sizeable minority of the schools we were concerned with, the decision to become involved in TVEI was influenced by this threat. Some of the headteachers reasoned that they could not be closed when such large sums of money that had been lavished on them, others that the various 'goodies' which came with TVEI would make them so attractive to parents that any threat to their futures would disappear under popular pressure. However, though this was an extremely serious issue for the schools involved, the existence or not of TVEI in a school was very rarely considered a major element in the school's attractiveness to parents. It was certainly never considered as important as the school's record in 'O' and 'A' levels. Consequently, whenever there appeared to be a clash of priorities between the requirements of TVEI and the requirements of obtaining exam passes, TVEI lost out. The extreme example of the effect of this occurred in one of the LEAs we looked at where the schools involved were all in the same locality and where the historical competition between them had been further sharpened by the very real threat that one of them would be closed. This competition had been based on a 'league table' of exam results. Maintaining their position in the league table was each headteacher's main priority. Though TVEI was an unknown quantity, all of the head teachers considered it too risky to invest a great deal of effort in it, because it might detract from the main objective of their schools. TVEI in this LEA was very much a marginal affair despite the efforts of the scheme co-ordinator, whose attempts to implement a more radical version of TVEI were rejected out of hand by the headteachers.

The hegemony of the 'O' level had, of course, been recognized by all of those involved in TVEI from the start and a great deal of effort was put into getting 'respectable' accreditation for TVEI courses. Despite the great flexibility and goodwill of the various examination boards involved, this inevitably had a somewhat conservative effect on the TVEI curriculum. Courses were created with the awareness that they would have to meet external criteria, i.e. they were not created on the basis of what would be best for the school, pupils and teachers alone, but in the recognition also that they would have to demonstrate their comparability with other courses elsewhere, especially when a potentially lengthy approval period could be anticipated (and one with a very clear end-point). At least one school we looked at had the unfortunate experience of announcing at the end of one school year that a particular TVEI course would carry an 'O' level qualification, only to fail to achieve approval for it from the examination board. This produced considerable pressure towards the incorporation of features that it was fairly clear would be uncontroversial for the examination board.

This process altered somewhat, though not fundamentally, with the arrival in the middle of the pilot phase of the GCSE in place of 'O' level and CSE. This involved the whole school and not just those on TVEI in creating or selecting syllabuses that conformed with a set of national criteria. Here the TVEI experience seems to have been particularly valuable. It had certainly made schools much more able to respond quickly and efficiently to the kinds of demands made by GCSE – another educational innovation that was introduced with far less preparation time than schools would have wished (this does reinforce a central feature of the TVEI story – the enormous work load it places on teachers). GCSE brought about the kind of reappraisal of the curriculum in the whole range of subjects that TVEI had required in the particular areas where it was introduced. It was, too, for all pupils, and centrally rather than incidentally, concerned with the critical question of public examination success. For these reasons, many teachers we spoke to – including some who had been very heavily involved in TVEI – felt that GCSE had had a considerably greater impact on the curriculum than had TVEI, a very interesting view given the subsequent tension between TVEI and a National Curriculum that was introduced in apparent ignorance that TVEI had ever existed.

One final point should be made about the impact of accreditation on TVEI. It was not just schools' needs for exam passes that pressed TVEI in the accrediting direction, but the explicit requirement that TVEI pupils be prepared for appropriate qualifications. One latent consequence of this was to reinforce other pressures that squeezed TVEI towards concentration on the middle levels of pupil ability. At the one end, for the academic pupils, TVEI constituted no effective alternative to examination passes in the high-status subjects that would ensure their entry to university (some parents even prevented their children from taking part in TVEI on the grounds that time spent on work experience and residential education would be time when they could not study for their 'O' levels). At the other end were the groups who were unlikely to pass any external examination and thus excluded themselves from TVEI if the accreditation requirement were taken seriously. One story exemplifies this effect usefully. In one of the schools we looked at, the Motor Vehicle course that had been very popular with the lowest stream boys was reconstructed as a result of TVEI. In its new form it included an examination. Its former clients regarded this as quite sufficient reason not to take it – 'It's a grammar subject, now.'

The change TVEI brought about in internal school politics was quantitative rather than qualitative. Inter-department competition for resources, appointments, accommodation and pupils are intrinsic to all schools; what TVEI did was both to raise the stakes and to change the rules. It raised the stakes through the provision of a larger 'pot' of resources to compete for, especially through the threat it apparently posed to the very survival of some departments and individuals. It changed the rules both through the creation of an outside arbiter over what should happen in the school, and through the set of criteria it introduced. This had the effect of shaking the existing status hierarchy of the school from top to bottom. Those formerly at the bottom of this hierarchy appeared to be the pupils most eligible to receive the enormous extra resources TVEI promised. This created some very interesting scenes in staffrooms, typified by one head of Technical Studies walking into the staffroom at the start of the pilot phase and proclaiming 'Next year, they'll all be mine', and by one very traditional head of English who never became reconciled to what he saw as 'those brown-coated buggers taking over the school'.

Of course, the 'brown coated buggers' never did take over the school. This was partly because only a minority of pupils was involved in TVEI. More importantly, though, it was because the existing struggles carried on with the same players and the same histories even with the stakes raised and the rules altered. The sudden largess was often as much a threat to those who seemed likely to receive it as it was to those who thought it might mean the end for their subject. From teaching Cinderella subjects operating on minimal resources at the margins of the school with a predictable clientele, some technical teachers suddenly found themselves expected to transform their subjects and their clientele aided (or threatened) by the possibility of having very large amounts of money to spend. It is little wonder that very many of them did not want to know.

So, constructions of a TVEI curriculum did not proceed according to a rational assessment of how the objectives set could be met most effectively and efficiently, but on the basis of confused attempts to retrieve some conceptual clarity from the guidelines offered, and the filtering of these attempts through the politics of the school and of the staffroom.

These circumstances produced a particular set of organizational problems for schools and LEAs in creating TVEI curricula. Schools' general reactions to taking on TVEI are discussed elsewhere in the book. In the curriculum area specifically, besides the universal problems of pressure and work load the problem was three-fold. It meant getting a quart into a pint pot. It meant changing courses very rapidly. And it meant coming to terms with running two parallel programmes – the mainstream and the TVEI – and the responses to these problems were shaped by the stance of the school as a whole and the individuals involved in TVEI, but the overall effect of these problems was to curtail the extent of curriculum change.

There were many ingenious attempts to fit the quart into the pint pot. The best known of these, whose strength was that they also seemed to offer a solution to the problem of the integration of TVEI, though intensifying its problem of rapid course development, were various initiatives that can be grouped together under the heading of the modular curriculum. The basic ideas behind breaking down the curriculum into modules much shorter than the typical 1- or 2-year course in the secondary school, were that the more digestible modules would increase student motivation and commitment and provide greater flexibility in what could be taught. It thus offered an attractive way out of the dilemma of ever-proliferating lists of options and restricted combinations thereof available to 14- to 16-year-olds. The arrival of TVEI had done nothing to instigate or simplify this, as the most common form of its incorporation within the schools was originally – and remained throughout the pilot phase – as another set of options to be chosen at the beginning of the 2-year run up to the 16+ examination. Its devotees talked of flexibility, the facilitation of curriculum development and the facility for rapid response to future change. Students could defer important decisions and achieve greater motivation by negotiation/discussion of learning objectives.

This 'experiential learning approach' allegedly led to more relaxed teacher–pupil relationships, increased motivation, encouraged 'creative teaching' and facilitated cross-curriculum thinking/planning. The short-term commitment of modular choice was claimed to reduce sex stereotyping by enabling 'cross-gender tasters' in the form of options (rather than requiring a 2-year commitment), the formation of unviable groups, and at a time of falling roles to be more economical for the schools and allow them to preserve threatened subjects. However, though it continued as a significant organizational form throughout the pilot phase of TVEI, the modular curriculum never became fully embedded in the Initiative. There were a number of reasons for this. Some were intrinsic to the idea. Critics talked of a lack of coherence and the latent danger of curriculum fragmentation, for instance. They maintained that the vital question of whether modules should be independent or sequential had been largely ignored. And they pointed to problems of assessment (e.g. links with profiles and graded tests) and finding the balance between pupil-choice and common course elements. Furthermore, it could not be guaranteed to be a less complex or more comprehensible system than the options system it replaced – or sometimes ran alongside. It was no more insulated from the need to lead to qualifications than any other form of organization, but its novelty did nothing to lessen the time it took to obtain accreditation through an examination board. And, finally, it did nothing to solve the 'political' problems associated with the entry of TVEI into the curriculum. Departments were no more likely to yield ground in the form of modules than they were in the form of extended courses; consequently, the modular curriculum could only change the terrain of such struggles, rather than their purpose or intensity.

Rapid change in course content overlapped as an organizational problem with the wider problem of how to accommodate TVEI. It was, in fact, as much a political matter, concerning priorities in the allocation of personnel and resources, as it was an organizational one. Rapid change in the content of what was taught could only be obtained by the transfer of resources – specifically of teachers' time from other non-TVEI-related activities. While, as we have stated a number of times in this book, schools were willing to do this to a far greater extent than the level of funding in it would require, there were limits to what could be done, and these limits were inevitably reflected in the nature and extent of TVEI curriculum development that took place in schools. This is not for a moment to belittle the efforts made by the teachers. Indeed, the main cause of schools putting such inordinate amounts of effort behind TVEI was teachers' enthusiasm to be involved in curriculum development. Throughout its history, TVEI has stood out in a period of low morale and poor funding of schools, as the only reasonably funded basis for curriculum development. This exclusivity enabled it to capitalize on the professional talents, abilities and commitments of very many teachers attracted by the opportunity to be involved in curriculum development; a position of strength that may, paradoxically, in attracting a range of teachers, by no means be confined to technical and vocational areas, have weakened the message it was set up to promulgate.

The major organizational problems created by the requirement to create a TVEI curriculum, however, were to be found not in the schools but in the LEAs, who, after all, signed the contracts promising what the schools would deliver. They had overall responsibility for the construction of TVEI curricula. In this, they faced similar problems to the schools. The conceptual issues were scarcely any clearer for LEAs than for schools. They had their own 'political' problems, chiefly that of the relationship between the existing advisory/inspection service and TVEI. This issue is discussed elsewhere in the book, and we shall allude to it in the following section, but it is important to note that, *mutatis mutandis*, the issues and their effects were very similar at LEA and school. A second and distinct political problem for the LEAs was that they had to advise and implement a policy that in some degree at least would be common to all the participating schools. Here, the traditional autonomy of schools, the typical absence of any history of inter-school cooperation – or even of exchange visits – to say nothing of the competition between schools created or intensified by falling rolls, were the kinds of difficulties LEAs had to face that set distinct limits to what it was possible to achieve. The successes achieved in this area, through TVEI and the TVEI-Related In-Service Education for Teachers (TRIST) scheme, are indeed one of the most important legacies of TVEI.

Faced with the 'technical' problems of an uneven distribution of relevant professional knowledge and expertise across schools, and the political problem with little inter-school cooperation, the solutions most LEAs opted for were centralized curriculum development (whether in the form of individual curriculum development officers or through the facilitation of curriculum development groups made up of teachers from the participating schools, or some combination of these) and intensive programmes of in-service education for teachers in the scheme. These were particularly aimed at building up expertise in 'obviously TVEI' areas, such as CDT and Business Studies, where existing teacher numbers were inadequate to permit the kind of expansion TVEI would require, and existing knowledge and approaches inappropriate to the requirements of TVEI. The teacher supply problem was also acute in the area of IT where, in addition to the difficulties encountered in CDT and Business Studies, there was sometimes a particular problem of 'poaching' by industry. One school we observed, for instance, lost three IT teachers – two of whom left 'overnight', breaking their contracts – to industry in one year. In another authority, an IT teacher we spoke to who took a party of TVEI pupils to see how IT was used in a real organization, was offered a job there on the spot at twice what the director involved initially refused to believe was his salary in teaching. He did not accept the offer, but these instances do point to a neglected issue in the development of an initiative like TVEI. The upgrading of teachers' knowledge and skills makes them attractive to other employers, not only outside teaching, but to other LEAs and schools. We know of a number of cases where the expansion of TVEI across the country placed such a premium on their skills and knowledge, that some teachers who had been involved in the earlier pilot schemes achieved extremely rapid promotion and salary increases – moves from scale 1 to scale 4 were not unknown.

As well as providing a solution to the LEAs' problem of how to meet their commitment to provide a TVEI curriculum, the centralization of curriculum development and INSET had other incidental but important consequences. It provided legitimation for project directors, who were often seen as parasites, an unnecessary drain on funds that would have been better employed in schools. It also provided a means, or at least a model, for fulfilling another contractual requirement – that the programmes be 'readily replicable'. Although as the final chapter shows, this requirement became watered down in the course of the pilot phase to 'dissemination' and 'generalization', that chapter also demonstrates how both the work of curriculum development officers and INSET programmes was not only extended to cover schools not participating in this pilot phase of the schemes, but that the central units in fact became what remained of TVEI in the extension phase.

The effects of the use of centrally based mechanisms for the development and underpinning of TVEI curricula inevitably had implications for this kind of curriculum development. Most importantly, this strategy was not able wholly to avoid all the disadvantages traditionally associated with INSET and authority-based curriculum development. These are, crudely, that the message becomes diluted and the messengers isolated when they return to the reality of their own school. Even the enthusiasm generated in the best organized INSET courses tends to be dissipated as the practical difficulties and external politics and organization ramifications of doing so become evident. This is especially so when, as is frequently the case, only one teacher per school attends INSET courses. One other factor inhibiting the success of this strategy that was especially noticeable in the TVEI case was teachers' reluctance to go on INSET courses. This reluctance did not stem from any lack of professional commitment. On the contrary, it was stimulated by teachers' unwillingness to leave their classes to be taught by supply teachers in whom they typically had little faith. This was a particular problem for TVEI both because the extent of the INSET commitments required tended to be greater than previous INSET courses, and because TVEI-related INSET was usually devoted to subject areas where it was especially difficult to find effective, or even adequate, supply cover (see Shilling, 1990). The extent of the time commitment problem can be gauged from the fact that in the first full year of TVEI in one of the LEAs we looked at, there was *less* time devoted to teaching CDT in the participating schools than there had been in the previous year, due entirely to the absence of CDT teachers on INSET courses.

However, if the demands of TVEI exacerbated the historical problems of INSET, its resources and its style of operation more than compensated. The historical problems were well known to TVEI personnel and they sought to use their resources to overcome them. So, for instance, in the authority where the impact of INSET on what happened in schools was probably greatest, it was unusual for only one teacher from each school to be sent on a course. In most cases, it was part of the remit of curriculum development officers to provide continuing support in the schools for the initiatives they set in motion. And considerable TVEI funds were often devoted to the search for more – and more effective – supply cover in the geographical and curriculum areas where they were most needed. All these 'solutions', however, brought with them further problems. Sending more than one teacher from the same school department on an INSET course multiplied the problem of supply cover. There were limits to what a small group of curriculum development officers could achieve; but there were also political limits to the appointment of more of them because that would inevitably have meant a further centralizing of TVEI resources at the expense of individual schools. And while TVEI might unearth new sources of supply cover, it was even more difficult to prevent them being 'poached' by other non-TVEI schools.

The possibility of installing TVEI curricula in schools by means of central initiatives, then, ran into a set of problems that like so many of the issues we discuss in this book, were essentially nothing to do with TVEI, but embedded in parts of the system through which it had to operate.

In one respect, however, TVEI INSET did represent a clear advance over what had gone before. To oversimplify, unlike traditional INSET, it was tailored to the needs of the school rather than of the individual teacher. For what seemed to be the first time in many LEAs, INSET was put on a relatively systematic footing that took its shape from the need to install, support and develop particular curriculum initiatives in a range of schools. Of course, something of this nature had occurred pre-TVEI as local advisers/inspectors provided INSET courses to back up current curriculum trends. The difference was that in most cases the schools themselves were not involved. Individual teachers decided whether or not to go on such courses, as often with a view to embellishing their CVs as with the intention of radically altering what or how they taught. Under TVEI, on the other hand, it sometimes became close to a requirement of some teachers that they attended INSET courses aimed at supporting TVEI curriculum development. And as with TVEI as a whole, the broader impact of its INSET strategy was in the form it took rather than in the curriculum changes it brought about. The 'needs analysis' strategy for deciding the shape of INSET programmes became the basis of the TRIST programme. It was further developed there, and is now quite clearly the dominant, if not the only, form of INSET in English education.

Conclusion

We stated in the introduction that TVEI had to be considered a failure in curriculum terms, i.e. in achieving a clear and permanent shift in the balance of the secondary school curriculum. The main evidence for that contention was the form taken by the

National Curriculum, which far from reflecting any influence of TVEI, could on some interpretation appear to make a full TVEI programme in schools impossible. There is, though, other evidence which we have gathered that confirms the argument of this chapter that relatively little change was brought about in the curriculum as a result of TVEI. The first evidence comes from the schools in TVEI authorities that were not involved in the scheme. Some of us, as part of our local evaluations, looked at such 'control' schools in our TVEI authorities. The reaction of these schools to what occurred in the curriculum area was consistent, almost unanimous and, most significantly, persisted throughout the pilot phase. It was, in a nutshell, 'they're doing nothing we couldn't do tomorrow if we had the resources'. Now two objections might be made to this as a piece of evidence. It might be argued that 'ready replicability' was to be a feature of all TVEI programmes, and that it was no part of the purpose of the pilot phase to create any sort of 'magic', 'mystique' or 'mastery' that could not be emulated by others. This is true, but it is not really the point. The feeling among the non-participating schools was that there was nothing 'new' about TVEI; what changes it brought about were quantitative and dependent on additional resources rather than anything qualitatively different. While certainly by the end of the pilot phase this was becoming more difficult to sustain in some authorities, especially as some schools moved into an expansion mode, the overwhelming feeling remained among the non-TVEI schools that they would be able to take their place in the extension phase of TVEI without undue difficulty, effort or need to change. This brings us to the second objection – that 'they would say that, wouldn't they?' Again, this objection has some weight. There was certainly in some cases a sufficient degree of envy, hostility and anger at what was seen as exclusion, among the schools not chosen for TVEI at the start of each pilot scheme, for them to want to belittle if not denigrate the efforts of those who were chosen. It was the case, though, that long after those initial reactions had cooled and the non-TVEI schools had become supportive of the pilot scheme, they retained the feeling that there was nothing going on that they could not have done. As if to prove this, a few non-TVEI schools did in fact start their own 'unofficial' TVEI programmes, that paralleled those in the pilot schools but without any additional funding.

However, the most compelling evidence for TVEI's relative lack of curriculum impact is to be found in the programme of a fourth-round pilot scheme that began to operate only as the original 14 schemes were nearing the end of their pilot phase. With 4 years experience of TVEI pilot schemes to draw on, the programme offers Business Studies, Community Studies, CDT, IT, Modular Science and Food Studies. Only Modular Science (itself a reaction to the needs of the National Curriculum rather than TVEI) would not have been found in the first-round pilot schemes 4 years before. Without specifying what is actually taught in these courses, pupils in any one school found their curriculum changed only to the extent of being able to choose two from the following options: Business Studies, IT, CDT, Community Studies, Modular Science, Food Studies and in another school two from Business Studies, Community Studies, Modular Science and CDT. It is significant that this programme shows little evidence of the kind of good practice examples promulgated through the various publications of the TVEI Unit. It shows that their influence was distinctly limited, at least as they were appraised by those responsible for setting up this scheme. But it also demonstrates the relatively low expectations for curriculum change that the TVEI Unit held after 4 years with its pilot phase. They had, after all, to approve the scheme.

We have attempted to show in this chapter why a scheme introduced under such favourable conditions – well resourced, allowing time for teachers to become involved in curriculum development, and with improved teacher – pupil ratios – did not produce more in the way of visible impact on the curriculum, though inevitably that impact varied across both schemes and schools. Some of these reasons are not confined to TVEI, e.g. those emanating from the political and technical difficulties of bringing about quick and effective change of whatever kind in schools. Other reasons have their roots in the speed with which the initiative was set up and the consequent lack of clarity about what TVEI could, should and would entail for the curriculum. Both these sets of factors militated against both the possibility of creating distinctive TVEI curricula and the possibility of their being implemented in relatively undiluted forms. These two factors also represented the main dimensions of the difference between the schemes where TVEI had the greatest and the least impact.

However, it would be a serious mistake, and cause unjustified complacency or despair among opponents or supporters of TVEI, to conclude that nothing changed in the curriculum area as a result of TVEI, or even that nothing very much happened. Though that impact may not have been as dramatic or as visible as might have been hoped (or feared), it was nevertheless profound.

What did this impact amount to, then, and, given what we have said in this chapter, where did it come from? Essentially, it was possible because in the end it was the MSC/TVEI Unit who set and policed the boundaries of TVEI, who defined the terrain on which negotiations, developments and initiatives would be fought through. Not everything was possible under TVEI. There were limits, however unclear, broad and flexible they may have been. And if teachers became adept at writing proposals for the extension and expansion of TVEI into seemingly non-technical/vocational areas – and they did – those proposals nevertheless had to conform to, certainly not challenge, the assumptions about the nature and purpose of education contained, however vaguely, in the guidelines and criteria. That is to say, they had to employ a vocabulary of motives possibly different from that they would have employed outside TVEI. Again while no headteacher we spoke to felt she or he had done anything that they would not have wanted to do anyway, it is certainly not the case that they would have used the resources available in ways that conformed to TVEI requirements, if they had been given a free hand.

Furthermore, some curricular areas, especially those traditionally on the margins of the school, were seriously affected, sometimes to a point close to extinction. Certainly, TVEI created in some schools a transformation in the content, pedagogy and rationale of some subjects like Music and Drama. In addition, TVEI led to all subjects feeling under some obligation to demonstrate how they could be 'applied'. This meant, to put it simply, that English departments, for instance, might find themselves expected to justify *not* teaching Business English, or Maths departments to justify *not* having courses in basic numeracy, rather than having to make out cases for doing so.

It is easy to overlook the direct curriculum effect of TVEI. Its clearest visible impact has been on subjects that are unequivocally technical and vocational. As we pointed out above, the quantitative 'beefing up' of subjects like CDT and Business Studies led in many cases to qualitative changes in content and pedagogy. Though it may have accelerated trends that were already present, TVEI certainly both hastened the demise of woodwork, needlework and typing and created clear pointers to what should succeed them.

But overall, TVEIs most important effect on the curriculum was probably the way that it raised teachers' consciousness of the alternative purposes for education to the traditional liberal academic. Few teachers who had anything to do with TVEI can have escaped some level of contact with, even infection from, the idea that what they taught in schools had at some stage and in some way to be justified in terms of its relations to the 'world of work'. This emphatically did not mean that training in specific occupational skills was initiated (it was not even desired), or even that the long cherished ambition to combine the academic and the technical was high on the agenda. What it did mean was, as we have just noted, their vocabularies of motive changed, especially in what it became necessary to justify *not* doing.

If, then, TVEI did not bring about the supplanting of the academic by the technical/vocational as the centre of gravity of the secondary curriculum, it did make some progress towards dislodging the academic from its perch or taken-for-granted pre-eminence. It was bidding to establish a parallel, if not yet equal, set of justifications, contents and practices – but whether or not it would have succeeded will never be known following the installation of a National Curriculum based on a different set of principles and seemingly indifferent to, if not ignorant of, the albeit largely latent curriculum advances made under the auspices of TVEI.

CHAPTER 8

Work experience in TVEI

Introduction

In examining the role of work experience in the Technical and Vocational Education Initiative (TVEI), it is useful to look at the recent history of this activity. The changing reasons which have been given by the state for sending school students into the workplace for short periods of time, tell us much about the current purposes of TVEI work experience.[1]

Work experience played an important part in the school curriculum well before the introduction of TVEI. Indeed, in the early 1970s, the government recognized the growing number of schools that were organizing work placements for their students by introducing the Education (Work Experience) Act of 1973 and issuing the subsequent DES circular on work-experience schemes (DES, 1974). However, TVEI had an important impact on the contemporary development of work experience. It was the first national school-based scheme to make work experience a *mandatory* part of the education of students, and it served to reorientate the aims and objectives of this activity. So, while TVEI did not 'invent' work experience, it was an important force in shaping its meaning as an educational activity.

In this chapter, we will examine the development of work experience in schools, before analysing in more detail its operation as part of TVEI.

The development of work experience

It would be a mistake to think that there has ever been a complete consensus concerning the 'function' of work experience as part of the school curriculum. For example, those who have written about the organization and effects of work experience, have variously seen it as something to educate, socialize and even control young people. For example, Eggleston (1982, Watts (1983), Kerry (1983) and Montgomery (1983) have illustrated the educative potential of work programmes. In contrast, critical educationalists have viewed work experience as an activity which has changed the curriculum in order to *occupy* large sections of youth who face a jobless future (Stronach, 1984), and to reinforce 'the perception that the burden of adjustment to the labour force is the individual's responsibility' (Cole, 1983: 24). Others have pointed to the radical educational possibilities of an activity which can stimulate in students a 'greater understanding of the attempts to control workers and the oppositional forces which occasionally arise to contest these controls' (Watkins, 1987: 34).

There is, then, considerable disagreement about the effects that work experience can have on participating students. However, since the Great Debate, the dominant State view of work experience has changed. In particular, the *intended aims* of this activity were reformulated as a result of the changing responsibilities of the DES and the MSC.

The DES traditionally took a *reactive* role in relation to school-based work experience. It was not in the business of determining the precise nature of schemes, nor passing detailed value judgements on their worth. These were seen as decisions best left to LEAs and schools. Instead, the DES has sought to ensure through 'general guidance' that work experience remained an educational activity and was not used by employers as a recruiting strategy or a short-term form of free labour:

> The principle which should underlie any work-experience is that pupils should be given an insight into the world of work . . . schemes for pupils of compulsory school age must form part of an educational programme. . . . Employers should be made fully aware of the [educational] aims of the scheme and should be invited to plan their part in cooperation with the schools (DES, 1974).

The DES was concerned to promote a consensus around the educational aims of work experience. Stipulating in fine detail how this activity should operate may not have been essential. However, it was important that the organization and operation of work experience should involve *educational* rather than employment criteria.

The DES approach towards work experience did not remain static, though, but changed in the political climate established by the Great Debate (Centre for Contemporary Cultural Studies, 1981). During this time, the government and a number of employers had expressed concern about the 'relevance' of schooling to an industrial economy. This concern was reflected by the DES who, in the year after the Great Debate had begun, issued a circular in which local authorities were asked what steps they had taken to 'promote the development of work-experience' in relation to the 'needs of an industrial society' (DES, 1977). Work experience no longer had to be part of a purely *educational* programme. Rather, it should also be used as an activity which could be related to the needs of an industrial, capitalist economy (DES, 1977; Saunders, 1987).

The DES signalled a change in the State's official view of work experience, and this was developed further as a result of the MSC's responsibility for TVEI. In its promotion of the Initiative, the MSC focused more clearly on the relationship between work experience and 'economic need', and went much further than the DES in linking the aims of work experience to the performance of the economy. Work experience was to be more than simply industrially relevant. In the context of TVEI, it was to play an integral role in providing an 'early' and 'permanent bridge between school and work' (MSC, 1984b). This 'bridge' was concerned with preparing young people for work by equipping them with industrially relevant knowledge, skills and attitudes which they would be able to exchange for jobs in the marketplace (Shilling, 1988).

The MSC's approach towards work experience had two major components. First, work experience was to familiarize students with a job environment in order that they should 'adapt' to the demands of work in a 'changing occupational environment' (MSC, 1984b). Secondly, students were to be better equipped to enter full-time employment through the actual acquisition of specific and, in particular, *generic* work-related skills (MSC, 1984b; see also Jamieson, 1985). While work experience was not expected to achieve this by itself, it was to play a central part in realizing this aim through TVEI. In marked contrast to the initial DES guidelines, the MSC invested the aims of work experience with a content drawn largely from the *employment* rather than the education system. Work experience had become a 'transitional' activity which was to facilitate the move of students from school to work.

The official rationale of work experience had shifted from being education-driven in the early 1970s, to becoming an employment-driven activity as part of TVEI. However, there was considerable variation in how work experience was presented as part of the school curriculum in LEA submissions. In some cases, work experience was to form the core element of students' programmes of study. In others, it constituted just one of several elements which were equally important to the education of students. Similarly, there were differences in the degree to which work experience was portrayed as an employment-driven activity. However, it is important to remember that there were limits to the degree of variation permitted by the MSC. As has been mentioned, work experience is a *mandatory* part of TVEI. LEAs had no option but to include work experience in their submissions if they were to have any chance of success. They also had to elaborate on the relationship that would exist between work experience and other components of the TVEI curriculum. Moreover, the submission and monitoring procedures that participating LEAs were subject to, provided a framework with at least the 'potential for control over the direction and detail' of work experience in each local scheme (Dale, 1986: 36).

The MSC did much to raise the profile of work experience in TVEI schools. None the less, this was still no guarantee that the *actual* consequences of work experience would be the same as those intended by the MSC. Indeed, our findings suggested that whether work experience could help facilitate the transition of students from school to work ultimately remained outside of the *direct* control of the MSC, LEAs and schools.

The supply and quality of work experience

Much of the TVEI curriculum can be seen as a relative 'constant', in that once resources were provided by the MSC, teachers employed and timetabling decisions made, a course existed which was ready to be delivered to students. Once these decisions had been approved and taken, there were few variables outside the control of schools to interfere with this situation.[2] However, in the case of work experience, suitable firms needed to be sought out by those responsible not once, but each time a group of students required work placements (cf. Kerry, 1983, for an attempt to regulate this situation through Project Trident). The participation of industry, and hence the ability of schools to deliver TVEI, depended upon the willingness and ability of firms to supply appropriate placements. In contrast to youth and adult training schemes, industry received no subsidies from the State to provide schools with work placements. The State did not socialize this cost (O'Connor, 1973), nor were there sanctions which could have been used against firms refusing to participate with schools. As a consequence of these conditions, teachers had to rely on public and private firms in the marketplace to deliver fully a school-based curriculum (see Shilling, 1987).

The MSC changed the intended aims of work experience to include facilitating the transition of young people from school to work. However, in establishing a material basis on which these aims could be realized, the MSC relied on a source outside of its direct control. Given a constant and plentiful supply of placements, this might not have been a problem. Teachers could conceivably have selected suitable placements from a long list of employers prepared to offer work experience to students. However, the dynamic nature of the capitalist economy in which firms operate made this degree of stability impossible in the long term (Offe, 1984, 1985). In the recessions which the British economy has been through in recent years, large numbers of companies have been forced to close and many others had to rationalize their operations to survive. Such events affected the supply of TVEI work placements in a number of ways. In many LEAs, economic pressures reduced the total number of placements available as a result of bankruptcy and closures. Similarly, a large number of firms were forced to reduce the extent of their involvement with schools. Furthermore, these pressures had unequal effects on different sectors of the economy, and even when schools or an LEA did not experience an overall shortage of placements, it usually suffered from a lack of particular types of work experience. This depended crucially on the structure of local labour markets. For example, in certain local authorities, a buoyant manufacturing sector provided schools with placements that were in short supply across the rest of the country. Other placements whose supply varied dramatically between local labour markets included agricultural, engineering, information technology and computing work experience. However, despite these local variations, it remained the case that most LEAs found a variety of manufacturing placements harder to come by than service or commercial placements. Another experience across LEAs was a variation in the supply of work-experience placements over the course of the academic year in response to stock-taking and particularly busy periods of business (e.g. sales).

The fact that LEAs had to deal with shortages of work placements illustrated the MSC's limited control over work experience. While the MSC changed the official aims of this activity, it was the material base of the economy, mediated by the ability and willingness of particular firms to supply work placements, which was a prerequisite for the operation of work experience. In attempting to forge a work experience which would facilitate transition from school to work, the MSC itself had to depend on the *capacity* of the economy. For most of the local authorities we have experience of, this created problems for teachers and schools struggling to find sufficient numbers of TVEI work placements. 'Solutions' to this problem included students spending less time than originally intended in work placements, TVEI students taking work placements originally intended for students on other courses, and the use of local authority 'skill centres' as a substitute for work experience.

The supply of work experience was not the only variable outside of the MSC's control. There was often a 'hidden' *selectivity* built into a firm's involvement with a school. For example, the majority of firms were unable to take disabled students for placements. In fact, our experience suggests that students with a variety of special needs have been poorly catered for by work experience, just as they have been by many TVEI programmes as a whole.

It is not just students with special needs who were inadequately catered for by work experience. We also found examples of how the gender, racial, social class and age divisions which characterize local labour markets operated to exclude other students from particular work placements. For example, there were reports of employers refusing to take girls or boys for work experience for a variety of spurious reasons such as the lack of suitable toilet facilities. Employers have also expressed preferences for older, sixth-form students to fill placements. This could be for a variety of reasons, such as a desire for 'responsible' students, and a hope that older students of 'high ability' would be attracted through work experience to a career with the firm (see Moore, 1986).

Such practices did not necessarily exclude students from work experience altogether. However, in our LEAs, students were often confined to certain sectors of the economy, and certain firms and jobs within these sectors, solely on the basis of socially ascribed characteristics (see also Barnes *et al.* 1989). This problem was exacerbated by general shortages of work experience placements. With work experience in short supply, it was difficult for schools to be selective in their participation with firms. It should be made clear that such differentiation is not a problem confined to TVEI. For example, there is plenty of evidence showing that gender and racial discrimination takes place in the government's Youth Training Scheme (e.g. Benn and Fairley, 1986; Walker and Barton, 1986; Cockburn, 1987).

In short, there were cases where the involvement of industry with schools *transported discriminatory labour market practices into the education of young people*. When such discrimination took place, it had serious implications for the ability of work experience to help students adapt to the demands of work in a changing occupational environment, and acquire specific and generic work-related skills. The value of work experience which provided students with a limited range of placements and on-the-job tasks, can be questioned in terms of its ability to help equip young people with the skills and characteristics required for what the MSC sees as a rapidly changing economy. For example, when work experience simply provided girls with experience of traditionally female occupations, it was difficult to see how it could contribute to the creation of a 'flexible' labour force so prized by many industrialists (Pollert, 1988).

However, the supply of work placements was not determined in an unmediated manner by industrialists. The policies of local authorities and schools, and the actions of teachers, also affected the availability of work experience placements.

The organization of work experience

In organizing work experience for TVEI students, LEAs and schools were in the position of mediating social divisions in local labour markets. Organizational issues faced LEAs and schools well before TVEI elevated the position of work experience in the curriculum. However, the intended role of TVEI work experience as a 'transitional' activity which should contribute to the provision of *equal opportunities* increased the importance of questions concerning the demand and quality of placements (MSC, 1984b).

There were several major ways in which TVEI work experience was organized in our LEAs. The most common of these was a centralized approach, and in the early years of TVEI, Project Trident was a popular way of arranging work placements. Here, a single body was in charge of recruiting, allocating and monitoring work experience, and there were significant advantages to this for achieving and maintaining a sufficient supply of work placements. Project Trident provided someone *exclusively* in charge of organizing and supervising work experience (see Kerry, 1983). The job was not left to overworked teachers. Furthermore, there was a single point of organizational contact for firms and they were promised 'minimal paperwork' and the chance to participate on a 'trial basis' (Trident, 1986). However, several disadvantages also faced LEAs using Project Trident. First, there were three prongs to the full Project Trident (the other two being 'challenging pursuits' and 'voluntary service') and most local authorities were only interested in the Project's organizational capabilities with regard to work experience. Secondly, Project Trident insisted on work placements being 3 weeks long. As Kerry (1983: 29) notes, 'the need for work-experience to be for three continuous weeks is an article of faith in Trident'. For many schools and LEAs who desired a more flexible arrangement, this was an obvious problem. Thirdly, Project Trident traditionally catered for students considered of low academic 'ability'. As TVEI work experience had to cater for students across the ability range, questions were raised concerning the continued appropriateness of this body. Fourthly, by having Project Trident, the organization of work experience was outside of the direct control of LEAs. To change any element of the policy or practice of TVEI work experience, LEAs had to work through an individual co-ordinator employed by a body outside of their direct control. As a result of these problems, several of the LEAs in our study stopped using Project

Trident to organize their work experience. Instead, they assumed direct responsibility for organizing work placements across the authority.

A significant advantage of a centralized approach (with or without Trident) was its potential to maximize the total number of placements available to schools, and in being well placed to meet rising demands for work experience. For example, a single organizational centre prevented firms being disturbed by increasing numbers of competing demands on their time and could, as a consequence, reduce the pressure on them to lessen their involvement, or 'pair' with a single school. Local authorities who delivered work experience to schools and students in this way, generally reported their satisfaction with the efficiency of this type of organization. Furthermore, when schools were not competing against each other for placements, there should have been a better chance of negotiating or imposing selection standards on participating firms. A centralized recruitment structure could have enabled effective negotiation to achieve equal opportunities, and a refusal to work with firms who did not allow students of different race, gender, class and academic ability to work in non-traditional jobs. Here, the effects of maintaining standards would not have been felt disproportionately by individual schools, as sub-standard employers would be prevented from participating with *any* school. Those responsible for work placements in an area could, through negotiation with schools, have set standards for firms to meet before they participated in work experience. However, *in practice*, this did not represent the reality of centralized structures in our LEAs.

The growth in demand for work experience as a result of TVEI tended to dominate concerns for quality, and centrally organized schemes emphasized what they could do for participating *firms*, rather than students and schools. For example, when Project Trident noted that firms could participate on a trial basis, it was not the firm that was on trial but the education system. It was for firms to see what it was like participating with schools, rather than the other way around. Furthermore, Trident tended to reinforce, rather than combat, the gender division of labour. In some LEAs, Trident booklets of placements for students included the comments 'suitable for girls' or 'suitable for boys' next to job descriptions. Trident also stressed the choice which was available to firms in terms of the acceptability of students. For Trident work experience, the students who are 'acceptable to the employer will be discussed and agreed upon prior to entry into the scheme'. The implications are clear. The criteria of employers concerning the appropriateness of students for particular placements entered into the selection process. For example, if employers did not want to offer placements to girls, there was no pressure on them to do so.

Centralization may have been an efficient way of *organizing* TVEI work experience in an authority, but there is little evidence that this was used to provide equal opportunities to students. Even when several LEAs abandoned Project Trident as a way of organizing TVEI work experience, the evidence suggests that questions of quantity continued to receive priority over those of quality. This was despite the fact that securing placements for TVEI work experience was usually given priority over other work experience schemes within both LEAs and individual schools.

The centralized organization of work experience was not the only structure through which firms were brought into contact with schools. Some LEAs centralized organization for a set of schools in one geographical locality, while leaving other schools to arrange their own work placements. The reasons that schools fell into one category or other depended on a variety of factors, such as the available supply of placements in a local labour market, and the willingness of schools to be co-ordinated centrally.

Other authorities 'organized' their work experience wholly on a *laissez-faire* basis. Here, individual teachers from each TVEI school made contact with local firms, negotiated with them the nature of work placements they were able to offer, arranged the duration and timing of placements, and visited students during their placement. This approach was satisfactory for certain individual schools. However, looked at from the perspective of the local authority/area within an LEA as a whole, it caused a number of problems. In the areas where a *laissez-faire* approach existed in our authorities, there was a substantial duplication of effort. Several teachers often found themselves searching for identical work-experience placements. With schools effectively competing among each other for placements, there were also shortages in particular occupational areas as a result of their unequal allocation. This is despite individual schools giving priority to TVEI work experience over other work experience programmes they were involved in. Such shortages were also exacerbated as a result of firms 'pairing' with particular schools as a way of minimizing the time and effort expended in organizing multiple placements. This was illustrated by the comments of a personnel manager of a large public utility:

> Most of our placements go to [. . .] school. I've got to know the teacher there well, and this arrangement works. It makes organization a lot easier – you know who you'll be working with.

Other problems caused by this *laissez-faire* approach included the 'poaching of placements' (causing bad feeling between schools in an area), and a worsening of supply problems (as schools often looked for placements at the same time of year). Without the central organization of work experience, it was all too easy for a number of schools to chase after a limited supply of placements at the same time of the year.

Even in times of an abundant supply of work placements, a *laissez-faire* approach appeared less than ideal for the delivery of TVEI work experience. However, at times of shortage, the process of school competition for placements had particularly detrimental consequences for the education of students. The fact that schools were in competition with each other meant that their first priority was to find sufficient placements, rather than to check carefully the quality of firms willing to provide work experience. In this context, demands of competition made schools reluctant to exclude all but the most obviously unsuitable firms from work experience. Similarly, in this situation, schools had little bargaining power to negotiate with firms the type and variety of jobs that students should be given. This demand/supply position created circumstances in which schools often unwittingly reinforced social divisions in the labour market. In a free market scramble for work placements, while individual schools occasionally refused to become involved with firms that embodied extreme racial or gender divisions of labour, they were disadvantaged in comparison with the total number of work placements gained by schools not practising this selectivity.

Evidence from the LEAs we were involved with suggests that both centralized and *laissez-faire* methods of delivering TVEI work experience operated to reinforce pre-existing social divisions within the economy. This had important implications for the MSC's stated view of work experience as a transitional activity. The feasibility of a work experience which was to help students adapt to the demands of work in a changing economy, depended upon the capacity of firms to provide an appropriate supply of work placements, and the capacity of schools to manage those placements. When this supply was inadequate, or highly differentiated, then it was unlikely that work experience could function as a *general* transitional activity for students of all backgrounds. At most, it might have provided a vehicle for transition to the labour market which was stratified. Put crudely, if work placements were meant to aid transition for all students to a wide range of jobs, this was unlikely to have been accomplished for students confined to a limited range of occupations.

So far in this chapter, we have looked at how the *organization* of work experience affected its potential for helping to provide students with an 'early' and 'permanent bridge between school and work' (MSC, 1984b). However, the actual *experiences* of students can be seen as of even greater importance to the outcomes of work experience. The responses we gained from a series of interviews with students in our LEAs demonstrated the impact of these social divisions in the economy on students' experiences of work placements. Employer perceptions of the academic ability of students also affected the experiences of young people on placements. However, before examining the actual experiences of students on work experience, it is important to say something about their expectations. In our LEAs, it was generally the case that students about to attend a placement similar to a job they were considering as a post-school option, showed great interest in and enthusiasm for their work experience. In contrast, those not using their placement as a 'taster' for possible future work, tended to be bored by the prospect of work experience. These expectations were often, though not always, confirmed by students' experiences of placements. However, the experiences of the majority of those interested in a placement, *actually led them to decide against working in a similar area after they had left school.*

Students' experiences of work placements could be seen to result from an interaction of three major features of the school–work relationship: the school organization of work experience, the social relations of production which exist in the site of work, and the labour processes they were confronted with. These factors did not operate separately. Rather, they combined and shaped each other in processes of interaction which had different consequences for various groups of students. It is for analytical purposes that they will be examined in turn.

The experiences of students on work placements

The school's role: preparation, monitoring and debriefing

The role of the school in affecting the overall *supply* of work experience has already been mentioned. However, a school's involvement rarely stopped once a sufficient number of work placements had been secured. For example, teachers often made decisions concerning placements deemed 'suitable' or 'unsuitable' for particular students. In a number of schools, students were actually prevented from going on work experience as they were seen as 'troublemakers' who were too great a risk to place with firms. In these cases, concern for the public image and reputation of the school, and the need not to alienate firms from future participation with the school, played an important part in determining who should participate in work experience. Even when these concerns did not exclude certain students, they usually dominated schools' preparation for work experience. As a result, it was rare for schools to provide students with a comprehensive briefing programme which enabled them to gain the maximum educational benefit from their work experience. Here, our findings agree with those contained in the report written for the MSC by Douglas Barnes and his colleagues:

> In preparing students to go out on the first work experience placement many schools place major emphasis upon the practicalities of attendance and upon ensuring that the student's general demenour and behaviour is acceptable in the workplace. . . . Important as all these matters are, they do not go far to ensure that students gain as much as possible from the experience (Barnes *et al.* 1989: 98–9).

The domination of these 'practicalities' had an important impact on the way in which students interpreted their experiences of work placements. As schools seldom provided any kind of framework in which to contextualize or evaluate the experiences offered by placements, individual students were dependent upon their own resources to make sense of their time at work. This is not to suggest that these resources would be 'inadequate'. However, this situation meant that the influence of schools in shaping the educational meanings of work experience was diminished. As will be made clear later, it also meant that students seldom returned from work placements with comparable findings which could serve as the basis on which to integrate work experience into the curriculum.

Teachers' perceptions regarding the suitability of placements had other implications for the operation of work experience. For example, a number of teachers placed students in work experience which related to TVEI courses they had been taking at school (e.g. Catering, Information Technology). However, others felt that the type of placements students participated in were unimportant so long as they experienced some sort of work environment.

The above examples concern the affects teacher perceptions had on the participation of students in (particular types of) work experience and the preparation they received for their time at a place of work. However, the degree of student choice allowed by schools was also a vital element in affecting their exposure to social divisions in the workforce. Here, the demands of employers were not the only factor which excluded students from certain placements. For example, when given the opportunity, a large number of girls chose traditional work placements. They often made these decisions as a result of previous life-experiences which illustrated the costs faced in making non-traditional decisions (cf. Stanworth, 1983; Cockburn, 1987).[3] It will take careful counselling by schools to alter such choices; a counselling which can only even hope to succeed if it is made clear that steps have been taken to *remove or reduce the obstacles young women may expect to be faced with at home and in a place of work.* Unfortunately, we have few examples of 'good practice' to report on here and our findings again concur with those of Barnes *et al.*'s report:

> there is little sign of progress in breaking down gender stereotypes in employment; these are powerfully entrenched both in families and in workplaces, and schools only occasionally make any serious effort to challenge them (Barnes *et al.*, 1989: 98).

As well as affecting the preparation and selection of students for placements, schools usually played some role in monitoring the quality of work experience. Teacher visits to students during their placements was one method by which this was achieved. Visits also allowed students to air any grievances they had to a familiar figure outside of the work environment. For example, the following students illustrated how useful the teacher visit could be:

> I was having problems with one of the other older boys who worked there. I had a word with the teacher when she came to visit and she got things sorted out. I didn't have any trouble after that.
>
> I really didn't like it [the work]. They were getting me to do the same thing all the time. I said that to the teacher and [. . .] told me just to stick it for the rest of the week. That wasn't what I really wanted but I felt better about it having spoken to [the teacher]. She said they wouldn't put anyone there again.
>
> I was getting teased a lot and I complained to [the visiting teacher]. They had a word with the manager and got me moved to another department. It was much better there.

In addition to monitoring the quality of placements, teacher visits were sometimes used to actively improve them through building good relations with firms. When this was accomplished, teachers made effective suggestions concerning how to improve placements. In certain cases, they were even able to increase a firm's involvement with a school by enlisting the help of employers in such activities as mock interviews. However, teacher visits could also lead to problems when they were poorly timed or irregular. In most of our LEAs, several firms complained that named schools were not taking enough interest in their pupils. This is illustrated by the owner of a medium-sized firm who had participated in work experience for 2 years:

> I need to see more teachers here. Pupils from certain schools I could mention never get to see their teachers during the week. I don't know what else [teachers] are up to, but it's a poor show if they can't get here at least once.

Poorly timed visits also caused problems, as the following comment from the personnel manager of a utility illustrates:

> I'm glad they visit, but oh the inconvenience! They'll turn up here, unannounced, and I'll be dragged from some meeting and have to take the teacher to where they [students] are working. This doesn't just happen once – again and again, it's a right pain.

Teacher visits also caused problems for students in a number of instances. On the one hand, if they did not take place, or did not allow for a *private* chat between student and teacher, students were unable to relay directly to the school any problems they were experiencing. Similarly, if teacher visits occurred too near the beginning of work experience, students often had insufficient time in the placement to judge its worth. For example:

> Well, Mr [. . .] came and visited after three days. It was alright then . . . it only got really bad near the end of the first week and I still had two more weeks to do . . . only there was no-one to complain to then, so I left and just went back to school.

> Teacher visits are good, I think, only Miss [. . .] came at the beginning before I knew what it was really like. I couldn't say anything to anyone about it then. I told Dad and he phoned up the school and got it sorted out. He told them.

On the other hand, when students were content in their placements, teacher visits sometimes served to replace them in an educationally subordinate relationship just as they were in the process of negotiating a subordinate workplace relationship. We have reports from several students relating how their attempts to gain credibility and acceptance among work colleagues, had been damaged by the arrival of a teacher who had come to see how they were getting on. Such factors have led to the decision of some LEAs to visit only when there are problems with students. However, this decision carried with it all the problems of being unable to keep a close check on the quality of work experience. Indeed, in most of our LEAs, students have walked out of placements because they were not happy with them and felt they had no-one to approach outside of the firm. As one student remarked, 'nobody took any notice of me at all, so I left'.

The dilemmas facing schools did not stop with the monitoring of work-experience placements. Most schools in our LEAs involved students in some form of 'follow-up' or 'debriefing' activities. Here, students were to discuss, compare and evaluate their experiences of work. However, in the large majority of cases, these activities were fragmentary. Usually, students were allowed only a period or two in which to express their opinions of work experience. Sometimes they would be set an essay or discussion exercises in an English or Personal and Social Education lesson. Furthermore, as schools' preparation for work experience was often minimal, the extent to which students could search for possible common or contrasting causes of their experiences, was rather limited. There were rare exceptions, but it was unusual to find schools where students were provided with a structured programme which gave them the opportunity to interpret and critically examine their work environment.

The social relations of production

Although not engaged as full-time waged-labourers, students still experienced the social relations of production in their firm. As students were almost universally placed into work experience through a relationship between a teacher and manager/ supervisor, rather than a worker representative, their relations with this authority figure assumed particular importance. There was often no-one else available to help with problems, and it was usual for the manager/supervisor to report back to the school on student performance. As a consequence, it was particularly disturbing when we heard of cases where this position of power was abused. Unfortunately, examples of such abuse were not exceptional and ranged from sexual harassment to physical assault. Others include a boy who was teased constantly and used to do the fetching and carrying on the building site while others sat and drank tea. A girl on a clerical placement was made to do 3 days solid photocopying and was warned that any complaints would earn her a bad school report. An Asian boy walked out of his placement because he was ignored and given no work to do.

Not all students, of course, report negative experiences of the work relations they experienced during their placements. In many cases, students developed positive relationships with their supervisors which aided the role of work experience as a developer of positive work identities. Students have completed their work placements with a renewed determination to enter a particular occupation. This is illustrated by a boy's experiences of a computer placement which confirmed his ambition to enter such work after school:

> They treated me like an adult. It was good, not like a school. I could do what I wanted and they [supervisors] spent a lot of time helping me.

However, it cannot be deduced from this that the process of transition to full-time work has necessarily been helped. For example, the development of a positive personal relationship with a work supervisor can serve to mystify the power relationship which exists behind it, ill-equipping students for future work which did not offer such humanitarian relationships. The experiences of the student in the above example, may have done nothing to adapt or prepare him for work in a more disciplined environment.

The reported experiences of many sixth-formers on TVEI placements, provided a further example of the diversity of social relations that students became involved in. In certain sectors of the economy, it is clear that employers organized a carefully supervised and quite specific programme of work experience for older students considered to be of higher ability than fifth-formers and potential recruits. For example, firms who recruit technicians and engineers often spend a portion of work placements providing careers information to participating sixth-formers. This is sometimes coupled with additional measures in the hope of attracting individuals back to the firm. Such practices are illustrated by the personnel manager of a microelectronics company:

> Some of the older students we have interested in this area of work, who might be going to university or college the following year, we offer summer jobs to. It benefits them and

> we hope they will keep in contact with us, ultimately to possibly come and work here in the future.

The particular interest in sixth-formers taken by a number of companies illustrates how skill shortages and the academic stage students have reached, can affect the meaning of work experience for firms.

The labour process

The labour process is made up of three elements which surround the production of surplus value in our economy: the process of working itself, the objects on which that work is performed, and the instruments used to facilitate that work. The increased use of high technology in parts of the production process, is causing a great many changes to the labour processes experienced by workers. In order to prepare young people for these changes, the MSC invested work experience with the objective of aiding the acquisition of specific and *generic* skills. However, in our LEAs, the reality of students' experiences of placements did little to help them acquire these competencies. Indeed, the experiences of many students support Watts' (1983: 13) argument that in short-term placements, 'participation tends to be confined to completely unskilled or routine operations'. For example, students on hairdressing, painting and decorating, plumbing and mechanics placements reported the following:

> I was looked after alright, but I wasn't allowed to do much and I spent my time watching or making tea, or sweeping the floor.
>
> Boring, I was meant to do painting and decorating but I just sat on the truck all day. They said I couldn't do anything.
>
> I didn't get up to much, just sat and drank tea most of the day. They didn't have anything for me to do.
>
> It was boring and I didn't get to do much when they were fixing things; held tools, that sort o' thing. It was better when the radio was on.

Students with positive experiences of learning often report the acquisition of so-called skills which are hard to justify as constituting a preparation for what the MSC sees as a rapidly changing hi-tech society (MSC, 1984b). For example, students reported that they have acquired such skills as 'how to answer the phone', 'put addresses on envelopes', 'how to sweep a floor' and how to 'make coffee properly'. One can only wonder at what contribution being able to make coffee, for example, in a variety of situations, will make to a high-technology economy.

The examples cited above illustrate that the tasks students complete during work experience are not determined solely by the labour process of a particular occupation. Rather, they are mediated crucially by the limited time allocated to work experience (usually between 1 and 3 weeks) and, more importantly, by the social relations that exist in the workplace. For example, the number of girls entering non-traditional male areas of work who report that much of their time was spent making the tea suggests not, of course, that this is representative of the tasks necessary to be a mechanic or engineer, but that it is the result of a gender division of labour which operates not only between sectors of work but *within* occupations and workplaces (Cockburn, 1987).

We are not arguing that these social relations of work and labour processes are representative of those experienced by *all* students. Again, the example of sixth-formers on work experience provides a contrast. Although the actual skills they learn on placements may be minimal, older students often had considerably more time and attention spent on them than their younger counterparts. However, the fact remains that students on work experience were subject to work practices that teachers had little or no control over. As student experiences of work placements have demonstrated, they may be subject to sexual harassment and a variety of other exploitative relations in an environment where they are likely to be and feel relatively powerless. The tasks students were expected to complete could also serve to limit the efficacy of work experience as a 'transitional' activity. For example, when used to make the tea, girls are not only allocated to tasks which are traditionally seen as 'women's work' in a firm. This gender division of labour also reflects a domestic role where women are placed in a position of serving others. Such experiences do not represent the positive taste of traditionally male occupations that were required for work experience to contribute towards a policy of equal opportunities (see Shilling 1989c).

One consequence of these negative experiences is that far from aiding the transition from school to work, work experience exposed many students to a set of social relations and a labour process which led them to develop negative work identities. For example, a number of previous surveys of students on work experience have illustrated how negative work identities and even alienation can follow work placements (e.g. Stronach and Weir, 1980; Institute of Careers Officers, 1974; Watkins, 1987). As has been mentioned, in our LEAs, the majority of even those students initially interested in their work placements had experiences which served to alienate them from considering future work in a similar area. For example:

> I wanted to be a secretary before but it was too boring sitting in an office all day. I don't know what I want to do now.
>
> The best bits were the tea breaks! I'm not going to work in a bank now. My mother said it was good work but I couldn't stick it – they all looked half dead working there.
>
> I've changed my mind now. Building seemed like a good idea but when it rains . . . and you're on your feet all day. I'm leaving [school] soon and my uncle had a job fixed up for me. But I don't want to go on a site now.

The experiences of students during placements have been seen as the result of a combination of the school's role (in interaction with local labour markets and the agendas of specific firms), the social relations of work and the labour process. The way in which these factors interact depended upon the structure of each specific firm, and determined the extent to which divisions within the labour market and workforce were mediated or reinforced. For example, a number of teachers sought to shield female students from 'making the tea all day' or far worse experiences, by directing them into 'safe', traditional areas of work. This humanitarian response, however, had the unintended consequence of reinforcing the gender division of labour.

The future of work experience in TVEI

The major themes of this chapter have been concerned with how the MSC has invested TVEI work experience with a role which seeks to facilitate the transition of young people from school to work. However, we have argued that this does not guarantee that the actual consequences of work experience will be in line with its intended aims. Rather, they are dependent upon interorganizational and inter-individual relations which remain *outside* of the direct control of the State. Indeed, because the existing labour market is marked by a number of social divisions, it is unlikely that work experience will be able to serve as a *general* transitional activity in terms of the effects it has on participating students.

The national extension of TVEI programmes is likely to increase the demand for placements at a time when industry and commerce are facing unprecedented pressures to become involved in education–industry relations. For example, in 1988, the government further reaffirmed its commitment to work experience when the DES announced that all students should participate in this activity during their secondary schooling. For this to become a reality, though, required an extra 200 000 work placements (DES, 1988a, b). As a number of LEAs and schools are already having problems securing sufficient work placements, it is probable that shortages of work experience may spread. In certain parts of the country, there is just not a sufficient quantity of work placements to include this activity in the education of increasing numbers of participating students. A major reason that shortages have not become *more* severe *is* related to recent demographic trends. After over a decade of large-scale youth unemployment, many employers in the Midlands and South of England are finding it increasingly difficult to attract sufficient numbers of school leavers. The size of the 16- to 19-year-age group entering the labour market fell from 3.7 million in 1982 to below 3.4 million in the early months of 1988. It is only expected to start rising again after reaching a low of under 2.6 million in 1994. In this context, work experience represents for an increasing number of employers one method of attracting young people to a firm as they approach school leaving age. As John Banham (Director General of the CBI) states in his foreword to the DES's guide to employers, no business can ignore the opportunities provided by work experience, 'particularly in the light of the sharp reduction in the number of school leavers that is in prospect over the next few years. 'Effective links with local schools will be an important competitive advantage in the tighter labour market of the early 1990s (DES 1988a). The full implications of this 'competitive advantage' in relation to employer participation remains to be seen, but we doubt that it alone will provide the extra 200 000 work-experience places sought by the DES.

The increasing demand for work-experience is likely to increase the attraction of two major responses for LEAs and schools, a centralization in the organization of work experience, and a redefinition of work experience away from the traditional activity of spending time working in a firm.

As mentioned earlier, there are considerable organizational benefits to be gained from a centralized approach to work experience within an authority. These are likely to be increased when greater numbers of placements are required. Furthermore, recent developments in the field of school–industry liaison may serve to reinforce any trends towards centralization. For example, the Department of Trade and Industry have funded a number of 'signposter' positions whose purpose is to liaise with and advise firms involved in education–industry activities, and search for work-experience placements. Over most of the country, there will be one signposter to each education authority (*Times Education Supplement*, 17 June 1988). With increasing demand for work placements, it may well be that such developments are used to encourage and facilitate the central organization of work experience.

In addition to a possible trend towards centralization, an increased demand for work placements may encourage the development of alternatives to replace or supplement traditional work experience. These alternatives include work shadowing (where students are assigned to an individual working adult and observe them at work for a brief but continuous period), work observation (where students/groups of students visit a workplace to observe an organization of a specific sector of industry/commerce), and work training centres (where specialists are hired to supervise students working in a local authority training workshop). The dissemination of mini-companies in schools across the country by the Department of Trade and Industry's Mini-Enterprise in Schools Project (MESP) may also help provide a popular alternative to traditional style work experience (see Shilling, 1989b). Mini-enterprises provide school-based experiences of making and marketing a product, and do not require the degree of organization involved in firm-based work-experience programmes. As a result, it is likely to make it an attractive alternative for teachers seeking some sort of work experience for growing numbers of students.

Over 400 000 school students a year presently undertake work experience (DES, 1988a). The national extension of TVEI requires a considerable increase in the number of available work-experience placements. In order to meet this demand, it is likely that there will be a considerable change in the organization and definition of future work experience in TVEI.

Notes

[1] Work experience is defined as the experience by a student of work tasks in a work environment without them taking on the full identity of a worker. 'They key distinctions are that an individual on work-experience is "employed" on a short-term basis and is not (officially) paid by the "employer" (apart perhaps from covering travelling expenses, etc.)' (Watts, 1983: 3).

[2] In its early days, TVEI residential experience often shared this characteristic with work experience. However, many authorities have now made regular provision for this activity which has removed the uncertainty associated with having to arrange a new residential for each year's TVEI intake.

[3] For example, the 'soft porn' often found on the walls of engineering and mechanic workshop walls, provide an indication of the type of cultural atmosphere that might confront a girl on a non-traditional work placement.

CHAPTER 9

Equal opportunities in TVEI

Equal opportunities are not only worthy of closer investigation because they were among the original criteria issued by the TVEI in 1983 as guidelines for implementation but because, above all others, they had arguably the most lasting impact on education. To a large extent, as a result of TVEI, equal opportunities and considerations of what that means in terms of student (and staff) entitlement are firmly on the educational agenda among both theorists and practitioners. Few, if any, authorities and institutions can now continue to ignore the issues and their implications.

None the less, of those original criteria set by the MSC for TVEI pilot development, equal opportunities (gender) remains among the most problematic and controversial. Initial debates concentrated on the motivations of the MSC in including it as its number one TVEI criterion – whether economic, social, political or educational. Regardless of intention, it soon became obvious that the 'problem' was more difficult and complex than had been envisaged. It was almost impossible to evaluate progress or success when outcomes were unspecified and aims, objectives, methods and strategies were unclear to many participants at all levels of implementation; equal opportunities was a perfect example of the initial 'underformulation' of the programme as a whole.

This chapter will attempt to investigate the various interpretations made of equal opportunities at various levels of implementation by the MSC, LEAs, schools and colleges, teachers and pupils. These levels, in themselves, are artificially divided. They are so closely and integrally related it is often difficult to differentiate between them. The same vast range of attitudes, opinions, views, values, experiences, expectations, beliefs and behaviours occur and exist within each level. It will be possible to do little more than raise certain issues and begin to speculate on the impact the criteria may have had in affecting actual change, behavioural and/or attitudinal, and in extending educational provision for all, but more specifically for girls, in this brief analysis.

Some background information

Debate concerning 'equality' and the role education plays in extending or restricting opportunities has occurred for many years in most countries by philosophers, economists, political scientists, sociologists, educationalists and others. In Britain, the 1944 Education Act gave formal recognition to the concept of equal education opportunities and its relationship to the provision of secondary education. During the 1950s and 1960s, there was an increasing awareness that, despite the compulsory nature of education, it was not of equal benefit to working-class pupils. It was not until the 1970s in Britain, following the growth of civil rights and women's movements in the USA during the 1960s, that disadvantage within and beyond the system was associated with gender and race. More recently, it has been recognized by the Warnock Report that pupils with 'special educational needs' (ranging from the least to most able at various phases of development) and those with physical disability have not had adequate benefit from their educational experiences.

The reorganization and conversion of schools to comprehensives by LEAs in the 1960s and 1970s, which was designed to improve provision for working-class children, appeared to increase disadvantage for girls and female staff. As single-sex schools (with predominantly female management and staff) often closed or amalgamated, traditional avenues for promotion decreased. Moreover, girls and boys appeared to develop even more stereotyped approaches to subject choices and career aspirations when taught together, and girls were reported to be academically less successful in mixed schools (Kelly, 1981).

The 1975 Sex Discrimination, the 1976 Race Relations Acts and the setting up of the Equal Opportunities Commission (EOC) and the Commission for Racial Equality (CRE) gave legal precedence and nominal enforcement procedures concerning educational provision. The Sex Discrimination Act of 1975 required that co-educational institutions give equal access to 'any benefits, facilities or services' in education in recognition of the realization that girls were excluded from certain areas of the curriculum and that this was affecting their long-term achievement in employment. It did not, however, advocate or encourage positive discrimination despite subsequent publications from the DES and the EOC highlighting the extent and nature of 'sex differentiation and stereotyping in schools and its pedagogic and administrative implications' (see, e.g. DES, 1975, 1980, 1981, EOC, 1979). These reports examined the different educational experiences of girls and boys but tended to reflect a deficit model of 'blaming the victims', the girls, who could overcome their problem by changing their attitudes and motivation and acquire that which they previously lacked. They attempted to explain the nature, genesis and extent of the *problem* of girls' underachievement which became increasingly evident beyond 16 and in certain areas of the curriculum (e.g. maths, science and technology). More recent government reports have begun to recognize that ensuring equal access (and breaking down some of the more overt barriers to subject selection) has not, in itself, alleviated the educational disadvantage of girls. The Women's National Commission (WNC), the EOC, educational researchers and certain feminist writers began, and continue to, investigate the structure of the existing educational system, examining the real and ideological barriers that face girls. While a great deal of debate still exists about the origins and institutionalization of sex differentiation in education and society in general (from liberal progressive to Marxist and radical interpretations), there is, at least, a 'clear commitment in government policy statement of the need to promote equal opportunities in schools and to encourage girls in particular' (Whyte *et al.*, 1985: 7). This may have to some extent influenced the MSC to focus more heavily on 'gender' among TVEI equal opportunities criteria.

The MSC

The Sex Discrimination Act of 1975 not only recognized and outlawed discrimination in education, but also in training and employment. It mentioned the specific responsibilities of the MSC to help redress existing imbalances. The MSC was therefore committed in law to provide equal opportunities within YOP and YTS programmes. Although the realization (through monitoring outcomes) of their failure to break down stereotypical choice and behaviour has more recently encouraged increased funding for special compensatory (and often single-sex) programmes for adults (often females), particularly in non-traditional areas of employment, no such programmes have been *specifically* funded at secondary level. While MSC's entry into the educational arena in the early 1980s with the arrival of the 'new vocationalism' theoretically brought the equal opportunities criteria (and their links between education/training and employment) with them, there appeared to be little initial guidance given by the MSC about how and to what extent this would and could be achieved through TVEI.

In its interpretations of equal opportunities, TVEI conforms to the 'liberal' educational tradition which believes that progressive reforms in education can lead to real and substantial change without the need for 'revolutionary changes in the economic, political or cultural realms' (Bouchier, 1984: 66). Within this perspective, existing structures constitute successful conditions for reform that can be brought about primarily by changing social training and challenging stereotypes. The outcome or goal is a fairer and more egalitarian apportionment of existing social and economic rewards through better, wider or different provision and attainment. Though the MSC did not clarify its theoretical framework in this way, it none the less appeared to operate within this perspective in relation to equal opportunities.

The original criteria issued by the MSC (1984b) simply stated that:

> Each project should comprise one or more sets of full time programmes with the following characteristics – equal opportunities should be available to young people of both sexes and they should be educated together on courses within each project. Care should be taken to avoid sex stereotyping.

It was further stated that TVEI should be available to 'all students across the ability range'. This was interpreted by a few to include provision for students with special educational needs (another equal opportunities issue) and formed a focus for development in some educational authorities, particularly those already involved with, or committed to, special educational needs programmes.

However, the MSC's initial main focus for equal opportunities was on gender. A major aim of TVEI was to produce 'more skilled youngsters' hoping that 'the schemes we set up will act as a catalyst to increase the pace of change' (stated David Young, then Chair of the MSC, concerning TVEI) in the growing realization that most pupils were 'failing' within an academically oriented educational system, that vocational training was reduced both inside education and in employment, and that youngsters were, therefore, increasingly ill-prepared for entry into the world of work. Much of the early TVEI literature and speeches by representatives of the central government concerning TVEI stated that the 'needs of industry' were not being met. Speculation about those needs led some to hypothesize that a better quality and quantity of students would be required in technological areas by the 1990s. With the increasing overall reduction in numbers of young people, 'industry' would have to tap into the 'unexploited potential' of those who had previously not been attracted to such areas as engineering (or other projected growth areas), e.g. girls. They would have to be encouraged to enter these expanding areas of employment for 'their own good' with the 'to some extent unexamined assumption that there are more good jobs available in science and technology and so women would have a bigger bite of the cherry' (Orr in Whyte *et al.*, 1985: 10).

In 1983, the Secretary of State had also given clear recognition of the fact that 'girls education must reflect the fact that most women will be working for much of their lives and that many will be the sole or principal breadwinner of the family' (Orr in Whyte *et al.*, 1985: 10). This may have also indicated the government's awareness of societal shifts and female underemployment alongside growing pressure from some employers and trade unions.

This initial MSC interpretation of equal opportunities as a 'need to shift more girls towards technological areas of the curriculum and employment' to fulfil the needs of industry reflected an homogeneous view of industry that often conflicted with the realities of the local employment situation. It also failed to acknowledge sufficiently the full range of obstacles presented by schools, peers, parents, less enlightened employers, the community and society at large, that would confront girls attempting to enter non-traditional areas. This underestimation of the magnitude and complexity of the problems of implementing the massive change of attitudes and orientations needed to achieve a significant flow of girls into technological areas, may have encouraged the MSC to later reinterpret their definitions and change their expectations.

TVEI's equal opportunities criteria (and subsequent emphasis on gender) may also have been the government's response to pressure by national bodies such as the EOC and the WNC to provide more opportunities for girls and women. The EOC and WNC were involved with MSC in an advisory capacity prior to the inception of TVEI. They were well aware that the vocational nature of the initiative could potentially create highly sex-segregated and sex-stereotyped programmes without 'adequate safeguards' rather than a vehicle for change. Prior to the selection of first-round authorities, the WNC spelt out to the MSC chairman its own interpretation of 'good equal opportunities practice' (Millman in Whyte *et al.*,

1985: 60). Despite this involvement, and the participation of both girls and boys nationally, most local programmes were initially clearly sex-stereotyped.

Six months into the project, the MSC stated that:

> Local Authorities . . . are to be asked to provide hard evidence that they are trying to phase out traditional boy–girl divisions within their programmes . . . the MSC is to write to all 14 authorities now running schemes to tell them it wants to see an improvement in the numbers of boys and girls taking non-traditional options. It will expect firm evidence that authorities are developing strategies to overcome sex stereo-typing (Wilce, 1984).

A one-day seminar on equal opportunities (gender) was held in February 1984 in Clwyd LEA for pilot project directors run by the EOC and the WNC. In June 1984, in Birmingham, a DES conference on equal opportunities was held and attended by large numbers of TVEI staff from all over the country.

Although this indicated some commitment by the MSC (and the DES) to equal opportunities for both girls and boys in non-traditional areas of the curriculum the MSC was, at the same time, adamant that it should not appear to be too prescriptive to the LEAs and intervene or interfere too far in local TVEI implementation in this initial phase.

Prior to the selection of the second-round authorities, however, the EOC and WNC again requested that the MSC provide 'more detailed central guidance' that 'would commit local authorities firmly and specifically to equal opportunities' (Millman in Whyte *et al.*, 1985: 60). While the MSC continued to make exhortations at this time about equal opportunities, it did not appear to actually insist on the production of firm evidence of strategies that would indicate 'contract compliance' (part of the mandate of TVEI as a whole). The MSC did not issue clear long-term perspectives and indications of expected outcomes.

The MSC, however, did continue to request yearly statistical monitoring of TVEI students by gender and race through Trent Polytechnic. It not only became increasingly clear that, on the whole, girls were not opting for non-traditional areas of programmes but that, in some LEAs, there was an actual deterioration in the numbers of girls taking CDT/Technology and science-based courses by the second and third years of the first-round projects. According to one director, TVEI did not solve the 'problem of boys and girls choosing traditional educational and vocational pathways but *highlighted* it'. Others stated that change would be 'evolutionary'. The evident failure of TVEI to attract girls into technological programmes may have shifted some to focus on the increased movement of boys into TVEI Business or Catering courses as a measure of some success in helping to break down sex-stereotyping.

During 1985–6 (the third and fourth year of first-round projects), many of the authorities engaged in a single high-profile event or conference which usually resulted in a TVEI policy statement being written. It was suggested to some local evaluators that they begin to 'investigate the problem' and propose some solutions. The national evaluators in Leeds and NFER, a small national study and small local studies, were funded to conduct some limited research on equal opportunities. PhD,

MA, MEd and MPhil students were also encouraged to carry out additional research which could be of use to the projects or the LEA. The first of two national residential conferences involving those active or interested in equal opportunities was funded by the MSC. Many reports by the MSC to local authorities during this period failed to mention equal opportunities to the extent they had in the previous 2 years (if at all). The thrust appears to shift to issues involving 'management' and the 'management of change', as though these would provide solutions to all the unanswered problems unearthed by TVEI. The MSC may have also become frustrated by the enormity of the equal opportunities issues, the limited progress made by TVEI in effecting change in this area in a climate of continuing uncertainty about how far the authorities could and should be accountable for this and other issues.

Some regional advisers continued to look for 'simple solutions' to the problem through modular programmes or compulsory common core curriculums. Many still appeared to believe that the single key to change lay somewhere to be discovered – a perspective doomed to failure.

There was some indication that interpretation of equal opportunities gender and desired outcomes began again to be redefined. Jack Cross (MSC, n.d.) made this statement:

> An unqualified over acceptance of the imperative to open up "male" opportunities to girls may be deceptive and dangerous; it can so easily lead to the presumption that the traditional female occupations are less significant and, properly less desirable and more poorly rewarded. Equal opportunities will only exist when jobs are valued according to the education, skill, training and responsibility they require, and the contribution they make to society and/or the economy, no matter by whom they are performed.

Some representatives of the MSC may have begun to also recognize that the status and expectations of girls (and boys) in traditional areas must be also raised alongside those in non-traditional areas. This may suggest that the concept of equal opportunities (gender) was changing from the narrower one of attracting girls into technology and physics (boys into catering, business and modern languages) to one of providing an overall broader and enhanced education for all which could widen the range of experience and encourage better informed choices and increased expectations.

There certainly is evidence that MSC's commitment to equal opportunities both revived and extended its definition. The equal opportunities criterion still remains an essential element of TVEI Extension. The MSC appear to have demanded in the extension the inclusion of clearer strategies for implementation from the onset (although clear outcomes were not yet defined) and greater accountability at all levels. MSC, at the same time, produced better guidelines and support by means of its increasingly active Equal Opportunities National and Regional Networks, increased publications and more nationally funded conferences. One equal opportunities and industry conference funded by the MSC included both gender and race issues, and also, although less prominently, considerations of those with special educational needs. The MSC appears to be looking for an *overall* awareness of the range of equal opportunities issues within Extension proposals as well as specific compensatory strategies and programmes. This may indicate an increasing awareness of the issues and a widening in the interpretation of equal opportunities.

The LEAs

In 1983, the LEAs were at very different starting points and levels of receptivity to TVEI generally, but more specifically, to the equal opportunities criterion. The following model may be useful in attempting to identify the various states of readiness within the LEAs and among those individuals which made up the LEAs:

1 Interested, committed and/or motivated with previous experience in one or more areas of equal opportunities.
2 Interested, committed and or motivated (whether for ethical, educational, political or economic reasons) but with little or no previous experience in equal opportunities.
3 Had not thought about or investigated the issues to any large extent, if at all, but not unresponsive (to one or more aspects of equal opportunities).
4 Had not thought about or investigated the issues to any large extent, if at all, and were unresponsive (e.g. did not recognize 'a problem' and saw current iniquities in outcomes as natural or right, or felt that education had little capacity to effect change).

Indications of commitment might include the existence of written statements or policies concerning the promotion of equal opportunities either within city councils and/or specifically within education. According to Patrick Orr of HMI (in Whyte *et al.*, 1985: 16):

> These statements vary considerably in quality and even more in effectiveness. The best recognise the complexity of the problems to be faced, allow for long term strategies in meeting them, and set up sound methods for the gathering and dissemination of information concerning the performance, aspirations and choices of boys and girls. Equal opportunities (gender) is a major feature of policy in a small number of LEAs, and in most this is a part of a larger programme also concerned with racial discrimination and underachievement among working class children. However, most authorities provide little practical support for reducing sex differentiation in schools; the issue is seen as one of a large number of causes arguing for priority treatment in the allocation of resources.

The level of practical support for reducing sex differentiation was indeed minimal in most authorities in 1983. Virtually no advisory teachers or curriculum advisers had, at that time, been appointed with the specific responsibility to oversee and guide development in the area of equal opportunities (gender), though more may have existed in some authorities in areas of multicultural education through Section 11 funding, or special needs through the DES Lower Achievers Programme (LAP) or other related projects. Few authorities had considered delivering staff development programmes to raise awareness of the gender issues among education officers or staff in schools. The development and/or availability of materials for use by staff and students was not given priority. Though some eduational research projects such as Girls into Science and Technology (GIST) and Women into Science and Engineering (WISE) were operating in 1984, virtually no funding was provided *by the LEAs themselves* for compensatory programmes or projects supporting positive action for girls. Some Certificate of Pre-Vocational Education (CPVE) and other pre-vocational education programmes had begun to consider ways of breaking down rigid sex-stereotyped choice in vocational options, though this activity tended to be limited to a few interested individuals.

There were various other activities occurring within education and employment areas on a local basis that may have influenced readiness for change. Some local trade unions and teacher associations were, at this time, beginning to question why their female members were either in a minority or experiencing limited career progressions. Certain other professional organizations (many associated with engineering at various levels) had begun to recognize the need to recruit more girls and women as did some other local employers. The careers service was beginning to examine its practices for levels of equal opportunity awareness. Women's organizations and groups were forming networks for personal and professional support.

The 'climate' or 'ethos' and receptivity to equal opportunities in the various authorities was also affected by their political orientations. Theoretically, Labour-controlled authorities with strong union ties were more receptive to equal opportunities gender issues if not to TVEI itself. Local employment markets and their needs (actual or perceived) helped dictate those employment opportunities which were at least theorectically available and receptive to women. Regional differences in traditional attitudes towards women and their expected roles at home and at work were significant, as were the demography and diversity of ethnic minorities. Urban and rural environments might have been quite disparate regarding their employment requirements and opportunities.

Given this vast and complex range of factors affecting levels of awareness of the issues, and receptivity – previous experience, political, economical and environmental factors within LEAs – it was hardly surprising that the original submissions to the MSC were varied in their interpretations, approaches and foci on equal opportunities. One submission contained a small section about special education, one mention of the 'multicultural urban environment' with no reference to gender at all. Another contained a long section about gender that promised to deliver outcomes that were not realistic and perhaps reflected a lack of understanding of the complexity of the issues. Most submissions failed to include *specific* strategies to achieve equal opportunities for girls or others disadvantaged within the system. An *overall* awareness of the issues throughout the submissions was even less in evidence. It is, however, difficult to determine how far these documents were representative of the views and priorities of the LEA, those of the authors of the document, or the result of the haste and uncertainty in which they were written. One submission according to its author 'told the MSC what [he thought] they wanted to hear, then we would worry about how to achieve projected outcomes later'; in our experience, this was by no means an untypical response. This initial confusion and lack of forward planning concerning equal opportunities, reflected in the submissions, may have created difficulties that would affect future development in various authorities. The fact that the MSC accepted even those submissions with no mention of gender may have shed doubt on their own level of awareness or the extent to which LEAs would be held accountable for equal opportunities within the contractual arrangements.

The 'cosmetic' nature of many of the references to gender equality is reflected in the fact that the original design (proposed in some submissions and implemented in 1983) of many TVEI programmes inevitably reinforced sex-stereotyped divisions between subject areas and perpetuated traditional patterns of choice by offering a rigid package with either business (secretarial) or CDT technology/science emphases (often with a higher priority attached to the latter 'boy-orientated' area):

> Not one LEA had counselled TVEI girls on non-traditional subject/career choice prior to making their course options. Two LEAs whose TVEI courses were based on traditional occupational families experienced the heaviest stereotyping (Millman in Whyte *et al.*, 1985: 62).

Ironically, even in LEAs (or schools) where TVEI students in the first cohort were specially selected rather than recruited, there were few girls and boys in non-traditional options (reflecting the sex-stereotyped attitudes and assumptions of selectors). With some early pressure from the MSC (through reports and monitoring), from the EOC and WNC (through their national co-ordinators' conference in Clwyd), and the increasing numbers of employers, unions, parents, teachers, pupils and governors, some LEAs and their members began to question traditional patterns and choices. Some TVEI projects began to experiment with different curriculum organizations and approaches. Some authorities (and their projects) experimented with compulsory core elements – hoping to break stereotyping by structuring the curriculum in a way that compelled girls and boys to take non-traditional courses such as core technology, world of business, community, life and parenting skills. Taster terms were designed to encourage students to blend the (previously rigid) TVEI programmes through sampling non-traditional options.

A few authorities adopted a 'carousel' system or circus ensuring that all pupils had a taste of all courses in their first years, though this, in practice, varied from one school to another. Modular approaches were developed (quite strongly in certain authorities) in a range of curriculum areas, as a possible vehicle for breaking down traditional patterns of choice by offering shorter-term commitments. Some units or modules on sex stereotyping were built into general education modules or included within (Personal, Moral and) Social Education programmes, work experience or careers and guidance programmes. Some of these were specifically for TVEI students; others were for the whole school.

Over the course of the pilot phase, many LEAs increased the general numbers of posts with responsibility for equal opportunities (gender), some specifically with TVEI-related briefs. Therefore, the level of expertise and equal opportunities staff development provision may have also expanded. Whereas many of the first-round authorities had relied on the 'Big Event' or a major conference alone to produce the policy for the LEA or TVEI project in 1985–6 that would 'solve the problem' of equal opportunities, it became more widely recognized that the *whole* of the education service must be aware of how educational provision can be widened for all. Some LEAs organized large-scale staff training programmes to help inform all members of the educational support services and advisors of the issues – generally and within specific curriculum areas. They used the results of national and local TVEI evaluation teams and research projects to call attention to the problems and suggest possible strategies for change.

In writing their own curriculum guidelines, many LEAs included gender considerations and strategies alongside those concerning race and special educational needs within their statements about the Educational Entitlements of All. More LEAs wrote equal opportunities policies with plans for implementation and some means of monitoring and evaluating progress. By creating LEA equal opportunities working parties or task groups, some authorities attempted to create firmer links between various aspects of equal opportunities gender, race, ethnicity, disability and special educational needs that had previously worked independently of each other. Many other curriculum development working parties began to reflect greater equal opportunities awareness in their constitution, respresentation and activities.

In 1983, many LEAs and TVEI projects were almost totally male dominated (though there were regional differences), particularly in top management posts and in certain areas of the curriculum. This not only may have affected the level of awareness and response of participants, but also created a 'male' ethos and a feeling of male exclusivity that may have transmitted itself to students and staff. There is some evidence that this situation changed slowly during the pilot phase. In one totally heavily male-dominated authority, there is now one female ACEO, one female principal of a further education (FE) college and two vice principals (of a total of eight colleges). Several TVEI programmes had female director/co-ordinators at central and institutional levels, though there was less progress in breaking down traditional male/female staffing in certain curriculum areas through initial teacher training, secondments or in-service training.

Though these activities and developments may not have been *directly* and solely attributable to TVEI, additional funding for time and staffing gave added flexibility. The existence of equal opportunities criteria, in some cases, provided a vehicle for change and did give some priority to gender issues. It also created a climate for greater experimentation in the organization, delivery and approach of the curriculum that had potential to open up more opportunities for girls while raising greater awareness in the LEA that there was indeed a problem or situation which required specific strategies and long-term planning alongside better and more balanced curriculum provision. Most LEAs appeared, on the whole, to have made considerable progress in *attitudinal* change from their original 1983 position in the model presented at the beginning of this chapter, though this was not clearly reflected in student uptake in non-traditional areas of the curriculum.

TVEI pilot projects

The local management of TVEI differed from one LEA to another in its degree of integration into the mainstream system. Therefore, it may be entirely inappropriate or inaccurate to examine TVEI separately from the LEA in situations where philosophies, developmental priorities, planning, training, etc., were consistent, complementary and integrated. However, in many authorities, for a variety of reasons including the management style of the authority (centralized or *laissez faire* at either end of the scale) and different funding and organizing requirements, TVEI was set up in distinct units with differing levels of autonomy from, and contact with, education officers on the one hand and the schools and colleges on the other. The local project co-ordinators or directors were also to varying extents responsible to both the local LEAs and the MSC and, at times, were unclear about their chain of command and decision-making powers. Some were, therefore, doubly (and sometimes conflictingly) accountable and this may have varied from one issue to the other. If the LEA and the MSC were in agreement in prioritizing equal opportunities, the director had a clear mandate and TVEI had the capacity to be a more effective vehicle for change. In some LEAs and projects, this may have encouraged earlier and better planned programmes enlisting existing expertise or additional funding for the development of strategies within the project (e.g. a person with the designated reponsibility for the equal opportunities of gender on the central team).

The degree of control over TVEI funding retained by the director and the extent to which he or she determined priorities also varied, particularly in those LEAs in which a consensus did not necessarily exist. The director with a great deal of personal power, for whatever reason, and an interest in or commitment to equal opportunities (whatever the motivation) and who invested specifically funded programmes and initiatives had the potential to accelerate progress even in an authority without previous experience of, or commitment to, equal opportunities. Similarly, an unmotivated director could be pressured by a strong LEA commitment (or fear of MSC accountability). A weak but committed director could be sabotaged by a disinterested authority. A weak director in an uncommitted authority was unlikely to promote substantial change despite pressures from others (e.g. grassroots teachers, employers, etc.).

Many of the TVEI central teams were, as stated previously, not only male dominated but developmentally focused on curriculum areas traditionally staffed by men (e.g. technology and CDT). These teams were less likely to recognize the importance of gender issues and 'problems' that existed within their own curriculum areas despite low female participation and under-achievement. These male-dominated teams may have also had the effect of conveying to staff and students that TVEI was more appropriate or open to males, despite the existence of literature that may have attempted to counter such messages. This is not to say that *all* TVEI teams were male dominated or heavily oriented towards technology or indeed that the male/female ratio did not change over the life of the pilot scheme. One team with a large number of careers officers (both male and female) committed to opening up career opportunities for girls and boys, produced drama programmes, videos and teaching packs the could be used in all of the schools within an authority (not just the pilot institutions). Another TVEI project in an northern mining area with a female director and a large number of women on the central team, managed to break down some of the traditional 'macho' culture of the region. A third project in a large urban environment had only one woman at any one time in the 'team' until, in the third year of the pilot phase, a female equal opportunities consultant was recruited. Because of the large size of the unit (16 members in total) and the lack of overall planning, most worked autonomously and rarely consulted or informed each other of their activities. This lack of communication made it very difficult for the consultant alone to ensure that individual projects within the programme had equal opportunities perspectives (and those issues were understood and owned by the members of the team).

The ideal TVEI team, in terms of maximizing equal opportunities (gender) development, would have had a director committed and informed of the issues, a team (50% male/female) equally committed to the development of programmes with an overall awareness of the different needs or orientations of girls as well as specifically girl-oriented projects. Individual projects would be part of an overall equal opportunities programme, with forward planning and projected targets and outcomes that would be evaluated and reviewed at regular intervals to check progress and identify barriers to change. This approach would possibly have provided the necessary cohesion and solidarity, at least within the team, to effect change even within an authority or schools uncommitted and/or unaware of the 'problem'. There is little evidence to indicate that many teams of this type actually existed, but some at least contained some individual(s) who attempted to promote equal opportunities.

The power of such motivated and interested individuals cannot be underestimated. During the third year of the first-round pilot projects, the MSC, certain LEAs and individual TVEI projects became very discouraged with the lack of progress in attracting girls into non-traditional areas and became desperate for guidance. During this period, anyone with any knowledge of gender issues – whether evaluators, researchers, advisers or teachers – became experts and sometimes integral members of the central team. In authorities with limited existing expertise, these people became quite influential: representing the issues at all levels; helping to formulate policy; providing materials, publicity and exhibits; organizing INSET (within the authority, the TVEI team, schools and colleges); and publishing books. Many helped organize equal opportunities working parties – cross-project, cross authority and/or within individual schools and colleges.

This new breed of 'expert' often managed not only to obtain high profiles for themselves and equal opportunities within certain authorities, but beyond to other LEAs and nationally through publications and the MSC equal opportunities network.

In certain authorities, the TVEI central team had enormous potential to encourage the breaking down of traditional sex-stereotyped barriers (or reinforce them) and to accelerate (or inhibit) developments within their programmes. Initiatives co-ordinated or produced by certain TVEI teams *aimed at students* included:

non-traditional work experience programmes (separately or allied with Trident); non-traditional careers packs, work shadowing (promoting female and non-traditional role models for boys and girls); various 'girls into engineering' conferences, residentials, sessions; college–school link days, sessions or conferences allowing girls to 'sample' non-traditional options and familiarize themselves with the sometimes forbidding atmosphere of the colleges; non-traditional speakers in classrooms, at conferences and on panels; 'modules' with equal opportunities perspectives or specifically about sex-stereotyping and gender issues. Many TVEI teams (or members of the team) actively supported the ongoing work or new strategies attempted by the staff in schools and colleges to help promote equal opportunities as well as raising levels of awareness through staff development (generally and in specific curriculum areas).

The institutional level

The schools and colleges, like the MSC and the LEAs, are organizations made up of *individuals* with a balance of corporate identity (in agreement with the 'culture' of the institution) and personal identity (adhering to their own values, ideas and experiences). While an individual may *seem* to support (or even promote) an aspect of the corporate, the personal could in actuality negate it (or vice versa). The 'school' or 'college' could have a stated commitment or policy regarding equal opportunities, while individuals – whether management or teachers – could consciously or unconsciously sabotage efforts in their areas of responsibilities or within the classroom.

The gaps between the rhetoric and the reality of what is said to be occurring and what is *actually* happening can be particularly wide when the issue is as complex and emotive as equal opportunities. Measuring attitudinal (and even behavioural) change is difficult and, to a large degree, speculative. With this proviso it is, however, possible to discuss some of the opportunities that were exploited as a result of TVEI and the equal opportunities criteria, while at the same time identifying some of the barriers to change.

The response of institutions to the MSC's equal opportunities criteria was as varied as their interpretations and organizations of TVEI and subject to some of the same factors. Each institution already had its own 'ethos', management systems, culture, philosophies, structures, aims, priorities, developmental patterns and levels of receptivity to change in general (dynamic ⟷ static), which may or may not have already begun to take account of equal opportunities (gender, race and/or special educational needs). Some schools and colleges and their members saw themselves as agents of change and innovation, whereas others – whether overtly or covertly – reinforced existing traditional patterns.

The same model previously used in this chapter to clarify the starting points of the LEAs can also be applied to the schools and colleges (without a necessary correlation between the position or starting point of the LEA and that of the individual school or college within it). Some schools may have participated in the Low Attainers Project, programmes of multicultural education and/or special educational needs. While in some cases this may have made them more receptive to gender issues, in others the links between common themes of disadvantage within the system were not made. The 'lessons' and existing expertise within institutions were not necessarily extended either to include gender issues or the TVEI project as a whole.

A few schools or colleges had been involved with specific intervention programmes aimed at attracting more girls into technological areas of the curriculum or, at least, knew of them. These included Girls into Science and Technology (GIST), and action research programme carried out in co-educational comprehensive schools in Greater Manchester from 1978–9 to 1984; the VISTA scheme, a programme of visits to schools by women working as scientists, technicians and craftspeople in industry, scientific research and government and educational establishments (Whyte *et al.*, 1985: 67) which worked as part of GIST; Girls and Technician Engineering (GATE), residential programmes organized by the Engineering Industry Training Board to encourage girls to consider technological areas; and other school-based, smaller-scale projects. For example, 1984 was designated Women into Science and Engineering (WISE) Year and many schools and colleges participated nationally in girls only programmes usually for one day or one week designed to actively encourage girls to consider those occupations requiring scientific and problem-solving approaches not traditionally attractive or open to women.

An increasing volume of feminist research with liberal progressive, marxist and radical perspectives were beginning to investigate the experiences of girls and female staff within schools and colleges. This body of research focused on the wide (and complex) range of issues defining the 'problems' of sex stereotyping and sex differentiation (in schools and the wider society) and their origins, proposing or testing a variety of 'solutions' either within existing societal and education structures or outside of them. These studies were not only influential in the institutions in which they were carried out but, when published (either commercially or by the MSC or EOC), were used as the basis of their own school-based research or planned intervention, eventually within some TVEI projects. Some of these projects were undertaken within the science/technology areas, those which were most problematic for girls and part of the TVEI remit.

In 1983, a few schools and colleges had begun to write equal opportunities policies, many of which had an emphasis on race or special needs rather than gender. In common with the LEA policies, they varied in their emphases and degrees of effectiveness in implementation. Despite the existence of increasing numbers of policy statements, commitment, understanding and 'ownership' of the issues varied considerably from institution to institution and individual to individual within the school/college. The existence of a policy may have at least indicated that the headteacher and/or senior management and/or committed individuals within the school or college gave some support for equal opportunities and provided some focus or impetus for future development and planning. Many more schools and particularly Non Advanced Further Education (NAFE) colleges (who were advised to do so) later wrote policies concerning race, gender and special educational needs with some positive action programmes, and some moved from policy writing to the planning stages of actual implementation within 5 years.

The headteachers, and to some degree their management teams, were very influential in determining whether equal opportunities became a priority within their schools or simply 'TVEI issues' which the TVEI school co-ordinator could 'deal with' or 'experiment with' in TVEI. Lessons learned may have subsequently become available for wider school dissemination or contained within the project alone. Those schools with committed headteachers and colleges with principals who had an interest in equal opportunities issues were more likely to make available provision for whole school/college staff development; provide time and staff to write policy statements and consider 'strategies'; sanction sessions with students about sex stereotyping or equal opportunities issues; encourage gender research by staff or external agents and encourage a range of strategies aimed at both staff and students. Some made changes in those structures and procedures which may have contributed to sex differentiation (e.g. attendance rolls by sex, different methods of discipline and control for girls and boys, subject option systems and structures which reinforced sex-stereotyped choice, a differentiated curriculum in the early years of secondary school, greater emphasis on the status of male sport and other accomplishments in assemblies or school displays). Others encouraged or supported positive action in the form of single sex groupings, particularly in non-traditional areas, modular curricula with non-traditional compulsory core elements, compulsory non-traditional components in general (core technology or 'parenting') for all, non-traditional careers programmes such as conferences or taster sessions, residential programmes for girls in engineering and a variety of other strategies designed to promote wider and better informed choice for girls (as well as boys). All of these types of whole school/college initiatives, often involving outside agents, required the permission, backing, encouragement and support of the management to take place (no matter where the ideas originated). Some motivated headteachers also saw the necessity to involve and better inform parents, governors, the community as a whole, local employers and industry in equal opportunities programmes through meetings, literature and publicity, and direct participation in tutorials with students.

This is not to say that there were not other powerful agents of institutional change within the school/college other than at the headteacher or senior management levels or externally through the advisorate, LEA, educational support services, researchers and the entire TVEI team, including its directors and the educational funding, staffing and measures of 'accountability' they brought with them. In some institutions, there was an increasing amount of 'grassroots' support for equal opportunities from mainstream staff, particularly in English, the creative and expressive arts, modern languages, social education and general studies, and within TVEI programmes. Some women teachers were also becoming discontent with patterns of staffing within their schools and colleges which traditionally gave more managerial responsibilities to men. Some TVEI school and college co-ordinators (and their 'teams' developed their own programmes of staff development and programmes aimed at increasing the options and personal development of students (e.g. non-traditional work experience, assertiveness sessions for girls and/or boys, more flexible TVEI programmes, modular approaches, additional or positive counselling and support and guidance for girls). These strategies were, in some instances, as stated previously, extended to all students in the school.

In those LEAs with a more supportive attitude towards equal opportunities, and as more advisers were appointed either with specific equal opportunities responsibilities or an equal opportunities awareness and perspective within their curriculum areas, an influence began to be felt within the schools – raising awareness within the school or college and mobilizing those internally who were interested and concerned. TVEI teams and those directors who prioritized the issues and provided additional support (e.g. staff time, materials, etc.), may also have accelerated 'changes' within the institutions. MSC regional advisers with equal opportunities perspectives through direct contact with some schools and colleges – through visits and conferences – often helped reinforce the importance of the criteria. Crucial to change was the combination of the perceived levels of institutional accountability to the LEA, MSC and TVEI (as a politically economic expedient), the levels of commitment at various levels within the schools, and the relationships (personal as well as professional) between participants (staff and students) at all levels, TVEI and non-TVEI, in the advancement and acknowledgement of the equal opportunities criteria in the schools and colleges.

A growing body of recognizable *individuals* with equal opportunities expertise (within and outside the institution) began to emerge during the pilot phase. In some cases, however, the existence of such 'experts' and perhaps writing a 'policy' may have allowed compartmentalization of the issues and even limited ownership of the problems and their possible solutions. 'Experts' may have had impact only as long as they were available to provide direct support.

Many schools/colleges, however, did begin to set up their own equal opportunities working parties and/or appointed people with designated responsibility for the equal opportunities within the institutions (sometimes with additional funding from capitation or TVEI). These groups of people engaged in a variety of tasks – analysing option choices and examination results by gender and for ethnic take up, and suggesting or helping organize strategies involving staff and students (parents, employers, the community).

The effect that these groups (and the other 'agents' or influences that have been involved) was at the very least, to widen recognition that there was a problem, i.e. that all students and some staff were not benefiting equally from the educational system and that some of the responsibility for this lay within the institutional procedures and practices as well as classroom organization, teaching methods and approaches, and the curriculum.

The complexity of the problems and their relationship to outside societal influences did, however, create a great deal of frustration for some. The pace of change in terms of student subject uptake and occupational choice was slow, despite a variety of strategies that may have already been implemented in some institutions. It was perhaps easier to write school policies and change some of the procedures and structures within the school/college than to effect the ways people treat each other and the perceptions and expectations they have of others and themselves (linked to gender, race, ethnicity and ability). One teacher (reflecting often stated views) said:

> TVEI has not solved the issues of sex stereotyping but has highlighted the problems and encouraged the development of some strategies to overcome them not only within TVEI but in the schools/colleges as a whole. It has made us realize that schools and teachers have an important role in effecting change but that we also have to involve parents, industry, the media and the community if opportunities are to be truly maximized by students. At least TVEI has provided more opportunities to do so and some additional training for teachers and students.

Conclusion

The MSC appears to be requiring closer accountability from the LEAs and the schools and colleges in the planning phase of the Extension of TVEI. These submissions must contain clear strategies for the implementation of criteria such as equal opportunities. The five-year pilot experience seems to have developed better interrelationships between the MSC, the LEAs and the schools and colleges. There are now national, regional and local equal opportunities networks to support TVEI – now a whole school/college development.

However, the effective implementation of TVEI can occur only if there is a common understanding and acceptance of its aims and objectives, with active support by participants at *all* levels of educational involvement, and positive interaction with outside agencies and influencers – the wider community, industry, employers, parents and governors.

Although equality of opportunity is now firmly on the educational agenda and this is, to some extent, the result of the TVEI experience (and its successes and failures), it is a long way from being achieved in many authorities. There is still an enormous variation in its definitions, interpretations and the levels of support it receives from all involved. If equality of opportunity is ever to become a reality, there must be an overall *awareness* of the impediments that exist within society (and particularly within the school/college experience) which inhibit individual development; and planned *strategies* to overcome these impediments based on a positive commitment to the improvement of educational entitlement.

The lessons of TVEI indicate that the following would ensure better preconditions for change:

1 All government-initiated programmes (and indeed all programmes) must have clear equal-opportunities philosophies, strategies and targets:

- with clear prioritization of initiatives and links between them;
- ensuring pilot to 'second phase' dissemination, and
- requiring accountability at all levels.

2 LEAs should have written policy statements with strategies for implementation backed by local funding, supported and monitored by trained and informed LEA officers, advisers and education support teachers – all requiring accountability from schools and colleges.

3 Headteachers and principals should provide overt support for equal opportunities issues through school/college policies, with planned implementation at institutional, departmental (divisional/faculty), and classroom levels. Progress should be internally monitored and evaluated.
4 Promotion systems in the schools, colleges and wider LEA should reflect commitment to equal opportunities by ensuring that women and black people are represented in posts of responsibility and decision-making.
5 Teachers and lecturers should demand better representation of women and black people at all levels while monitoring and evaluating their own attitudes and behaviour in relation to others.
6 Programmes should be developed at MSC, LEA, and institutional levels to ensure that staff and students receive information about available opportunities and widen individual expectation.
7 Specific programmes should encourage girls and boys equally to consider and experience all areas of the curriculum and careers (girls into CDT, physics, engineering; boys into modern languages, business, creative arts, catering).
8 Schools and colleges should monitor and evaluate whether they are providing real equal opportunities by taking into account and valuing the different experiences of students and by using a variety of teaching and learning strategies, approaches and materials within:

- *all* areas of the curriculum (including the 'hidden curriculum');
- subject-option choice and recruitment procedures, particularly in vocational areas and TVEI;
- profiling and Records of Achievement;
- work experience and observation;
- industrial tutor programmes and other work-related curriculum activities;
- social education programmes;
- tutorial, guidance and counselling programmes;
- residentials;
- careers programmes from 11 to 18 years, particularly at key choice stages.

9 All staff development and training should support equal-opportunities issues and encourage student-centred approaches.
10 Teacher training (initial, post-graduate, in-service) should raise equal opportunities awareness and help develop a range of strategies to implement change.
11 Parents and governors should be kept informed of equal-opportunities issues and developments and demand accountability and progress reports from the schools and colleges on these issues.
12 Governing bodies should be monitored to make sure that women, black people and those with special needs are represented.
13 Local employers, industry and community organizations should work together with schools and colleges to ensure equal opportunities.
14 External evaluation and further educational research in the area of equal opportunities should be encouraged, financially supported, and widely disseminated to inform change.

The climate and ethos for change, as well as some positive strategies, have already been implemented during TVEI Pilot. Extension has the potential to extend that development, but only if programmes are well formulated, planned, monitored and evaluated.

CHAPTER 10

The organization and management of TVEI

Introduction

Within the educational world, 'concern' about TVEI has concentrated upon its possible curricular and pedagogic implications (education *vs* training), and upon the role and the long-term intentions of the MSC in the educational arena. The latter was to be expected given that one of the original aims of TVEI stated the following:

> In conjunction with LEAs to explore and test ways of organising and managing the education of 14–18 year old young people across the ability range (MSC, 1983).

We want to begin by considering why the government and the MSC should have felt it necessary to investigate the management and organization of education, i.e. why were these topics on the TVEI agenda? We then want to consider the implied management structure and move on to look at that structure in operation. Finally, we want to examine the long-term impact of TVEI, in terms of the management and organization of education.

Organization, management and the TVEI 'agenda'

There appear to be two strands that contribute to the place of management and organization on TVEI's agenda. This signals a certain weakness in the government's educational interventions at the time, a tentativeness that reflected both uncertainty over how to translate economic policies into social policies and a difficulty over how to handle social institutions that still resonated strongly, internally and in the minds of the 'public' with the last vestiges of a social democratic ideology.

The concerted attack on education, throughout the mid- and late 1970s, for its apparent failure to maintain standards and move towards greater relevance to adult and working life, had quickly given way to an attack on the educational establishment itself, as defenders of an outdated system. Many of those attacking education saw themselves in broad agreement with Maurice Kogan, here writing about educational institutions:

> Each of them is allowed to develop organisational and educational styles of his [*sic*] own, and C.E.O.'s are resistant even to the notion that they 'manage' the heads and their schools. This system of delegated authority carries with it a corresponding power system which enables values to be stored and maintained at points sufficiently distant from and impervious to central government or other mechanisms by which society is governed (Kogan, 1975).

The view that the educational system and its practitioners were ill-equipped was expressed in the form of concern in government circles (both Labour and Conservative) and among industrialists, before and after the 'Great Debate', that the DES, the LEAs (in particular those controlled by the 'Left', the teaching profession (especially the trendy and left-wing elements), the Schools Council and other educational bodies, were inappropriate vehicles for changing education to meet what the government and others viewed as the growing need for students to learn about the 'real' worlds of employment and adulthood.

But, despite such expressions of concern, successive governments had been unable to claim a clear mandate for state interference in the educational curriculum. In the minds of many, including senior members of the Conservative Party, this was tantamount to 'political interference', and likely to set a dangerous precedence. The outcome was the call for education to become 'accountable' (Ranson *et al.*, 1986) to new constituencies. This rapidly became distilled in the eyes of many into two groups: employers (to ensure relevance) and parents (to check upon standards). The TVEI reflected the government's initial attempt to both shift educational control away from the educational lobby as well as drawing in the world of employment. Hence the management strand.

Furthermore, during and immediately after the Great Debate, the issue of a core curriculum had gained a certain prominence. Wide divergences over the precise content of any 'core' reflected more than the differences that people had over the purposes of education. While the mandate for educational change captured the purposes of education, it was singularly unable to define the way in which learning would be organized to fulfil these purposes. Consequently, the organization of education in TVEI was merely circumscribed by a set of aims that outlined a series of expected outcomes, i.e. that students would develop skills, knowledge and qualifications relevant to the world of work. In addition, authorities participating in TVEI were required to consider educational organization within the framework of a commitment to the enhancement of technical education.

The government and the MSC were aware that different, broad models of a technical and vocational curricular existed (see Chapter 3), but they were also conscious of the fact that how this was to be delivered, for all abilities, was still the subject of considerable debate within government circles, among employers and in the educational arena. Thus, unclear whether these purposes were to be best fulfilled via traditional curricular structures or new courses of study that cut across subject boundaries or changes in school organization to cater for the 'vocational', the 'academic' and the 'technical' students, they proposed to 'test and explore'. Hence the organizational strand.

However, we would suggest that the management structure implied by the MSC at the start of TVEI contradicted the aims of exploring and testing and this reflected the particular 'problem' the government was addressing by setting up the TVEI, i.e. how to move the control of education out of the hands of the 'educational lobby'.

In management terms, then, the interest in 'exploring and testing' was powerfully informed by a concern to involve employers in the management process and to investigate the extent to which different forms of central and local direction could deliver educational change. The MSC were to supply central direction via a contract with LEAs, based upon stated aims and criteria, and the local management was to include a steering group that was constituted in a manner not unlike a 'mini-MSC', thus ensuring the representation of local employers. This implies a management model that powerfully structures the aim of exploration and testing. It was most certainly not a continuation of the longstanding state commitment to approach social change via empirical studies of the 'various possibilities' (Karabel and Halsey, 1977).

The proposed management structure for TVEI

The precise management structure, at the national, local and institutional levels, was not clearly laid down in TVEI's original proposals. However, the 'bid and deliver' approach to funding, the existence of a central TVEI Unit, the drawing up of a contract between the Central TVEI Unit and the LEAs, and the constitution and responsibilities of the local steering groups, provides us with a picture of the underlying model. Furthermore, the idea of TVEI 'cohorts' within each educational institution closely mirrors the notion of control groups, drawn from a particular view of social science that emphasizes the measurement of the inputs and the consequent outputs.

The formal submission procedure required LEAs, after negotiation with the central MSC Unit, to produce a document setting out their intentions. Once accepted, this was to have contractual status. To quote from the contract:

> The project described in the Authority's proposal to take part in the Initiative [TVEI], will be carried out by the Authority in a manner acceptable to the Commission and in accordance with the Aims, Criteria and Guidelines contained in documents which were sent to Directors of Education in all Local Education Authorities in England and Wales by the Chairman of the Commission on 23rd September 1983.

The LEA was then to appoint a project director, and in conjunction they were to appoint a steering group, to take joint responsibility for the running of the Initiative, within the authority. Thus management lines were to flow from the MSC down, through the steering group and project director to the institutions and individuals. As John Woolhouse put it to an Assistant Masters and Mistresses Association (AMMA) TVEI conference in November 1983:

> The National Steering Group has the responsibility for advising the Commission. The Commission then enters into contractual arrangements with Local Education Authorities, and delivery is through the schools and colleges (AMMA, 1984).[1]

In the first year of the project, monitoring and evaluation was largely left to the local authorities; however, the MSC rapidly began to take this issue seriously and made significant changes for the second round of submissions. At the outset, it had not been clear whether the intention was to go for 'formative' or 'summative' forms of monitoring and evaluation or use it to assist in the process of contract compliance; or, indeed, a mixture of all three, i.e. not only offering advice and support, but also 'policing'.

At the conference mentioned above, Mr Woolhouse responded to a question on monitoring in the following way:

> So there will be monitoring in a number of senses – monitoring against the contract, monitoring the expenditure and its proper use, and monitoring by the Inspectorate of the educational implications (AMMA, 1984).

This implies monitoring via the contract and by some system of audit. The precise role of the Inspectorate remained unclear at this stage. However, he also indicated that 'There will be a team of advisers appointed by the Unit, one of whose jobs will be to monitor the progress of individual projects' (AMMA, 1984). Although it was not mentioned within this context, the Annual Review in each authority, involving top officials of the central TVEI Unit and representatives from the DES and Her Majesty's Inspectorate (HMI), was clearly intended to monitor progress. These quotations reflected the situation in November 1983, when the first 14 authorities had already started to 'deliver' their schemes.

Thus, the overall model implied not only a centrally directed initiative, but the reserved power of 'teeth' to pull wayward authorities into line. To quote from one of the second-round contracts:

> If the number [of students] in any such year falls below that specified . . . except where it does so without any fault attributable to the Authority, or any material variation is made by the Authority in the project as described in the above proposal without prior written agreement of the Commission, or the Authority is in breach of any fundamental term of this Agreement, the Commission may terminate the Agreement forthwith without prejudice to any other right or rights the Commission may otherwise have arising from or under this agreement.

In theory, the managerial structure placed great stress upon the original submission and the power of the steering groups/project directors to 'deliver the contract'. By the time the second-round authorities began their schemes, there was the additional layer of the regional advisers. This provides the following picture of the proposed formal management structure for TVEI.

Figure 10.1

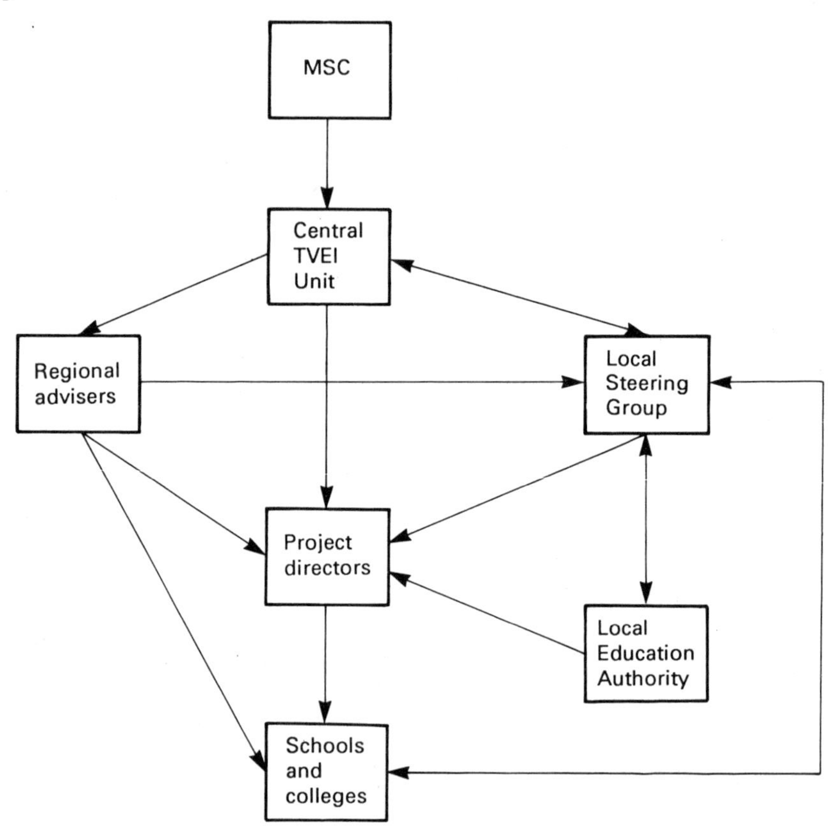

The relations between the MSC and the LEAs

'Becoming involved' in TVEI

Although, ultimately, they were responsible for deciding whether the authority would make a submission, we have no evidence of either individual councillors or councils asking the LEA to become involved. There is evidence that some both attempted and succeeded in blocking moves by others to gain acceptance for TVEI. Many Labour authorities viewed the acceptance of MSC finance as participating in the 'backdoor centralization' of education with the long-term aim of making training for employment a major element of the school curriculum. This suspicion was present to a far lesser extent in Tory authorities.

Not only were local politicians slow to call for involvement in TVEI, but so too were local employers. This general reticence and wariness partly reflected suspicion over the involvement of the MSC in the educational arena, and partly a lack of information about TVEI outside the educational world. However, for officers of the

LEA and senior staff in the educational institutions, the impact of the steady cutbacks in education since the early 1970s made the large sums of money on offer very inviting. It certainly appears at this stage that the 'educational lobby' took a far keener interest in TVEI than the constituency for which it was intended. Consequently, it was usually LEA officials (directors, deputy directors or members of the Inspectorate) or senior members of the teaching or lecturing (from the further education sector) profession who, sometimes individually and sometimes in concert, pressed for participation in TVEI.

Not surprisingly, this situation made it difficult for the MSC to circumvent the 'educational lobby' and they found themselves forced to accept that the initiative would be 'delivered' within the broader LEA context and the local management structures that were already operating. That is not to say that TVEI was simply 'hijacked' by the LEAs; it was, however, required to work within an existing management structure that operated upon a far less centralized model. Indeed, it was precisely this 'centralizing' perception of the MSC model that led to widespread suspicion in the educational world of a powerful 'quango' getting a foothold in the school curriculum and reorientating education to the extent that it would eventually becoming a training agency for industry. This made the early relationships between the local TVEI Units and the heads of the educational institutions very difficult.

Running the projects

The structures that have been operating in the authorities with which we are familiar, suggest that few LEAs found the MSC either willing or able to impose such a management structure. What emerged from the initial MSC/LEA negotiations were 'contracts' that, contrary to expectations, actually allowed considerable scope for LEAs and their individual institutions to explore the 'educational' implications of drawing technical and vocational elements into the curriculum.

Indeed, we would suggest that management structures that emerged had an in-built tension, the formal 'mechanistic' structure being continually pulled towards what Burns and Stalker (1961) refer to as the 'organismic' form of management. That is, one that is characterized by the sharing of specialized knowledge to meet the common tasks within a 'realistic' framework set by the particular context in which change is set. These tasks are thus continually redefined and the network structure of control, authority and communication lead to a spread of commitment across the management structure, where information and advice become the order of the day, rather than instructions and clear-cut decisions.

Thus while at the formal level the image of a 'mechanistic' model loomed large and bred suspicion, at the more informal level the structures and processes of an 'organismic' management model steadily emerged that has had long-term consequences for the different levels of management, the MSC, the LEAs and the educational institutions. However, developments external to TVEI have provided a further context around and within which the issues of organization and management have been restructured.

The relationship between the LEAs and the educational institutions and the MSC were 'managed' through the conduit of the local TVEI Units. This placed these Units and their directors/co-ordinators in a key position. At different times, project directors/co-ordinators used the MSC as a 'scapegoat' to force the hands of reluctant individuals. This was actually sanctioned by a least one of the regional advisers. However, overall, the regular use of such a tactic was recognized as counterproductive. The position was fraught with potential tensions emanating from the requirement to look towards the MSC, the LEA and the educational institutions as sources of highly differential and occasionally contradictory pressures. The NFER has recently published a study of these local Units that indicates some of these tensions:

> For instance, the salaries of team members, the cost of a centrally-equipped base and the establishment of an administrative machinery have to be weighed against the benefits of devolving extra equipment and staff to project schools. The need for schools to 'own' TVEI curriculum developments has to be set against the need for a degree of central control and direction by the LEA (NFER, 1988: 41).

This tension between the 'centre' and the periphery was of course exacerbated by the requirement of the local Units to be responsive to the MSC. Consequently, the directors/co-ordinators were continually 'squeezed' by the need to respond to centrally derived requests, often for information or justification of work undertaken or plans proposed, and at the same time the necessity to maintain good relations with the educational institutions. For the key people, this tension was a daily dilemma as they negotiated with the schools, colleges and individual teachers who took responsibility for 'delivering' TVEI. Such negotiations being made difficult by the need to be conscious of 'the latest MSC positions', while not appearing in the eyes of the 'deliverers' to have 'gone native'.

The relations between the LEAs, local TVEI Units, steering groups and local educational institutions

In view of the widespread suspicion of TVEI among the teaching profession, sometimes amounting to outright hostility, those who were promoting TVEI at the local authority level had to engage in delicate negotiations with the headteachers. Recruitment of the heads appears to have varied from invitation through to instructions from the officers of the LEA.

> . . . questionnaire findings suggest that in nearly 75% of the schools, LEA officers [rather than the heads] took the final decision as to which schools would offer a TVEI scheme, either by selecting the school directly or by initially asking for volunteers, negotiating with the heads and then, where necessary, making the selection (NFER, 1986).

This process of selection, rejection and the occasional use of 'strongly worded persuasion' meant that only the most strongly TVEI-committed heads were likely to fully embrace the aims of the local project. There was clear evidence in several authorities of the headteachers' cynicism ('we'll take the money and run'), as well as the view that the money was too useful to reject out of hand ('let's see what we can negotiate'). Where heads felt they had been pressured into participating in TVEI, there was a genuine fear of the power the MSC might choose to wield.

This was exacerbated by the fact that few (in some cases none!) of the heads were involved in the early negotiations. Most heads had no sense of 'ownership' of the first- and second-round projects and felt they were being asked to 'deliver' processes of change determined by others. Furthermore, the idea of an agency external to the educational world setting up a local Unit with power to affect developments, internal to the schools/colleges, was viewed as an attack on their long-held autonomy. Throughout the projects with which we are familiar, heads frequently commented on the erosion of their autonomy and regularly used this argument as grounds for baulking against the work of the local TVEI Unit.

The appointment of project directors varies, but it was not uncommon for them to be placed in post after the submission had been accepted; there are few cases of project directors being involved in the submission process. This is hardly surprising, given that the LEAs needed to know they would be receiving the finance from the MSC before they could appoint.

We have already indicated that most of the project directors had an educational background and few, if any, came from the industrial or commercial sector. Thus developments tended to look inwards, to the educational service for both their broad aims and the intended strategies for delivering these. In terms of the 'level of appointment':

> . . . 39 coordinators were on headship grades and five were on deputy headship grades. It is clear that most LEAs, the bodies responsible for setting the level of appointment for TVEI coordinators, have decided the position merits senior headship status (NFER, 1986).

However, few appear to have received any degree of training. As the NFER survey points out:

> When asked in what areas training would have been beneficial, 13 nominated management and administration, 13 identified LEA procedures and finance and three stated the management of curriculum development processes (NFER, 1986).

The impact of TVEI upon the relationships between the heads and the LEAs has varied considerably across the different authorities. For most, it has resulted in a far greater degree of contact between the heads and the officers/Inspectorate/advisers of the authority. However, it is the nature of that contact that is of interest. The difficulty in disentangling TVEI from other change agents is as evident here as elsewhere. It is apparent that many of the authorities brought the heads together as a 'planning group' to enable change to be on a project-wide basis. Where this did not happen, the MSC appear to have raised the question of doing so. Few heads appear to have grasped the implications of these planning groups and the power it could have given them to subvert the work of the project director and 'hijack' the projects. Instead, they used it as a wrecking and delaying device to block or delay change, and only rarely as a device to effect the changes they might have wished. However, in the later years of some projects, such an awareness did begin to emerge, but it was tempered by a far more cooperative stance as the working relationship between the heads and the directors/co-ordinators developed. This may reflect a weakness in the heads as 'operators' in a committee structure, or as individuals unused to long-term planning, or it may reflect the differences that existed between the heads and their institutions. The latter, in turn, may relate to the catchment area and the parents/students to be served, or the consitutent parts of what goes to make the 'ethos' of a school.

'Delivering' the contract

It has not been uncommon for the steering committee to have either disappeared or never to have materialized! Where steering committees have waxed and waned their limited role has tended to be that of a rubber stamping body. There is evidence of some steering committees having a limited impact. In one instance, they were able to require an authority to accept the appointment of temporary subject advisers, and there is little doubt that steering committees could have had considerable powers, had project directors chosen to use them or been able to promote their position. However, overall the response that, 'It ain't done no steering', has been a typical response of practitioners. This has largely been a problem of attracting and retaining the interest of local employers, politicians and others in being involved in TVEI. Yet again this has left the field clear for the educational lobby to pursue its interests, although with a wary eye on the potential powers of the MSC and the surrogate powers of the local TVEI Unit.

The work of developing the TVEI aspect of the curriculum rarely privileged the MSC or the local TVEI Units to delve deeply into the whole school curriculum. Some authorities chose a 'bolt on' model, keeping TVEI largely separate from the rest of the curriculum. This was particularly the case in the authorities that viewed the 'technical' and the 'vocational' in subject terms, i.e. technical = technology and vocational = business studies and the provision of an applications approach to certain other subject areas. In these cases, the money was often used to enhance the weaker subject areas, authorities unwilling to 'interfere' with the traditional and high-status parts of the curriculum. There was some evidence of authorities using 'the TVEI approach' across the school curriculum, introducing modularity or changing teaching and learning styles or starting work on profiling. However, it is difficult in all these cases to be clear how much of this was due to TVEI and how much other initiatives were the major sources of change.

The extent to which either the advisory service or the Inspectorate have been involved has varied considerably. Some projects took a conscious decision to try and keep the pilot phase out of the hands of the Inspectorate; this was particularly the case where authorities tried to marginalize the project and 'bolt it on' to the curriculum. As the pilot phase went on, it is apparent that the Inspectorate and individual advisers found themselves increasingly drawn into the process. Again, it is not easy to see the extent to which the impact of other initiatives began to shift the role of both the Inspectorate and the advisory services, e.g. the 'bid and deliver' approach to educational funding, the wide variety of initiatives, etc. What was clear was that these initiatives often made the members of the TVEI Unit, and those involved in TVEI, possessors of a new and highly valued knowledge base that certainly enhanced the standing of TVEI generally and acted as an 'enabler' in gaining influence elsewhere.

The working through of the relationships between the various educational posts has been continuous and remains in a state of flux. In some authorities, it has been a battleground throughout the pilot phase, only subsiding slightly towards the end but now being revived with the move to Extension.

The role of the director/co-ordinator clearly shifted over the period of the pilot phase and into Extension. Thus the management picture changes too. The key relationship has been seen by some to be that between the project co-ordinator/ director and the headteacher:

> All the evidence available suggests that the critical relationship in the implementation of TVEI is between the project coordinators and heads. Conflict is most likely to arise here if it occurs at all (MSC, 1986).

However, this is not entirely a power battle, and in most cases the directors/co-ordinators saw winning cooperation as a central aspect of their jobs. At the start of the projects, the 'heavy hand' of the MSC was seen by most heads to be in evidence in everything the directors/co-ordinators did. Over time this suspicion diminished, although at times of conflict the spectre of the MSC was frequently raised. A great deal depended upon the management style that was developed by the LEA, in conjunction with the director/co-ordinator, and the position of the local Unit with respect to the LEA and the educational institutions. Where they were 'detached' and discrete, the relationship was often difficult, and over the period of the projects merging into the educational setting became a necessary part of achieving any success for TVEI.

The headteachers varied in their responses to TVEI and this was not merely a result of their ideological views on the purposes and aims for which TVEI was set up. Neither did the heads only respond as individuals and there was ample evidence of groups of heads pursuing a particular 'line' in TVEI meetings. The picture that emerged was a complex micro-politics in which the various heads, the director/co-ordinator, officials of the LEA and the school/institutional co-ordinators man-oeuvred inside and outside the many TVEI-initiated meetings to gain advantages that reflected their particular concerns. These produced inflections in the TVEI projects and made the task of management an often frustrating and thankless activity.

The heads were always in a powerful position, possessing a detailed knowledge of the LEA and their own institutions as well as retaining a high level of autonomy over those institutions and their constituent parts. The management relationship between the directors/co-ordinators and their respective heads was more about the management of meetings and of meanings than about attempting to impose the decisions of a centralized management upon the heads.

Management and organization within the institutions

In this context, TVEI becomes a 'experience' for both teachers and lecturers and students. We have already suggested that this experience is differentiated as a result of factors outside the institution, such as the looseness of the contracts, the fractioned nature of the ideologies surrounding technical and vocational education. However, it is also differentiated by the varying experiences students and teachers bring into the institution and the particular features within institutions.

In management terms, the heads have often been 'aided' in their work in the school by the appointment of a TVEI institutional co-ordinator. The inverted commas signal the fact that this has not always suited heads and there are many examples of heads and institutional co-ordinators finding themselves out of sympathy on the delivery of certain aspects of TVEI. Adjusting the institutional management structure to accommodate the institutional co-ordinators was not always easy and occasionally resulted in difficulties over the scale/allowance balance. The extent and the nature of the participation of the institutional co-ordinators in the management team varies considerably. Some became key figures in their teams, whereas others were marginalized and deliberately excluded. Problems frequently arose with institutional co-ordinators and the heads feeling their 'territory' had been invaded by the other and specifying the role of the institutional co-ordinators became a major issue in some projects, at the outset, and this has been revived with the move into Extension.

There has also been the impact of TVEI upon the rest of the institution. The project has required staff cooperation – both inter-departmental and within departments, and even, on occasions, in an across-department or whole institution sense, e.g. the need to sort out timetabling problems. Securing this cooperation has meant another level of persuasion, even among some of the more autocratic heads. This has also been used strategically by individual heads of schools and colleges, claiming they cannot make changes without the consent of their management teams and the staff. The underlying difficulty being the continual question of the autonomy of the institution *vs* the autonomy of the project.

The changes in curriculum organization in the projects with which we were familiar support the observations of the Leeds University team in their 12 case studies, i.e. institutions responded with forms of adaptive extension (using TVEI to review and reshape the curriculum), accommodation (some innovative elements but largely a compromise between TVEI goals and the existing curriculum) and containment (funding confined and absorbed into the schools' existing practices) (Barnes *et al.*, 1987).

It was also evident that the notion of the TVEI cohort gave rise to a clash between the ideals of the comprehensive system and the idea of an educational experience being limited to a select group. This has often led schools to spread the TVEI experience across the school but identify a cohort of names for the benefit of the NFER student/teacher database returns. This has also been a way of managing the extent to which a TVEI enclave operates in the school (Saunders, 1985).

In general terms, the largest single impact on the institutions has been the high profile taken by management issues, both internally and externally. Heads, teachers and lecturers have become much more conscious of the managerial structure of their institutions and the various roles that this gives to the groupings and individuals that make it up.

Finally, it is vital to mention the increasing use the MSC made of the regional advisers. Originally, they did not feature in the management model and were 'added' at the time of the second-round submissions. For all those involved in TVEI, the regional advisers rapidly became the 'touchstone' for gauging the views of the MSC. They were able to have regular contact with directors/co-ordinators of TVEI Units, occasional contact with heads and institutional co-ordinators, and made visits to the institutions. In addition, they had contact with LEA officials.

Taken together, this placed them in a powerful position to influence change and to 'report back' upon work in progress. The opportunity to gain an overview of projects in different LEAs allowed contrasts to be made. However, it would appear that many of these regional advisers came from an educational background and 'understood' the views of educationalists. We were not aware of any of them acting in a 'policing' fashion and, although there is little doubt institutions made a considerable effort to smooth the visits of regional advisers, we have no evidence of institutions being told to make significant changes.

Part of the difficulty for the regional advisers lay in the massive work load they were expected to undertake. Covering several authorities and attempting to visit these regularly to get a clear impression of the projects that were running was a considerable task. It therefore tended to be the case that their impact was in the informal contact they made with people involved in TVEI and those they considered influential 'outsiders'. Regional advisers were often the source of spreading 'good TVEI practice' from authority to authority and making suggestions on how individuals might tackle specific aspects of change. This made them a 'resource' for participants in TVEI who would use them as 'sounding boards' and allies for pursuing particular proposals.

Discussion

We have already pointed out that the original proposals for TVEI appeared to promote a management system that was hierarchic in structure, tending to vertical interaction between units, and governed by superiors. This in turn implied a fairly rigid approach to delivering TVEI that bears a strong resemblance to Burns and Stalker's (1961) 'mechanistic' management system. It is somewhat ironic to note that Burns and Stalker viewed such a system as appropriate to stable conditions and unsuited to innovation. However, we indicated that the source of that structure reflected the particular problems it was aiming to solve. This resonated strongly with the state bureaucratic view of management:

> The solution governments adopt is to simplify in order to control: the form, the account and the statistic are all ways of coping with an over-complicated world, and are of course the very lifeblood of bureaucracy . . . it is better at treating people as things, in one dimension; it deals with quantifiable indicators (Mulgan, 1988).

That does not fit neatly with either the changing management structures of commercial and industrial concerns which are moving to weak power structures (Mulgan, 1988), or with the long-term political thrust of the present government: 'Across the board the market must be allowed to penetrate and replace administrative structures' (Mulgan, 1988).

Consequently, there was never any great pressure and certainly no mandate to operate the original model. In many ways, it is possible to see TVEI, in management terms, as a failure. However, this would be to miss the impact of the 'bid and deliver' approach to funding, the impact of management and auditing language on educational institutions (delivery, line managers, cost-effectiveness, cost-benefit analysis, audits, performance indicators, etc.) and the concerns that generates it, and it would be to miss the subtle introduction of an institutional market psychology. It remains to be seen whether the Educational Reform Act 1988 and the proposals contained therein will reap the benefits or find the educational world forewarned and forearmed.

Notes

[1] The projector slide that relates to this comment is reproduced in the back of the AMMA report. It shows arrows moving down through the lines articulated by the speaker.

CHAPTER 11

From pilot to extension: the consolidation of TVEI

So far, we have been largely concerned with the pilot phase of the TVEI. However, no commentary upon the pilot phase could be complete without some reference to Extension, for that is in effect where the pilot ends. What this chapter attempts is to highlight this transitional period and discuss some of the implications for schools and their local authorities.

Considering the furore which followed the original announcement of TVEI in 1982, the fact that within 6 years every LEA in England and Wales would be embarked upon the Initiative at one stage or another might be regarded as little short of phenomenal. By the end of the pilot phase, the widespread mistrust of the MSC by many educationalists, which was apparent at the outset of the Initiative, seemed to be drastically diminished and many of those who originally urged caution have been overtaken by the scheme's success. Indeed, the thrust of TVEI development was taken over by a committed legion of educationalists for whom TVEI had become their bread and butter and for whom the retention and expansion of the scheme had become vital to their career interests. As will be pointed out in this chapter, the successful attainment of 'Extension' status following the pilot phase became the focal point of their industry.

As we have stressed throughout this book, the TVEI pilot schools often went to great lengths to fulfil their duties as Comprehensives while at the same time fulfilling the administrative requirements of 'doing TVEI'. As a result, when the MSC came to call, they could reveal their 'identifiable cohort' and demonstrate their designated TVEI-enhanced curriculum while simultaneously continuing to avail all of their pupils of the TVEI-facilitated curriculum and equipment. A significant number of schools in our experience quickly discovered the ease with which they could use the TVEI funding to press ahead with developments in their schools which had hitherto been precluded due to a general lack of funding. Some of those schools privately prided themselves upon out-manoeuvring the MSC through deliberately ignoring the cohort-led principle and instead spreading the resourcing as far as possible throughout the whole school despite the fact that the MSC insisted upon the 'cohort' approach on the premise that it was necessary to monitor the effect of a substantial public investment upon a readily identifiable control group.

It is interesting to note the relationship between the commitment of an LEA to TVEI on the MSC's terms, and the degree and nature of curricular investment required of its cohort schools. At one end of the spectrum were schools where MSC guidelines were strictly adhered to. Here TVEI tended to be offered as a distinct curricular package of a technical and vocational nature, comprising a distinct option in the fourth year and an alternative to more traditional choices usually offering 'new' GCE and CSE opportunities (e.g. Business Language, Media Studies). Thus pupils had to apply at the end of their third year to be part of TVEI and risk a considerable degree of curricular investment in an initiative the outcomes of which were at that juncture totally unknown and equally unpredictable. In the early days of the project, these schools tended to accompany their TVEI publicity with carefully organized parents' evenings and a variety of literature provided by the MSC's TVEI Unit. Fearful of the consequences of not managing to attract sufficient pupils to constitute a cohort, the schools used what many pupils have referred to as 'hard sell' techniques including, for example, promises of privileged access to hi-tech equipment, heavily subsidized residential excursions and improved chances of employment upon leaving school.

At the other end of the spectrum were schools which devised a TVEI curriculum entirely extra to the normal and existing 14+ curriculum which would comply with the MSC guidelines regarding technical and vocational subjects but would interfere at most minimally with the established 14–16 school agenda. The cohort would comprise pupils who were *invited* to do TVEI upon criteria of suitability laid down by the staff involved and who could follow the course with minimal ramifications for their 14+ curriculum in school. Thus a low degree of commitment upon the part of the school to MSC guidelines resulted in a low degree of curricular investment upon the part of its *selected* cohort. Such an approach was intended to ensure that as far as possible TVEI staffing and equipment would benefit all of the school's fourth and fifth years rather than simply a select minority, thus minimizing the anti-egalitarian potential of the TVEI cohort-led principle. In such cases, pupils were generally unaware of their membership of TVEI, and in exceptional cases the actual existence of the scheme, until it became necessary for them to be identified, e.g. for purposes of evaluation.

Paradoxically, it was the schools employing the *latter* model of implementation, i.e. more or less ignoring the MSC for all but administrative purposes, which were laying the foundations for effective generalization and which were best placed to enter the extension phase when the opportunity arose. In effect, what was happening was that these schools were implementing their own unofficial programmes of replication and generalization from the very beginning, contrary to the strict implementation criteria laid down by the MSC at that time. Unbeknown to those schools which were going to some lengths to unofficially generalize their TVEI scheme, they were taking an important step in paving the way for the as yet unannounced extension phase of the Initiative. By contrast, those schools which had stuck to the letter of the MSC's criteria experienced the greatest difficulty in turning their high-profile, cohort-led pilot schemes into curriculum-wide initiatives which would have to be 'available' to all of their pupils under Extension.

Extension

In July 1986, the Secretary of State for Education and Science announced that the government had decided to extend the TVEI from a pilot into a national scheme. What was also made clear, however, was that 'interested' LEAs would still be required to undergo the necessary probationary period as 'pilot' schemes before being required to demonstrate their suitability for progession to 'Extension'. However, and as will be pointed out below, such progression was far from automatic but would rather involve several years of close partnership with the MSC at the end of which the authority would be required to submit a fesh bid for extension status. Furthermore, a pilot TVEI project's readiness for Extension did not necessarily depend upon successful completion of, or even adherence to, their original pilot contract, but depended rather upon a demonstration of its willingness and ability to switch to the revised criteria governing entry into this latest phase of the Initiative.

Thus the transition from pilot to extension status for projects never represented a mere formality; indeed, a number of first-round projects were refused such progression not necessarily through their inability to fulfil their original pilot contract but rather through their inability or unwillingness to meet the MSC's 'criteria for readiness' for entry into the new phase. By the same token, a number of second-round projects which had managed to meet those criteria, although not perhaps altogether intentionally, were granted early extension status and were thus effectively promoted above their first-round counterparts. The reasons given for failing to attain Extension were varied, but they illustrate the fundamental changes in approach and purpose that the new TVEI scheme was to represent. For example, Devon, which had often been held up as a model pilot scheme, was refused Extension on the grounds that they were not putting sufficient resources into staffing their advisory service. Staffordshire, another model scheme, was refused Extension upon much the same grounds, and Hereford and Worcester were told that there was insufficient coherence and co-ordination between institutions. It was clear that following the flexible and experimental approach of the pilot phase, far closer scrutiny and accountability to detail were to become hallmarks of the second phase of TVEI.

The growth of management

Whatever the emphases of the pilot phase regarding the curricula of schools, it was clear that the extension phase of the Initiative was equally concerned with the development and consolidation of an effective management and advisory team, as Devon and Staffordshire discovered to their cost.

But what also gradually became clear was that the increase in uptake of TVEI and consequent expansion of administration was not to be matched by an increase in funding. Rather, there appeared to be a need for a re-prioritization of funds, because for the MSC this next phase of the Initiative appeared to be more concerned with building and maintaining a central management team which could then become fused within the established LEA and which would ensure the successful growth of TVEI through an increased dependence upon its staff. There can be no doubt that a key factor affecting a particular project's failure or success in attaining 'extension' status was the ability to demonstrate to the MSC that the project was becoming inextricably bound within the overall LEA apparatus. Furthermore, the trend away from funding schools towards funding a central team facilitated both the initiation and appropriation of research and development projects into areas of concern that LEAs had increasingly been unable to address either due to the lack of a mandate or the lack of funds. As a result of having their fingers in so many pies at once, successful TVEI management teams had exploded out of all recognition in order to research and develop areas such as profiling, records of achievement, modular GCSE, equal opportunities, consortium networks, work experience, residential experience, science and technology, ITEC, YTS links, CPVE, etc., in addition to co-ordinating the growing ranks of TVEI institutions. However, such expansion upon the part of TVEI central management teams was not necessarily welcomed nor indeed totally anticipated by their LEA hosts.

The original negotiations with the MSC in bidding for inclusion in the pilot scheme was necessarily conducted through existing LEA channels. The success of those bids was partially dependent upon the LEA's plans for the management of the scheme which, the MSC insisted, must involve a distinct new tier of management accountable to a county steering group comprising representatives from the LEA, local politics, local industry, teacher unions, parents and the evaluation. Control of TVEI could not therefore simply be contained within the remit of an existing LEA department. Thus one LEA which proposed TVEI being managed half by the Low Attainer's Initiative co-ordinator and half by the proposed CPVE co-ordinator underwent lengthy negotiations with MSC before agreeing very reluctantly to initiate a brand new tier of TVEI management, albeit very small, within the LEA. This was clearly a major strategic move and indicated to many involved that the pilot was already primed to become more than simply a 5-year experiment. Furthermore, it seems probable that LEAs were rather reluctant to install this new level of management within their establishment, as they were concerned not only that this would be likely to result in a significant reduction of MSC funds actually reaching the schools, but also that come the end of the Initiative they would be saddled with a costly management team surplus to their requirements. As a result, in the early 'pilot' days, the TVEI management team often comprised a very low-profile and relatively powerless bolt-on department to the LEA, normally involving the co-ordinator and his secretary tucked well away from the real business of the authority.

In the event, it seems to have been one of the precise aims of the MSC that once installed the TVEI management team should forge strong and inseparable links within the LEA. This tactic was a very important one, because it is highly unlikely that the Initiative could have survived upon its MSC funding alone. Once the TVEI management was installed, it was carefully encouraged to grow both through the appointment of new co-ordination staff and through addressing a far-reaching range of issues which required the appointment of yet more personnel through whom the appropriate administration and research would be conducted. An examination of one project's financial records reveals quite clearly the process of moving from an exercise in generous pump-primed curriculum-funding with almost indecent haste to a predominantly management-funded model. In that particular scheme, the equipment budget for 1984–5 represented 60% of the overall budget, whereas the management, including co-ordination staff in schools, represented just 29%. In the following year, however, equipment accounted for 34% of funds and management 58%. During 1986–7, the third year of the project, despite two and half times the original official cohort, equipment accounted for just 15% of the budget, whereas management spending accounted for 77%. This dramatic increase in spending on management was to facilitate a broadening of the role of the TVEI management team rather than to simply compensate for the greater number of pupils involved. The growth in pupil numbers had to be absorbed by the schools themselves and many were forced to divert their own diminishing resources in order to compensate for the increasing demands of the Initiative. This move from a resource-led to a management-led initiative was consolidated further with TVEI Extension with the express direction of the MSC that TVEI funding could not be used to replace or update any of the equipment originally purchased for the project. The onus for the replacement of the much used, and in some cases now dated and broken, equipment lay with the schools and the LEA. A modest amount of new funds for Extension could be used in equipping incoming schools, but the vast majority of funding was now directed towards staff development and management of the Initiative. As the central management team expanded, so their infiltration became both more far reaching and effective. The shift in the allocation of resources allowed the management team not only to take on increasing amounts of the LEAs' work, but also placed them in an ideal position to manage the sudden influx of institutions that a successful bid for Extension would involve.

Not surprisingly, TVEI was also having a considerable impact within schools. The notion of TVEI in relation to teachers' objective and subjective careers has already been covered in some detail in this volume. Using such a model, there can be no doubt that TVEI was quickly seized upon by a significant number of teachers as a way of boosting their 'objective' career prospects. The Initiative represented a feasible alternative career route which, although perhaps temporary, was none the less one that many teachers stuck on the promotional ladder were willing to risk. This was an important factor in the success of TVEI, as it helped ensure that the Initiatives's growth within schools was supported by teams of staff committed to its success and who began to contribute to and facilitate developments which would have hitherto been considered unthinkable. As Chapter 7 shows, the original 'technical and vocational' brief gradually extended from, for example, Information Technology and Business Studies to include increasingly beleaguered areas such as the arts and humanities. As TVEI began to reprioritize traditional curricular hierarchies in favour of identified 'relevant' areas, so other previously non-TVEI departments began to realize that they could less and less afford not to become involved in the Initiative. Furthermore, the teachers themselves were persuaded that it was they who were controlling the Initiative through the 'ownership' of it, which, as will be pointed out later, constituted an oft repeated and very effective element of the MSC's legitmating rhetoric.

The successful consolidation and growth of the central management team, then, was an important contribution towards successful application for TVEI Extension. By way of illustration, one county's central team began in 1984 with one county director, who in status equalled a group 10 headship, and two part-time assistant area co-ordinators. By 1988, the team had grown to include a deputy director, four full-time area co-ordinators, seven full-time curriculum co-ordinators (each of whom directly linked into the county's advisory service), the equivalent of four full-time teacher secondments and a full-time evaluator. In addition, the county co-ordinator was elevated to the status of senior inspector and became county director. Within 4 years, the county TVEI scheme had outgrown its broom-cupboard status and had become firmly and irretrievably integrated within the everyday business of the LEA.

Replication

As is pointed out above, those projects which could demonstrate that TVEI could be readily generalized within schools stood a greater chance of attaining extension status than those which could not. Such a demonstration was an important prelude to Extension in which an increasing amount of commitment on the part of the schools and the LEA served to compensate for the decreased amount of funding received. Such a commitment paid dividends for one of our projects in particular, which as part of its original submission had set up a parallel scheme of 12 LEA-funded TVEI 'associate' schools which attempted to replicate and expand upon the efforts of the pilot schools with a fraction of the funding provided by the MSC. These schools tried, in many cases very successfully, to implement a complex TVEI curriculum covering additional curricular areas on just £1 000 per annum and 0.25 staffing, rising to 0.5 as the cohort grew.

The underlying rationale for replication originally centred around the notion of encouraging additional innovative work which complemented that being facilitated by the MSC through TVEI. When the possibility of Extension was officially announced, it was assumed by those associated schools that the same opportunities for experimentation would continue, only this time facilitated through direct and proportionally more generous MSC funding. However, it was at this time that the long-term intentions of MSC became apparent to many, in that they were not content with the experiment merely informing and assisting long awaited curricular change, but rather intended TVEI to actually *constitute* that change. What successful replication achieved was to demonstrate both the schools' willingness and ability to take on TVEI in more far-reaching ways than had ever been expected of the schools in the pilot project. This represented a crucial factor in this LEA's project achieving early extension status, because it had clearly demonstrated both a willingness and some success at delivering the Initiative at a far lower level of resourcing than that of the pilot; a very important step towards administering the proportionally far lower resourced extension phase. Thus TVEI expanded both in depth and breadth in order to incorporate its industrial and market-led principles not only into an increasing number of curricular areas but additionally managed to become transplanted into a number of schools which did not officially come under the TVEI remit.

It is clear from such evidence, therefore, that the Extension of TVEI represented less an 'extension' of the original scheme and more the expansion of a revised and newly defined scheme involving a set of quite different criteria. There is little doubt that, following the example of their pilot counterparts, a number of schools had expected to be able to use the MSC's money to implement long-awaited changes not wholly connected with the TVEI criteria. Indeed, the then president-elect of the Secondary Heads Association, Anne Jones (later to take charge of TVEI extension), confirmed that there had 'been an element of take the money and do what you like in the TVEI' (1987) when castigating some LEAs for not sticking to the MSC's criteria. As has been pointed out above, however, the eventual extension phase of TVEI was to require quite radical shifts in both philosophy and structure, not only in the majority of schools but also by many of the personnel who had been involved in the scheme since its very inception.

'Ownership'

From the very beginning of TVEI, the MSC had been at pains to stress that it was the individual projects themselves who 'owned' the scheme. The MSC portrayed themselves as mere facilitators who were required to keep track of a substantial investment of public money. However, during the short period of transition between the pilot and extension schemes, the 'ownership' of the scheme was taken by the MSC from those who they had previously urged to take responsibility for it, the conditions for membership reconstituted and then handed back to the schools as their property once again. It is important to note here one or two details involving one representative LEA to highlight the very effective manoeuvring upon the part of the MSC.

When Extension was originally announced, the revised conditions for entry into the scheme, although heavy with implication, were very few and laid down in the main by the local management teams in order to assist incoming schools in avoiding any of the mistakes experienced by their pilot colleagues. Accordingly, the MSC maintained a distinctly back-seat approach while the aspiring extension schools began to plan, what for many were, quite fundamental changes to their 14–16 curriculum. For several months, they worked upon the premise that they were required to provide a TVEI-type curriculum which had to include 20% science and 10% technology and which must, in the words of the MSC, be *accessible* to all pupils. It was made clear that mere bolt-on courses of a technical and vocational nature, as per the original pilot contract, would not suffice and that TVEI must be fully integrated into existing option arrangements.

A characteristic feature of TVEI was always the speed with which change was required of its participants. However, the length of time between the announcement of Extension and subsequent submissions from schools and authorities appeared to be relatively generous. Guided by their local management teams, with the apparently distant attention of the MSC, proposals were drawn up and submitted. The timing of this phase is important, occurring as it did during the early part of the spring term when schools were simultaneously drawing up whole-school plans for the following academic year. Naturally, this provided a useful opportunity for schools to incorporate their proposed TVEI curriculum into their existing 14–16 option arrangements, which they generally managed to achieve very successfully, assisted by the local TVEI management teams.

A number of schools had been so assured of their success that they printed out and distributed their post-14 option booklets to parents of their third-year pupils. All that was required was the MSC's official approval which, the local managers of the scheme assured them, would be merely a formality. Thus in March of the spring term, each school had, at much self-expense, drawn up an integrated TVEI curriculum (incorporating an innovative Modular GCSE curriculum), including 20% science and 10% technology which was accessible to any pupil aged 14–16 who might wish to participate in any part of it. In addition, they had been assured that a minimum sum of £25 000 per school would be allocated to assist the implementation of their plans.

In late March, however, the MSC took the unexpected step of pointing out in no uncertain terms that the project being 'accessible' actually meant 'compulsory'. The wording remained the same but the meaning was drastically altered. All bids in which the TVEI curriculum did not represent part of the *core* curriculum were turned down and given a 2-week deadline within which to resubmit. Not surprisingly, perhaps, this came as something of a nasty shock to the schools, as well as the project management. The vast majority of schools were too far down the TVEI road to turn back and they were thus effectively committed to making the changes. Those which could not make the changes were granted a year's 'development funds' with which to ready themselves for coming on stream at the beginning of the following academic year. Equally surprising to all involved, was the announcement that the schools involved in the pilot project, which had been pioneering the Initiative in one form or another since its inception, were not to be included in the extension project. In the event, the pilot was totally superseded by a brand new TVEI project which was to involve the remainder of the LEA's secondary schools spearheaded by the previously non-TVEI-associated school project. The pilot schools were simply left to wind up their original TVEI projects, many of them involving a very substantial commitment, and prepare themselves to tag on to the end of the phased extension project in a further 3 years' time. Thus the extent to which a scheme might require redefining depended both upon its preparedness to take on the new TVEI and its ability to fulfil what the MSC liked to call their 'criteria for readiness'. It is at this crucial point that the 'ownership' of the scheme, which had ostensibly been that of the project and its teachers, was temporarily appropriated by the MSC and later handed back to them in a different form. Thus as was pointed out at the outset, it was not necessarily those pilot projects which could demonstrate strict adherence to their original contract which were in the best position to achieve extension status, but rather those which were best prepared to meet the revised criteria for this second and new phase of the Initiative.

It is interesting to note that the LEA, despite becoming increasingly involved in the TVEI through their inspectoral and advisory service links, had up until then kept a distance from such blatant interferences by the MSC. However, there is evidence to suggest that pressure was actually brought to bear upon schools threatening to opt out of the scheme to stay put on the basis that extension submissions must be 'whole authority' bids. At one particular TVEI conference instigated by the LEA itself, a senior inspector, who had sensed a degree of unease among delegates, informed the assembled representatives of schools which had been allotted to a particular phase of the Initiative that the LEA could not tolerate any school proposing to withdraw from participation. Furthermore, it is also interesting to note that despite the onset of Local Management of Schools (LMS), TVEI central teams, which have increasingly become fused with the LEA through extension, were still to be responsible for the distribution of MSC moneys. Indeed, TVEI is one of the very few areas of funding where it appears that schools will remain dependent upon the LEA. What is also clear is that the eventual extension funding itself was not a sufficient inducement for schools to participate in TVEI. As is pointed out above, originally schools were led to expect £25 000 to spend on much needed equipment and drew up their bids accordingly, but the sum eventually received was less than half of that amount. Indeed, that funding has become much reduced to the extent that in relation to per-capita allocations it is relatively insignificant and in the view of many schools certainly doesn't warrant the upheaval that TVEI has come to demand. It also became apparent that local projects would only be granted Extension if their plans proposed the eventual inclusion of *all* schools within the LEA and to *all* 14- to 18-year-olds in full-time education. Much to the consternation of some head-teachers who were being 'invited' to become involved in Extension, this bore little resemblance to the spirit of the original pilot scheme and it is highly unlikely that any TVEI local management team would have the powers to pursue such a policy without the full support of its LEA.

An examination of the extension phase suggests that despite the nurturing of the concept of 'ownership', TVEI was not in the end the property of the schools nor of the local project management teams and their LEAs, but ultimately that of the MSC. Local management was granted a certain degree of licence in formulating their response to the scheme, and they in turn granted a degree of licence to their schools, but control of the initiative rested firmly and unequivocally with the MSC. Pilot, Extension and Generalization is likely to be phased over 15 years and represents a series of contractual stages which projects must successfully negotiate in order to be granted admission into the subsequent stage. Those projects for whom this process has been relatively painless might be forgiven for assuming that they have ultimate responsibility for, and ownership of, 'their' scheme, but the fact that a number of projects have been repeatedly refused admission into Extension would suggest a different story. The 'criteria for readiness' are formulated by the MSC and include not only significant changes in the curriculum, but also quite major attitudinal changes on the parts of both the TVEI management and the LEA. TVEI has, as one project director frequently stressed, been as much about nurturing 'quite radical changes in the cultures of schools' as anything else.

The notion of 'ownership' represents just one part of what might be described as a well-developed and legitmating rhetoric which has underpinned TVEI from the start. It is a fairly straightforward task to tease out the rhetoric through an examination of the inconsistencies in attention to certain details. It might be argued that the MSC successfully ameliorated a negative response to its ideologically led project through the contractual requirement of schemes to address a number of quite laudable educational issues. Notable among these was the requirement to attend to the question of 'equality of opportunity', as has been pointed out earlier in this volume.

Probably, an even more powerful legitimating device was the involvement of a huge programme of TVEI evaluation ranging from nationwide studies to small, individually commissioned research contracts. Every local project from the second round onwards was contractually obliged to devote a minimum of 1% of its annual funding towards a local and independent evaluation which would monitor and assist the project in its development. But there exists very little evidence that the plethora of evaluative studies of TVEI informed its progress whatsoever. Indeed, many local evaluators have been actively discouraged and in a number of cases directly prevented from disseminating critical information regarding, what they consider to be, some of the more negative aspects of the scheme. Indeed, Simons (1987) claimed that:

> We should not be surprised if Lord Young, in announcing the extension of TVEI to all secondary schools as a result of the 'success' of the pilot scheme, entertained few fears of contradiction from a substantial investment in evaluation. None has so far been forthcoming.

But that is not to suggest that none were made, for, as would be expected, evaluators *have* been critical as well as supportive in their formative evaluation roles. What became clear was that, by and large, only the supportive was disseminated by projects and the MSC and that as a result any less auspicious developments within the scheme did not become widespread knowledge. It was only when the scheme was well established throughout the country and with the majority of LEAs committed to seeing their project through that the dissemination of critical evaluation began to trickle through via more independent channels. Such work, however, did not pose any threat to the proponents of TVEI and is likely to prove useful only in historical debates of the scheme. In particular, there is no evidence to suggest that the huge programme of TVEI evaluations, both local and national, in any way informed the setting up of the Extension, lending support to the opinions of a significant number of local evaluators that their work has comprised little more than a symbolic and legitimating exercise.

Consolidation

Within 5 years, then, TVEI was transformed from a cohort-led and lavishly resourced curriculum experiment piloted in selected schools and regarded with some suspicion by educationalists, to a scarcely adequately funded compulsory core curriculum involving all 14- to 18-year-olds in all schools with support from the increasing number of teachers and administrators who had vested interests in the project. It became consolidated within those original LEAs to such effect that it was increasingly difficult to distinguish from the authorities' everyday business; and TVEI management teams are talking of letting the acronym fade away for all but basic administrative purposes. Thus the experiment was, publicly at least, a widespread success. Under the pressure of contemporary economic stringencies, schools and their staff took on TVEI as a means of developing their curricula and careers, respectively. Much was achieved in the way of curriculum development, but it would be mistaken to conclude that LEAs, schools and their staff had ultimate control over that development. As more and more projects approached extension, so their extensive management teams had to prioritize developments in relation to proportionally less funding and the MSC-determined 'criteria for readiness'.

But a new piece of rhetoric must now be added to the TVEI vocabulary. It has already been pointed out how the scheme, which should at 14–16 have been 'accessible' to all pupils, actually became part of their core curriculum. Now, what had originally been explicitly a voluntary initiative at 16–18 became one of 'entitlement'. The rationale central to this new concept was that if the TVEI administration determined that pupils were 'entitled' to certain experiences and to acquire 'appropriate attitudes, skills, concepts and values necessary for personal effectiveness in adult and working life in a rapidly changing society', then they would all be provided with them regardless of their individual wishes. Entitlement at 16–18 was to be a contractual requirement of LEAs and thus comprised a mandatory aspect of what had hitherto represented a totally voluntary stage of education. Furthermore, the introduction of pupil profiling, again pioneered in many areas through TVEI, as an integral method of assessment *and* accredition, would ensure that the assessment and recording of the appropriate attitudes, skills and concepts upon which the whole entitlement framework was based would become a necessary and normal component of youngsters' standard leaving documentation.

But there are at least two major developments which further consolidated the work of the MSC through TVEI. First, the move from Extension towards full Generalization was to be a phased development requiring further submissions from LEAs and their TVEI administrations for participation during the next 5–10 years. As with the transition from pilot to extension, this will provide the MSC with a rationale with which to monitor developments and, if required, yet again set TVEI on an altered course for subsequent contractual stages.

Secondly, a good deal of attention was paid to formulating a range of 'performance criteria' through which TVEI management teams would be enabled to appraise the progress of their schools and colleges and the MSC their individual projects. The finalization of such criteria would ensure that the Initiative was closely policed to guarantee that schools really did provide all of their pupils with, what the MSC determined to be, an entitlement curriculum of appropriate 'breadth and balance'.

But perhaps the most important work of TVEI has been achieved. In a matter of half a decade, major gains have been made in altering the very terrain upon which schools and their teachers have been used to operating. TVEI was to prove irresistible to all but the strongest willed LEAs, and even they have now fallen into line. Practices which would have been totally alien to most teachers earlier in the decade, such as bidding against fellow schools for money or being required to teach and encourage children how to make profits, are now commonplace and widely accepted. In-service training has become bid-led, segmented and is under such scrutiny that only courses which are functional to current ideological preference are funded. Lump sums in the form of honoraria are offered to teachers to prime departments for entry into the Initiative and a new generation of teacher has emerged combining both the advisory and inspectorial role in the form of the TVEI central team member.

But as the scheme injected the ethics and practices of the business world into the world of schools, so may this be the undoing of its champions. TVEI is set to disappear. The chief proponents of TVEI within the LEAs are either scrambling for elevation on the ladder into the LEA establishment proper, or else launching themselves across to the more recent and therefore relatively more seaworthy sinking ships of the late-coming authorities. Either way their futures are less than assured in the current climate due, rather ironically, in no small way to their success in promulgating the ideology of the MSC.

For the MSC, TVEI was hugely, if not wholly always intentionally, successful. It was able to intervene directly in many of the educational issues which successive governments have construed as 'public concern', but have lacked the mandate or courage to address and, equally importantly, was simultaneously laying a foundation upon which to pursue its own ideologically led programme of reform. With the benefit of hindsight, it is a fairly straightforward project to tease out the fundamental ideology from the legitimating rhetoric. As we have attempted to illustrate, particular aspects of TVEI have warranted far closer scrutiny from its sponsors than have others and 'success' in TVEI, if indeed we can measure success in terms of qualifying for subsequent stages of the project and its attendant moneys, has had less to do with an LEA fulfilling the original criteria of the Initiative and more to do with readying themselves for subsequent and far more consequential stages of the ideological programme.

Many of those who originally urged caution in becoming involved in the Initiative appear to have been overtaken by its success. An initiative that was front loaded with relatively lavish funding is now successfully up and running largely on the commitment of schools, their teachers and the LEAs. As TVEI extends and eventually generalizes, the money and support is likely to dry up, but whether the MSC's intended project (i.e. to radically alter the established premises of curricular and institutional provision within the state secondary sector, with the fundamental ramifications for primary and higher education sectors that such alterations inevitably imply), will have been achieved is a question this book cannot answer. It is, though, an issue that seems unlikely to disappear, and we hope that this book will enable more adequate analyses of the forms it takes in the future.

Bibliography

Ahier, J. (1988). *Industry, Childhood and the Nation*. Lewes, Falmer Press.

AMMA (1984). *The TVEI: A Seminar on Progress*, AMMA.

Arnot, M. and Weiner, A. (1987). *Gender and the Politics of Schooling*. London, Hutchinson.

Apple, M. (1983). 'Work, class and teaching'. In Walker, S. and Barton, L. (eds), *Gender, Class and Education*. Lewes, Falmer Press.

Ashton, D., Maguire, M. and Garland, V. (1982). *Youth in the Labour Market*. Department of Employment Research Paper No, 34, London, HMSO.

Ball, S. (1987). *The Micro-Politics of the School: Towards a Theory of School Organization*. London, Methuen.

Ball, S. (1988). 'Schools of management'. *The English Magazine*, 2, summer, pp. 7–10.

Barnes, D. *et al.* (1987). *The TVEI Curriculum 14–16: An Interim Report Based on Case-Studies in Twelve Schools*. University of Leeds, School of Education for the MSC.

Barnes, D., Johnson, G. and Jordan, S. (1989). *Work-Experience in TVEI: 14–16*. Sheffield, Training Agency.

Barr-Greenfield, T. (1975). 'Theory about organisation: A new perspective and its implications for schools'. In Houghton, V., McHugh, R. and Morgan, C. (eds), *Management in Education: Reader* 2. London/Milton Keynes, Ward Lock/Open University Press.

Bates, I., Clarke, J. Cohen, P., Finn, D., Moore, R. and Willis, P. (1984). *Schooling for the Dole*. London, Macmillan.

Beck, J. (1983). 'Accountability, industry and education: Reflections on some aspects of educational and industrial policies of the labour administrations of 1974–9'. In Ahier, J. and Flude, M. (eds), *Contemporary Education Policy*, pp. 211–32. London, Croom Helm.

Bell, L. (1986). 'An investigation of a new role in schools: The case of the TVEI coordinator'. In Simkins, T. (ed.), *Research in the Management of Secondary Education*. Sheffield City Polytechnic for the British Educational Management and Administration Society.

Benn, C. and Fairley, J. (eds) (1986). *Challenging the MSC*. London, Pluto Press.

Bennet, C. (1985). 'Paints, pots or promotion?: Art teachers' attitudes towards their careers'. In Ball, S. and Goodson, I. (eds), *Teachers Lives and Careers*. Lewes, Falmer Press.

Bouchier, D. (1984). *The Feminist Challenge*. New York, Schoken Books.

Bosanquet, N. (1983). *After the New Right*. London, Heinemann.

Braverman, H. (1974). *Labor and Monopoly Capitalism*. New York, Monthly Review Press.

Brennan, E. (1985). 'On the eve of CPVE – some impressions on the changing pre-vocational scene'. *Cambridge Journal of Education*, 15, (1).

Broadfoot, P. (1987). *Interim Evaluation Report*. Open University/Bristol University, PRAISE.

Burns, T. and Stalker, G. (1961). *The Management of Innovation*. London, Tavistock.

Centre for Contemporary Cultural Studies (1981). *Unpopular Education*, London, Hutchinson.

Chitty, C. (1986). 'TVEI: The MSC's trojan horse'. In Benn, C. and Fairly, J. (eds), *Challenging the MSC*. London, Pluto Press.

Chitty, C. (1989). *Towards a New Education System: The Victory of the New Right?* Lewes, Falmer Press.

Cockburn, C. (1987). *Two-track Training*. London, Macmillan.

Cole, P. (1983). 'Work experience programs in schools: some suggestions for program reorientation'. *Discourse*, 3 (2).

Dale, R. (1979). 'The politicization of school deviance: The case of William Tyndale'. In Barton, L. and Meighan, R. (eds), *Schools, Pupils and Deviance*. London, Studies in Education Ltd.

Dale, R. (1981a). 'Control, accountability and William Tyndale'. In Dale, R., Esland, G., Fergusson, R. and MacDonald M. (eds), *Education and the State: Vol. 2; Politics, Patriarchy and Practice*. Lewes, Falmer Press.

Dale, R. (1981b). 'Education and the state: Contributions and contradictions'. In Apple, M. (ed.), *Economic and Cultural Reproduction in Education*. London, RKP.

Dale, R. (1983). 'Thatcherism and education'. In Ahier, J and Flude, J. (eds), *Contemporary Education Policy*. London, Croom Helm.

Dale, R. (1985). 'The background and inception of TVEI'. In Dale, R. (ed.), *Education, Training and Employment*. Oxford, Pergamon Press.

Dale, R. (1986). 'Examining the gift horse's teeth: A tentative analysis of TVEI'. In Walker, S. and Barton, L. (eds), *Youth, Unemployment and Schooling*. Milton Keynes, Open University Press.

Dale, R. (1989). *The State and Education Policy*. Milton Keynes, Open University Press.

Dale, R. (1990). 'The Thatcherite project in education: The case of the City Technology Colleges'. *Critical Social Policy*, 27, 4–19.

Dale, R. and Pires, E. (1984). 'Linking people and jobs: The indeterminate place of educational credentials'. In Broadfoot, P. (ed.), *Selection, Certification and Control: Social Issues in Educational Assessment*. Lewes, Falmer Press.

Dale, R., Harris, D., Loveys, M., Moore, R., Shilling, C., Sikes, P., Taylor, M., Trevitt, J. and Valsecchi, V. (1989). 'TVEI: A policy hybrid'. In Reynolds, D. and Hargreaves, A. (eds) *Education Policy: Contributions and Critiques*, Lewes, Falmer Press.

Dancy, J. (ed.) (1984). *TVEI Perspectives 14*. Exeter, Department of Education, University of Exeter.

Deem, R. (1981). 'State policy and ideology in the education of women, 1944–80. *British Journal of Sociology of Education*, 2 (2), 131–44.

Dennison, W. (1981). *Education in Jeopardy: Problems and Possibilities of Contraction*. Oxford, Basil Blackwell.

DES (1974). 'Work experience, circulars and administrative memoranda'. *Circular 7/74*. London, HMSO.
DES (1975). *Education Survey 21. Curricular Differences of Boys and Girls*. London, HMSO.
DES (1977). 'Local Education Authority arrangements for the school curriculum, circulars and administrative memoranda'. *Circular 14/77*. London, HMSO.
DES (1980). *Girls and Science*. HMI Matters for discussion 13. London, HMSO.
DES (1981). *Curricular 6. The School Curriculum*. London, HMSO.
DES (1983). *Draft Policy Statement on Records of Achievement*. London, HMSO.
DES (1984). *Records of Achievement: A Statement of Policy*. London, HMSO.
DES (1985). *Better Schools*. London, HMSO.
DES (1986a). *City Technology Colleges: A New Choice of School*. London, HMSO.
DES (1986b). *Working Together. London, HMSO*
DES (1988a). Education at Work: A Guide for Schools. London, HMSO.
DES (1988b). *Education at Work: A Guide for Employers*. London, HMSO.
DES (1989). *Reporting Pupil Achievement Under the National Curriculum*. DES Press Release.
DES/DoE (1984). Training for Jobs, London, HMSO.
Education (1982). 26 November.
Eggleston, J. (ed.) (1982). *Work Experience in Secondary Schools*. London, Routledge and Kegan Paul.
EOC (1979). *Do You Provide Equal Educational Opportunities?* Manchester, EOC.
Esland, G. and Cathcart, H. (1981). *Education and the Corporate Economy*, E353 Unit 2, Milton Keynes, Open University Press.
Evans, J. and Davies, B. (1988). 'The rise and fall of vocational education'. In Pollard, A., Purvis, J. and Walford, G. (eds), *Education Training and the New Vocationalism*. Milton Keynes, Open University Press.
Finn, D. (1985). 'The MSC and the YTS: A permanent bridge to work?' In Dale, R. (ed.), *Education, Training and Employment*. Oxford, Pergamon Press.
Finn, D. (1987). *Training Without Jobs*. London, Macmillan.
Flude, M. and Hammer, M. (eds) (1990). *The Education Reform Act. 1988: Its origins and Implications*. Lewes, Falmer Press.
Fowler, G. (1985). 'What is TVEI?' *Liberal Education*, 54.
Fowler, G. (1988). *Towards the National Curriculum*. London, Kogan Page.
FEU (1979). *A Basis for Choice* (The Mansell Report). London, FEU.
FEU (1982a). *Basic Skills*. London, FEU.
FEU (1982b). *Skills for Living*, London, FEU.
FEU/SCDC (1985). *Supporting TVEI*. London, FEU.
Fiddy, R. and Stronach, I. (eds) (1986). *TVEI Working Papers 2*. Norwich, CARE, University of East Anglia.
Fullan, M. (1982). *The Meaning of Educational Change*, New York, Teachers College Press.
Gamble, A. (1985). 'Smashing the state: Thatcher's radical crusade'. *Marxism Today*, June.
Gleeson, D. (ed.) (1988). *TVEI and Secondary Education*. Milton Keynes, Open University Press.
Gleeson, D. (ed.) (1990). *Training and Its Alternatives*. Milton Keynes, Open University Press.
Gleeson, D. and Maunders, A. (1985). *Curricular Issues in Local TVEI Evaluation*. TVEI Evaluation Unit, University of Keele.
Golby, M. (1985). 'The coming crisis at 14+. *Forum*, 27 (3).
Goodson, I. (1980). 'Life histories and the study of schooling'. *Interchange*. 11 (4).

Gorbutt, D. (1984). 'The new vocationalism: A critical note'. In Dancy, J. (ed.), *TVEI Perspectives 14*. Exeter, Department of Education, University of Exeter.
Grieco, M. (1987). *Keeping it in the Family*. London, Tavistock.
Griffin, C. (1985). *Typical Girls. Young Women from School to the Job Market*. London, RKP.
Grubb, W. and Lazerson, M. (1981). 'Vocational solutions to youth problems: The persistent frustrations of the American experience'. *Educational Analysis*, 3 (2), 91–103.
Halsey, A. (ed.) (1961). *Ability and Educational Opportunity*. Paris, OECD.
Hargreaves, A. (1985). 'Motivation versus selection: Some dilemmas for records of personal achievement'. In Lang, P. and Marland, M. (eds), *New Directions in Pastoral Care*. Oxford, Basil Blackwell.
Harland, J. (1987). 'The TVEI experience: Issues of control, response, and the professional role of teachers'. In Gleeson, D. (ed.), TVEI and Secondary Education. A Critical Appraisal. Milton Keynes, Open University Press.
Harris, D. (1987). 'Consulting the customers: A strategy for the development of TVEI'. *Evaluation and Research in Education*, 1 (3), 131–46.
Herbert, C. (1985). *TVEI: Equal Opportunities*. Norwich, CARE, University of East Anglia.
Hickox, M. and Moore, R. (1990). 'TVEI, vocationalism and the crisis of liberal education'. In Flude, M. and Hammer, M. (eds), *The Education Reform Act, 1988: Its Orgins and Implications*. Lewes, Falmer Press.
Hilsum, S. and Start, K. (1974). *Promotion and Careers in Teaching*. Windsor, NFER.
Holland, G. (1986). 'The MSC'. In Ranson, S. and Tomlinson, J. (eds), *The Changing Government of Education*, pp. 88–99, London, Allen and Unwin.
Holly, P. (1987). *The Dilemmas of Low Attainment*. London, FEU.
Holt, M. (1984). The high rise curriculum, *The Times Educational Supplement*, 12 October.
Holt, M. (1987a). 'Vocationalism on the hoof: Interim observations on the TVEI'. In Holt, M. (ed.), *Skills and Vocationalism: The Easy Answer*. Milton Keynes, Open University Press.
Holt, M. (ed.) (1987b). *Skills and Vocationalism: The Easy Answer*. Milton Keynes, Open University Press.
Hughes, E. (1937). 'Institutional office and the person'. *American Journal of Sociology*, 43 (Nov.), 404–13).
Hughes, E. (1958). 'Institutional office and the person'. In Hughes, E., *Men and Their Work*. New York, Free Press.
Hughes, E. (1963). 'Professions'. *Daedalus*.
Institute of Careers Officers (1974). *Work Experience in British Secondary Schools*. Stourbridge, ICO.
Jamieson, I. (1985). 'Corporate hegemony or pedagogic liberation?' In Dale, R. (ed.), *Education, Training and Employment*, pp. 23–40, Oxford, Pergamon Press.
Jessop, B. (1982). *The Capitalist State*. Oxford, Martin Robertson.
Johnson, R. (1976). 'Notes on the schooling of the English working-class, 1780–1850'. In Dale, R., Esland, G. and MacDonald, M. (eds), *Schooling and Capitalism*. London, RKP.
Jones, K. (1989). *Right Turn: The Conservative Revolution in Education*. London, Hutchinson.
Karabel, J. and Halsey, A. (1977). *Power and Ideology in Education*. Oxford, Oxford University Press.
Kelly, A. (1981). *The Missing Half: Girls and Science Education*. Manchester, Manchester University Press.
Kerry, J. (1983). 'Work experience: The Project Trident approach'. In Watts, A. (ed.), *Work Experience and Schools*. London, Heinemann.

Kogan, M. (1975). *Educational Policy-Making: A Study of Interest Groups and Parliament*. London, George Allen and Unwin.
Lyons, G. (1981). *Teacher Careers and Career Perceptions*. Windsor, NFER/Nelson.
MSC (1981). *A New Training Initiative*. London, MSC.
MSC (1983). *TVEI Manual*. London, MSC
MSC (1984a). *TVEI Operating Manual*. London, MSC.
MSC (1984b). *TVEI Review*. Sheffield, MSC.
MSC (1985a). *TVEI Review 1984*. London, MSC.
MSC (1985b). *TVEI National Pupil–Teacher Database Figures*. London, MSC.
MSC (1986). *TVEI Review 1985*. London, MSC.
MSC (n.d.). *TVEI Developments 2 – Equal Opportunities*. London, MSC.
McCabe, C. (1986a). 'The coordinator'. In McCabe, C. (ed.), *The Organisation of the Early Years of the Technical and Voational Education Initiative*. Avon, Multilingual Matters.
McCabe, C. (ed.) (1986b). *The Organisation of the Early Years of the Technical and Vocational Education Initiative*. Avon, Multilingual Matters.
McCulloch, G., Jenkins, E. and Layton, D. (1985). *Technological Revolution? The Politics of School Science and Technology in England and Wales Since 1945*. Lewes, Falmer Press.
McCulloch, G. (1986). 'Policy, politics and education: The TVEI'. *Journal of Education Policy*, 1 (1), 35–52.
McCulloch, G. (1989). 'City technology colleges: An old choice of school?' *British Journal of Educational Studies*, 37 (1) 30-43.
McGeever, P. (1988). *Graduates at Work*. London, Jessica Kingsley.
McGowan, E. and Cohen, D. (1977). 'Career education – reforming school through work'. *Public Interest*, 46, 23–47.
McNair, D. and MacDonald, A. (1976). 'The first years in physical education'. *Journal of Psycho-Social Aspects*, Dunfermline College.
Mathieson, M. and Bernbaum, G. (1988). 'The British diease: A British tradition?' *British Journal of Educational Studies*. 26 (2).
Millman, V. (1985). 'The new vocationalism in secondary schools: Its influence on girls'. In Whyte, J., Deem, R., Kant, L. and Cruickshank, M. (eds), *Girl Friendly Schooling*. London, Methuen.
Montgomery, R. (1983). 'Work experience: a school based approach'. In Watts, A. (ed.), *Work Experience and Schools*. London, Heinemann.
Moore, R. (1986). *Education, Training and Production*. London, South Bank Polytechnic.
Moore, R. (1988). 'Education, employment and recruitment'. In Dale, R., Fergusson, R. and Robinson, A. (eds), *Frameworks for Teaching*. London, Hodder and Stoughton.
Moore, R. (1990). 'Knowledge, practice and the construction of skill'. In Gleeson, D. (ed.), *Training and its Alternatives*. Milton Keynes, Open University Press.
Mulgan, G. (1988). 'The power of the weak'. *Marxism Today*. December.
Muller, D., Ringer, S. and Simon, B. (1987). *The Rise of the Modern Education System: Structural Change and Social Reproduction 1870–1920*. Cambridge, Cambridge University Press.
NFER (1985). *The Management of TVEI*. Sheffield, MSC.
NFER (1986). *The Management of TVEI: A Set of Papers on The Theme of 'Management Issues'*. Windsor, NFER/MSC.
NFER (1988). *Perspectives on TVEI: A Set of Papers Exploring Management Themes in TVEI*. Windsor, NFER/Training Commission.
Newman, G. (1985). 'Modules in TVEI'. *Times Educational Supplement*, 29 November.
O'Connor, J. (1973). *The Fiscal Crisis of the State*. New York, St Martin's Press.

Offe, C. (1981). 'The attribution of public status to interest groups: Observations on the West German case'. In Berger, S. (ed.), *Organizing Interests in Western Europe*, pp. 123–58). Cambridge, Cambridge University Press.
Offe, C. (1984). *Contradictions of the Welfare State*. London, Hutchinson.
Offe, C. (1985). *Disorganised Capitalism*. Oxford, Polity Press.
Owen, J. (1984). 'TVEI: Future control'. In Dancy, J. (ed.), *TVEI Perspectives 14*. Exeter, Department of Education, University of Exeter.
Pascall, G. (1986). *Social Policy: A Feminist Analysis*. London, Tavistock.
Pickard, J. (1985). 'The TVEI'. *The Times Educational Supplement*, 3 May.
Pole, C. (1986). 'The role of the school coordinator in the implementation of the TVEI'. In Stoney, S. *et al.* (eds), *The Management of TVEI*. Windsor, NFER for the MSC.
Pollert, A. (1988). 'The "flexible firm": fixation or fact?' *Work, Employment and Society*, 2 (3), 281–316.
Pratley, B. (1985). *Signposts '85: A Review of 16–19 Education*. London, FEU.
Pring, R. (1985). 'In defence of TVEI'. *Forum* 27 (3).
Pyart, B. (1985). 'An overview of TVEI' *School Organisation* 5 (4).
Ranson, S. (1985). 'Contradictions in the government of education'. *Political Studies*, 33 (1), 56–72.
Ranson, S. *et al.* (1986). 'Exams in context: Values and power in educational accountability'. In Nuttall, D. (ed.) *Assessing Educational Achievement*. Lewes, Falmer Press.
Reeder, D. (1979). 'A recurring debate: Education and industry'. In Bernbaum, G. (ed.), *Schooling in Decline*, pp. 115–48. London, Macmillan.
Reishe, D. (1972). *Women and Society*. New York, H. W. Wilson.
Saunders, M. (1985). *Emerging Issues for TVEI Implementation*. Lancaster, University of Lancaster TVEI Evaluation Programme.
Saunders, M. (1986a). 'Managing the enclave – teachers outside TVEI'. In McCabe, C. (ed.), *The Organisation of the Early Years of the Technical and Vocational Education Initiative*. Avon, Multilingual Matters.
Saunders, M. (1986b). 'The innovation enclave: Unintended effects of TVEI implementation'. *TVEI Working Papers No. 1*. Norwich, CARE, University of East Anglia/MSC.
Saunders, M. (1986c) 'TVEI – a tiger by the tail?' *Business Education*, November.
Saunders, M. (1987). 'At work in TVEI: Students' perceptions of their work-experience'. In Gleeson, D. (ed.), *TVEI and Secondary Education*. Milton Keynes, Open University Press.
Schwab, J. (1973). 'The practical 3: Translation into curriculum'. *School Review*. 81 (4) 501–522.
Shilling, C. (1987). 'Work experience and schools: Factors influencing the participation of industry'. *Journal of Education Policy*, 2 (2), 131–47.
Shilling, C. (1988). 'Thatcherism and education: The dialectics of political control'. Paper presented at the International Sociology of Education Conference, Westhill, January.
Shilling, C. (1989a). *Schooling for Work in Capitalist Britain*. Lewes, Falmer Press.
Shilling, C. (1989b). 'The Mini-enterprise in schools project: A new stage in education–industry relations?' *Journal of Education Policy*, 4 (2), 115–24.
Shilling, C. (1989c). 'Work-experience codes of practice: A critique and suggestions for reform'. *Journal of Education Policy*, 4 (4), 363–72.
Shilling, C. (1990). 'The organisation of supply workers in state schools and the National Health Service: A comparison'. *Journal of Education Policy*, 5 (2), 127–41.
Sikes, P. J. (1986a). 'The mid-career teacher; Adaptation and motivation in a contracting secondary school system'. Unpublished PhD thesis, University of Leeds.
Sikes, P. J. (1986b). 'Headteachers and the organisation and management of TVEI schemes'.

Paper presented at the conference on the Organisation and Management of TVEI, University of Newcastle. June.

Sikes, P. J. (1988). 'Growing old gracefully?: Age identity and physical education'. In Evans, J. (ed.). *Teachers, Teaching and Control in the PE Curriculum*. Lewes, Falmer Press.

Sikes, P. J., Measor, L. and Woods, P. (1985). *Teacher Careers: Crises and Continuities*. Lewes, Falmer Press.

Sikes, P. J. (1989). 'Imposed change and the experienced teacher', paper given at the International Conference of Teacher Development, OISE, Toronto, February.

Simons, H. (1987). *Getting to Know Schools in a Democracy: The Politics* and Process of Evaluation. Lewes, Falmer Press.

Smith, G. (1986). 'TVEI replication and FE'. *NATFHE Journal*, December.

Stanworth, M. (1983). *Gender and Schooling: A Study of Sexual Divisions in the Classroom*. London, Hutchinson.

Stronach, I. and Weir, D. (1980). *Experiences of Work: In, Out and Round About*. 2nd Evaluation Report on the Clydebank EEC Project, Glasgow, Jordanhill College of Higher Education.

Stronach, I. (1984). 'The sacred anvil of work-experience'. In Varlaam, C. (ed.), *Rethinking Transition: Educational Innovation and the Transition to Adult Life*. Lewes, Falmer Press.

Taylor, W. (1985). 'Productivity and educational values'. In Worswick, G. (ed.), *Education and Economic Performance*, pp. 101–12. Aldershot, Gower.

Thomas, W. and Znaniecki, F. (1919–20). *The Polish Peasant in Europe and America*. Chicago, University of Chicago Press.

The Times (1982). 'Tebbit starts technical education scheme', 13 November.

Training Agency (1988). *Developments 5: Profiles and Records of Achievement*. London, The Training Agency.

Trident (1986). *Project Trident Work Experience*. London, Project Trident.

Troyna, B. and Smith, D. (eds) (1983). *Racism, School and the Labour Market*. Leicester, National Youth Bureau.

Walker, S. and Barton, L. (eds) (1986). *Youth, Unemployment and Schooling*. Milton Keynes, Open University Press.

Watkins, P. (1987). *Modular Approaches to the Secondary Curriculum*. London, SCDC.

Watts, J. (1980). 'Sharing it out: The role of the head in participatory government'. In Bush, T. *et al.* (eds), *Approaches to School Management*. Milton Keynes, Open University Press.

Watts, A. (1983). 'Work experience: principles and practice'. In Watts, A. (ed.), *Work Experience and Schools*. London, Heinemann.

Weale, A. (1978). *Equality and Social Policy*. London, RKP.

Whyte, J. (1986). *Girls into Science and Technology*. London, RKP.

Whyte, J., Deem, R., Kent, L. and Cruickshank, M. (eds) (1985). *Girl Friendly Schooling*, London, Methuen.

Wickham, A. (1986). *Women and Training*. Milton Keynes, Open University Press.

Wiener, M. (1981). *English Culture and the Decline of the Industrial Spirit*. Middlesex, Penguin.

Wilce, H. (1984). 'Professor speaks out for sex equality'. *Times Educational Supplement*, 30 March.

Williams, G. (1981). 'The government's education policy during the first Parliamentary session'. *Education Policy Bulletin*, 8 (2), 127–44.

Williams, G. (1985). 'Graduate employment and vocationalism in higher education'. *European Journal of Education*, 20 (2–3), pp. 181–91.

Williams, R. (1965). *The Long Revolution*. Harmondsworth, Penguin.

Wragg, T. (1984). 'Evaluating TVEI programmes'. In Dancy, J. (ed.), *TVEI Perspectives 14.* Exeter, Department of Education, University of Exeter.
Wragg, T. (1986). 'The parliamentary version of the Great Debate'. In *Perspectives 26: Ruskin Plus Ten.* pp. 6–14. Exeter, Exeter School of Education.
Wragg, T. (1988). *Education in the Market Place: The Ideology Behind the 1988 Education Bill.* London, NUT.
Wyatt, H. (1985). 'TVEI and all that'. *Forum* 27 (3).
Young, M. (1971). *Knowledge and Control.* London, Collier Macmillan.

Index